NORTHROP FRYE AND THE PHENOMENOLOGY OF MYTH

In *Northrop Frye and the Phenomenology of Myth*, Glen Robert Gill compares Frye's theories about myth to those of three other major twentieth-century mythologists: C.G. Jung, Joseph Campbell, and Mircea Eliade. Gill explores the respective theories of these thinkers as they relate to Frye's views on the phenomenological nature of myth, as well as its religious, literary, and psychological significance.

Gill regards Frye's work as both more radical and more tenable than that of his three contemporaries. Eliade's writings are shown to have a metaphysical basis that does not support an understanding of myth as truly phenomenological, while Jung's theory of the collective unconscious emerges as similarly problematic. Likewise, Gill argues, Campbell's work, while incorporating some phenomenological progressions, settles on a questionable metaphysical foundation. Gill shows how, in contrast to the conceptions of these other thinkers, Frye's theory of myth – first articulated in *Fearful Symmetry* (1947) and culminating in *Words with Power* (1990) – is genuinely phenomenological.

With excursions into fields such as literary theory, depth psychology, theology, and anthropology, *Northrop Frye and the Phenomenology of Myth* is essential to the understanding of a crucial aspect of Frye's work.

(Frye Studies)

GLEN ROBERT GILL is an assistant professor in the Department of English at Troy University.

NORTHROP FRYE AND THE PHENOMENOLOGY OF MYTH

Glen Robert Gill

UNIVERSITY OF TORONTO PRESS
Toronto Buffalo London

Toronto Buffalo London
Printed in Canada

ISBN-13: 978-0-8020-9116-1 (cloth)
ISBN-10: 0-8020-9116-4 (cloth)
ISBN-13: 978-0-8020-9404-9 (paper)
ISBN-10: 0-8020-9404-X (paper)

Printed on acid-free paper

Library and Archives Canada Cataloguing in Publication

Gill, Glen Robert, 1969–
Northrop Frye and the phenomenology of myth / Glen Gill.

(Frye studies)
ISBN-13: 978-0-8020-9116-1 (bound)
ISBN-10: 0-8020-9116-4 (bound)
ISBN-13: 978-0-8020-9404-9 (pbk.)
ISBN-10: 0-8020-9404-X (pbk.)

1. Frye, Northrop, 1912–1991 – Criticism and interpretation. 2. Mythology in literature. I. Title. II. Series.

PN75.F7G55 2006 801′.95092 C2006-904923-8

This book has been published with the help of a grant from the DeGroote Trust for the Collected Works of Northrop Frye at McMaster University.

University of Toronto Press acknowledges the financial assistance to its publishing program of the Canada Council for the Arts and the Ontario Arts Council.

University of Toronto Press acknowledges the financial support for its publishing activities of the Government of Canada through the Book Publishing Industry Development Program (BPIDP).

For Alvin
from his students

Contents

Preface

I first read the work of Northrop Frye as an undergraduate and, as Frye once said of his reading of William Blake, I haven't been the same man since. I absorbed most of Frye's canon in graduate school, and then worked through the writings of the other mythologists discussed in this study, all the while reading liberally in literary theory and criticism and in the literature of various periods. Had this order of reading been different, this book might well have been. As it happened, I was struck with two impressions: first, that Frye's theories of myth were both more potent and more tenable than those of Eliade, Jung, and Campbell, each of whom had nevertheless become more influential in twentieth-century mythography; and second, that this field, particularly the branch concerned with archetypal theory and criticism, had been exiled from contemporary literary and cultural studies without due process. Taken together, these two impressions suggested to me that the baby of Frye's *theoria* had been thrown out with the disciplinary bathwater, and that I might do something to rectify this in a doctoral thesis *cum* first book. A serious, comparative philosophical consideration would, I felt, reveal what was problematic in the work of the three affiliated mythologists mentioned above, and demonstrate how Frye's work rested on a surer foundation. The fact that this sort of approach was precisely what was lacking in recent treatments of these thinkers (by both their defenders and their detractors) made it still more necessary. Not surprisingly, the specific philosophical orientation shared by the four mythologists, that of phenomenology, offered the best means of accomplishing this task, and it seemed only fair to judge these thinkers by their own rules. This required me to employ a good many ideas from that complex area of philosophy, and while I would even now make few claims of expertise in phenomenology proper, those ideas turned out to be most effective in facilitating the task at hand. Excursions into semiotics, depth psychology, theology, and anthropology provided other critical resources.

The task involved several challenges and compromises. One challenge was to avoid the artificially inflated cant that afflicts much postmodern philosophy and literary theory, which has done much to render it inaccessible to scholars and readers of other areas. I have therefore eschewed the conceptual jargon that often obscures writing in these fields while making good use of the concepts themselves, and it has been instructive to discover that they are not inseparable. One major compromise came as an inevitable side effect of comparative analysis: that only major lines of argument and major texts could be represented in my consideration of the theories of these thinkers. The substantial use of quotation in this study is partly intended to compensate for this effect, by keeping the reader as close as possible to the theories themselves. Students and scholars of Eliade, Jung, and Campbell in particular will doubtless be able to point out significant elements in their theories that I have overlooked. On the whole, however, I believe that I have been judicious in surveying their theories and in measuring those theories against each other and against those of Frye. Another compromise involved the deliberate and careful structuring of the discussion; some will find the symmetries here to be fearful, and will suggest that this study exhibits signs of what Frye jokingly called 'schematosis.' Insofar as myth and mythography tend to be meticulously structured, however, and as this study is in some ways about the heuristic value of structure, it seemed appropriate to order the book as thoroughly as possible.

Some limitations and sacrifices could not be avoided or offset. I regret that I have not been able to take stock of some significant works about Northrop Frye that were published during and shortly after the composition of this one. János Kenyeres's *Revolving around the Bible: A Study of Northrop Frye* (Budapest: Anonymus, 2003) appeared as I was writing, and Robert D. Denham's *Northrop Frye: Religious Visionary and Architect of the Spiritual World* (Charlottesville: University of Virginia Press, 2004) as I was revising. I would have liked to avail myself particularly of the latter, as Denham explores many of the radical elements of Frye's thought that I examine here, but time, as per its nature, did not cooperate. Even so, as I have been fortunate to know Dr Denham for some years, his benefaction is evident here in the form of suggested quotations, useful critiques taken into account, and the like. I was similarly ill-positioned to absorb the scholarly introductions to the new editions of *Fearful Symmetry* and

Words with Power (by Ian Singer and Michael Dolzani, respectively) which have recently been and are about to be published as part of the Collected Works of Northrop Frye. Alas, these too would have informed the present study to its betterment if there was world enough and time. The same condition, naturally, applies to my consideration of the other mythologists; there are doubtless dozens of essays and studies on Eliade, Jung, and Campbell that I was forced to overlook as well.

More positively on the matter of content, I am pleased to say that the vast majority of this study is new. However, elements of two previous publications of mine reappear in the final chapter: Parts of 'The Flesh Made Word: Body and Spirit in the New Archetypology of Northrop Frye' from *Frye and the Word: Religious Contexts in the Criticism of Northrop Frye,* edited by Jeffrey Donaldson and Alan Mendelson (Toronto: University of Toronto Press, 2004), and 'Beyond Anagogy: Northrop Frye's Existential (Re)visions' from *Northrop Frye: Eastern and Western Perspectives,* edited by Jean O'Grady (Toronto: University of Toronto Press, 2003), have been borrowed in the conclusion. While providing these citations, I should also comment on the unusual documentation formats that are occasionally used in this study: the extensive list and use of abbreviations of book titles was necessary in a comparative study of this scope to allow scholars and frequent readers of Frye and the other mythologists to expeditiously track quotations. For the most part, I have followed the citation practices that are most common in studies of Frye, Eliade, Jung, and Campbell, respectively. Students of Blake may find my citation of pages from Erdman's edition of his poetry and prose (rather than of title and line number) to be strange, but this was necessary because in many cases I wanted to cross-reference passages from Frye's *Fearful Symmetry* in parenthetical citations without their becoming distractingly long. Biblical quotations are from the Authorized Version.

I would be remiss, finally, if I did not extend my thanks to the many people who supported this work with material aid, advice, time, and goodwill. The sheer array of personae and energies that are required to bring a scholarly work into being, through the labyrinth of editing and production and into the promised land of publication, has been a revelation, one which typifies the power of faith as the substantiation of the hoped-for and the evidencing of things unseen. I should begin where I began, and thank my parents, John and Arlene Gill, who have been unflagging in their support of my academic and scholarly endeavours. Special thanks are also owed to Jeffery Donaldson, whose scholarly advice and gift of friendship were essential in the completion of this study. Robert Denham and Michael Dolzani, whose groundbreaking work on Frye has been invaluable and inspiring to me, were supportive and encouraging at every turn. Many others in Frye studies, and in my academic life more broadly, were similarly generous with their time and resources, particularly Joseph Adamson, Alan Mendelson, Jean O'Grady, Margaret Burgess, Imre Salusinzky, Nicholas Graham, Joseph Velaidum, Graham Forst, and Nicholas Halmi. The University of Toronto Press lived up to its reputation in the work and support of Ron Schoeffel, Anne Laughlin, and Judy Williams. Jeff Sprang graciously granted us permission to use his painting of Frye on the cover. Several others provided important personal and moral support, including Barbara and Ken McKim, Kerry Matthews, Richard Outram (R.I.P.), and Elizabeth Loveland. My deepest thanks, however, go to Alvin A. Lee, whose guiding hand has been providential, both for my own studies and in the fields in which they have taken place. My highest hope for this work is that it may live up to his uncompromising standards of scholarship and be understood as following, however falteringly, the example set by his ongoing intellectual and imaginative work. It is to him that this work is dedicated, with gratitude, on behalf of myself and all the students who have been enriched by his wisdom and teaching.

G.R.G.

Abbreviations

The following abbreviations have been used for parenthetical reference within the text.

Works by Northrop Frye

AC *Anatomy of Criticism: Four Essays.* Princeton: Princeton University Press, 1957.

CP *The Critical Path: An Essay on the Social Context of Literary Criticism.* Bloomington: Indiana University Press, 1971.

CR *Creation and Recreation.* Toronto: University of Toronto Press, 1980.

D *The Diaries of Northrop Frye, 1942–1955.* Collected Works of Northrop Frye, vol. 8. Ed. Robert D. Denham. Toronto: University of Toronto Press, 2001.

DV *The Double Vision: Language and Meaning in Religion.* Toronto: University of Toronto Press, 1991.

EAC *The Eternal Act of Creation: Essays, 1979–1990.* Ed. Robert D. Denham. Bloomington: Indiana University Press, 1993.

FI *Fables of Identity: Studies in Poetic Mythology.* New York. Harcourt, Brace and World, 1963.

FS *Fearful Symmetry: A Study of William Blake.* Princeton: Princeton University Press, 1947.

GC *The Great Code: The Bible and Literature.* New York: Harcourt Brace Jovanovich, 1982.

LN *Northrop Frye's Late Notebooks, 1982–1990: The Architecture of the Spiritual World.* 2 vols. Collected Works of Northrop Frye, vols. 5 and 6. Ed. Robert D. Denham. Toronto: University of Toronto Press, 2000.

MM *Myth and Metaphor: Selected Essays, 1974–1988.* Ed. Robert D. Denham. Charlottesville: University Press of Virginia, 1990.

NB Notebook (unpublished). Numbers refer to notebook and paragraph respectively.

NFC *Northrop Frye in Conversation.* Ed. David Cayley. Concord, Ont.: Anansi, 1992.

NFCL *Northrop Frye on Culture and Literature: A Collection of Review Essays.* Ed. Robert D. Denham. Chicago: University of Chicago Press, 1978.

NFHK *The Correspondence of Northrop Frye and Helen Kemp, 1932–1939.* 2 vols. Collected Works of Northrop Frye, vols. 1 and 2. Ed. Robert D. Denham. Toronto: University of Toronto Press, 1996.

NFLS *Northrop Frye on Literature and Society, 1936–1989.* Collected Works of Northrop Frye, vol. 10. Ed. Robert D. Denham. Toronto: University of Toronto Press, 2002.

NFR *Northrop Frye on Religion: Excluding 'The Great Code' and 'Words with Power.'* Collected Works of Northrop Frye, vol. 4. Ed. Alvin A. Lee and Jean O'Grady. Toronto: University of Toronto Press, 2000.

RT *Northrop Frye's Notebooks and Lectures on the Bible and Other Religious Texts.* Collected Works of Northrop Frye, vol. 13. Ed. Robert D. Denham. Toronto: University of Toronto Press, 2003.

RW *Reading The World: Selected Writings. 1935–1976.* Ed. Robert D. Denham. New York: Peter Lang, 1990.

SE *Northrop Frye's Student Essays, 1932–1938.* Collected Works of Northrop Frye, vol. 3. Ed. Robert D. Denham. Toronto: University of Toronto Press, 1997.

SeS *The Secular Scripture: A Study of the Structure of Romance.* Cambridge, Mass.: Harvard University Press, 1976.

SM *Spiritus Mundi: Essays on Myth, Literature, and Society.* Bloomington: Indiana University Press, 1976.

SR *A Study of English Romanticism.* Chicago: University of Chicago, 1968.

StS *The Stubborn Structure: Essays on Criticism and Society.* Ithaca: Cornell University Press, 1970.

TBN *The 'Third Book' Notebooks of Northrop Frye, 1964–1972: The Critical Comedy.* Collected Works of Northrop Frye, vol. 9. Ed. Michael Dolzani. Toronto: University of Toronto Press, 2002.

WGS *A World in a Grain of Sand: Twenty-Two Interviews with Northrop Frye.* Ed. Robert Denham. New York: Peter Lang, 1991.

WP *Words with Power: Being a Second Study of the Bible and Literature.* New York: Harcourt Brace Jovanovich, 1990.

Works by Mircea Eliade

Encyclopedia	*The Encyclopedia of Religion.* Vol. 6. New York: Macmillan, 1987.
Eternal Return	*The Myth of the Eternal Return: or, Cosmos and History.* Princeton: Princeton University Press, 1954.
Images and Symbols	*Images and Symbols: Studies in Religious Symbolism.* Princeton: Princeton University Press, 1991.
Patterns	*Patterns in Comparative Religion.* New York: Sheed and Ward, 1958.
The Sacred	*The Sacred and the Profane: The Nature of Religion.* New York: Harcourt Brace, 1959.
Shamanism	*Shamanism: Archaic Techniques of Ecstasy.* Princeton: Princeton University Press, 1964.

Works by C.G. Jung

CW 2	*Experimental Researches.* Princeton: Princeton University Press, 1973.
CW 4	*Freud and Psychoanalysis.* Princeton: Princeton University Press, 1967.
CW 5	*Symbols of Transformation.* Princeton: Princeton University Press, 1956.
CW 6	*Psychological Types.* Princeton: Princeton University Press, 1921.
CW 7	*Two Essays on Analytical Psychology.* Princeton: Princeton University Press, 1953.
CW 8	*The Structure and Dynamics of the Psyche.* Princeton: Princeton University Press, 1960.
CW 9i	*The Archetypes and the Collective Unconscious.* Princeton: Princeton University Press, 1958.
CW 10	*Civilization in Transition.* Princeton: Princeton University Press, 1964.
CW 11	*Psychology and Religion: East and West.* Princeton: Princeton University Press, 1958.
CW 12	*Psychology and Alchemy.* Princeton: Princeton University Press, 1944.
CW 13	*Alchemical Studies.* Princeton: Princeton University Press, 1968.
CW 14	*Mysterium Coniunctionis.* Princeton: Princeton University Press, 1970.
CW 16	*The Practice of Psychotherapy.* Princeton: Princeton University Press, 1954.

CW 18 *The Symbolic Life: Miscellaneous Writings.* Princeton: Princeton University Press, 1955.

Letters *Letters, Volume I: 1906–1950.* Princeton: Princeton University Press, 1973.

Memories *Memories, Dreams, Reflections.* Ed. Aniela Jaffé. New York: Vintage, 1965.

Works by Joseph Campbell

Flight *The Flight of the Wild Gander: Explorations in the Mythological Dimension.* New York: Viking, 1969.

Hero *The Hero with a Thousand Faces.* Princeton: Princeton University Press, 1949.

Inner *The Inner Reaches of Outer Space: Metaphor as Myth and as Religion.* New York: Harper and Row, 1986.

Journey *The Hero's Journey: The World of Joseph Campbell.* Ed. Phil Cousineau. San Francisco: Harper and Row, 1990.

Power *The Power of Myth.* Ed. Betty Sue Flowers. New York: Doubleday, 1988.

Primitive Mythology *The Masks of God: Primitive Mythology.* New York: Viking Press, 1959.

NORTHROP FRYE AND THE PHENOMENOLOGY OF MYTH

Introduction

Phenomenology and Modern Mythography: Northrop Frye in Context and Contrast

There must be in society a continuous fight between radical and conservative imagination.

Northrop Frye, *Fearful Symmetry* (68)

The twentieth century saw the appearance of a remarkable array of influential thinkers and theorists of the subject of myth. The middle of the century, in particular, witnessed the advent of several figures whose contributions to the study of myth are among the most significant in history. The most sophisticated and radical of these figures, Northrop Frye, has been overshadowed by some others, however, owing to a complex of pseudo-causes which include the relatively non-controversial nature of his persona and politics, a slightly narrower readership, and the misapprehension of his specific field of research (literature) as peripheral rather than central to myth studies. These extraneous factors have combined to create a false impression of Frye as a secondary or derivative thinker whose ideas about myth, insofar as they are to be discussed at all, should be discussed in relation to the ideas of other, more prominent mythologists. Chief among the objects of the present study is a redress of this misapprehension, and a reconsideration of the landscape of mid- and late twentieth-century mythography from the unexplored vistas of his revolutionary yet cogent theories.

Northrop Frye's career as a mythologist (a designation he might have resisted unless it was equated with that of literary critic) effectively begins with the writing and publication of his first book, *Fearful Symmetry* (1947), as it is there he articulates his first comprehensive theory of myth. His interest in myth considerably predates this, however, having taken root in his early academic life alongside his interest in William Blake, whose poetry is the ostensible topic of the book. Frye's encounter in 1931 with the work of Oswald Spengler, a philosopher who observed mythic patterns in history, was 'the first of several epiphanic experiences which turned vague personal ambitions into one great vision,' and led to a period of 'several years' where he 'practically slept' with Spengler's *Decline of the West* 'under his pillow' (Ayre 65, *RW* 321). Frye would later describe the encounter as yielding a sudden 'vision of coherence' in which 'things began to form patterns and make sense': a set of phrases and a tone he would later repeat when reporting similar peak experiences while studying Blake and James Frazer in 1934 (*NFC* 47–9). Of the insight and inspiration he derived from Frazer's massive study of myth, *The Golden Bough*, Frye confided:

> It's a whole new world opening out ... [this] sort of thing is the very lifeblood of art, and the historical basis of art. My ideas are expanding and taking shape so quickly that they frighten me; I get seized with terror sometimes that somebody else will think them out before I do, or that I shan't live long enough to complete anything. I shan't live very long in any case, of course; but that doesn't matter if I make the contribution I seem destined to make. (*NFHK* 355)

With Frazer as his departure point and Blake as his guide, Frye began developing what eventually became the theory of *Fearful Symmetry*, a 'contribution' that took another thirteen years to appear but which was in the end faithful to its epiphanic origins. Along the way, Frye made smaller forays into the study of myth, writing graduate student papers on the concept of religious sacrifice, fertility cults, the Augustinian interpretation of history, and other myth-related topics,[1] and reading the work of those other major figures in twentieth-century mythography, Sigmund Freud and C.G. Jung. So interested was he in the theories of Jung in particular that he forced himself to read them only cursorily until he could finish his own book, to ensure that it would not be 'overwhelmed by Jungian thought' (Ayre 425).[2] When *Fearful Symmetry* finally appeared in print in 1947, it was greeted as 'the inaugural example of what was soon to be codified in literary studies as "archetypal" or "myth" criticism' (Balfour 1). For many the book was not merely of critical interest, but struck the deeper chord usually reserved for religious awakenings or existential realizations. Stories abounded of students and readers staying up all night to study it, carrying copies of it wherever they went, and reading them to tatters (Ayre 204–5). In her review of it, English poet and critic Edith Sitwell announced:

> The book is of extraordinary importance, not only for the light it throws on Blake, but also philosophically and religiously ... It is a book of great wisdom, and every page opens fresh doors on to the universe of reality and that universe of the transfusion of reality which is called art.[3]

More than simply a study of William Blake, *Fearful Symmetry* is a presentation of a theory of the mythic source and unity of literature, which is underwritten by its compelling discussion of the broader human potential for mythic states of consciousness. In the book Frye presents Blake's corpus of poetry as a prime example of how myth provides the basis and structure of literature, and of how literature is the primary discourse generated by and constitutive of mythic consciousness. His other major theoretical statements, as well as several shorter books and dozens of essays, are concerned, in one way or another, with the development of the principles introduced in *Fearful Symmetry*. It contains, as Daniel O'Hara suggests, 'the essential Frye' (O'Hara 152).

The notion that myth is its own mode of thought, and constitutes the matrix of literature, did not originate with Frye, of course, but is quite ancient. One finds it debated in the earliest philosophy of the West, the writings of Plato and Aristotle, which in turn influenced the theologies of the Church fathers. This deep rooting of the issue of myth in the foundations of western culture ensured that it would be a perennial if diffuse concern of major thinkers ever after. Medieval writers consistently allegorized the myths of the ancient world, and the artists and philosophers of the Renaissance and Romantic periods were deeply involved in the study of myth as they reinterpreted the texts and ideas of the classical and early Christian traditions. The outset of the twentieth century, however, saw the study of myth consolidated and invigorated by the anthropological and psychological speculations of James Frazer and Sigmund Freud, and their students and followers. The simultaneous appearance in 1912 of the third and final edition of Frazer's *The Golden Bough*, Freud's *Totem and Taboo*, Jane Harrison's *Themis*, and Jung's *Symbols of Transformation*[4] has led many to regard this year as the watershed date in modern mythography, and it is worth noting that it is also the year of Northrop Frye's birth. Literary critics were quick to draw upon this proliferation of new theories of myth and immediately put them to work in their own field. By 1914, Gilbert Murray and Francis Cornford had unleashed Frazer's and Harrison's ideas upon Greek comedy and the plays of Shakespeare, establishing what was to become known as the Cambridge Ritual School. Other important theoretical statements and applications followed, including Jessie Weston's *From Ritual to Romance* (1920), which represented a major Frazerian effort to substantiate the connections between myth and literature (and was itself an inspiration for several major works of literature, most notably T.S. Eliot's *The Waste Land*). The psychological theories of Freud and Jung took longer for critics to digest than the mythic anthropology of Frazer, but their dissemination into literary studies soon developed a comparable momentum. Maud Bodkin's *Archetypal Patterns in Poetry* demonstrated the applicability of Jung's early theories to literature and attained a huge readership after its publication in 1934, by which time Freudian studies of literature had accumulated in numbers too great to warrant enumeration. The young Northrop Frye was more than just an avid reader of these works; he had tangible connections to some of them. He befriended G. Wilson Knight at the University of Toronto, whose *Wheel of Fire* (1931) and *The Starlit Dome* (1941) were major early contributions to mythopoetics, and he visited Knight's brother Jackson in England in 1936 while Jackson was writing *The Cumaean Gates: A Reference of the Sixth Aeneid to the Initiation Pattern* (Ayre 127).

A wide range of theories, disciplines, and applications was involved in this first wave of modern mythography, but an element common to them was the methodological tendency to objectify myth, as both a mode of thought and a cultural discourse, for empirical study. This general theoretical disposition resulted from the implicit assumption that myth was someone else's practice, if not someone else's problem. While there certainly were signs of admiration and nostalgia in the writings of these foundational modern mythologists, myth for them predominantly was an aspect of an Other, an immature if not problematic habit of mind exhibited by cultures distant in time and space, or manifested by a patient or analysand under therapy. Whether it was presented as primitive, as it was in Frazer, or pathological, as it was in Freud, myth was something to be outgrown, sublimated, or otherwise negotiated, as demonstrated in *The Golden Bough*'s tripartite cultural progression of magic, religion, and science, or *Totem and Taboo*'s association of mythic thought with neurosis.[5] This assumption was neatly reflected in the work of the first generation of mythopoeic critics, who scrupulously applied Frazerian, Freudian, and early Jungian methodologies. Poems and plays were interpreted as the faint echoes of primitive rites and rituals through the Frazerian 'comparativist method.' The mythic compulsions and neuroses of authors and fictional characters were diligently diagnosed through the developing principles of Freudian psychoanalysis. The appeal of the so-called 'classics' was determined to be a function of their uniform allegorical depiction of descents into the Jungian unconscious, their manifestation of vague patterns of death and rebirth.

This objectifying methodological tendency was reversed in the second phase of modern mythography, which saw not only an influx of new mythologists but also an updating of approach by the youngest of the major foundational theorists. While the empirical disposition continued in the 'functionalist' approaches of anthropology (persisting in the works of Bronislaw Malinowski and Claude Lévi-Strauss, for instance), the most influential new theories of myth in psychology, literary criticism, and religious studies were distinguished by their inquiries into the concrete, lived experience of myth. The ostensible focus of their attention was myth's phenomenological nature and structure, if not its existential priority, and the possibility of a modern restoration of it. Theirs were renewed inquiries into myth as an alternative if not 'higher' form of consciousness, with access to or constitutive of an ultimate 'reality' or 'being,' questions that had not been openly posed since the poetry of the great Romantics and the idealist philosophy of Kant and Schelling. Such queries had re-emerged from beneath the Victorian veneer of rationalism and progressivism that had informed Frazer's[6] and Freud's approaches to myth, at least partly in response to a cultural need to mitigate the painful collective experience of two world wars and the global onset of various ideologies of materialism and political extremism. To note this practical, historically rooted imperative, however, takes nothing away from the theoretical legitimacy of these inquiries.

For the second generation of modern mythologists, this new context meant that simply recognizing and identifying the latent structures and logic of mythic thought (which was the revelatory appeal of Frazer and Freud) was not enough. They wished to develop an understanding of the actual experience of myth, and enhance participation in it. Their working assumption was that myth endured in psychology, religion, and literature, not because such discourses were the lingering residual aftereffects of mythic consciousness, but because they were the modern cultural manifestations of it. For them myth was the voice of a perennial or eternal human spirit or condition that continually whispered through the vagaries of history. It was an undercurrent of wisdom that served as the guiding principle behind whatever essential continuities could be observed in human life and culture, and which offered opportunities for fuller experience if one only bothered to learn its language. As such, myth served as the dialectical complement, if not the outright opposite, of the various discourses of modernism that had fuelled the vast cultural conflicts of the first half of the twentieth century, and which had ironically limited the mythography of the previous generation. Thus the focus of study for the second-generation mythologists became the experience of mythic reality and the reality of mythic experience. Their self-appointed Promethean task was to secure for humanity an awareness of the creative 'power' of myth, as it was variously defined and theorized in their writings. This high degree of existential concern meant that the work of these younger mythologists enjoyed, even more than that of their predecessors, the rare coincidence of academic influence and popular acclaim.

Methodologically, this approach was, as we have suggested, phenomenological in nature, both generally and specifically, informed as it was by a general regard for the phenomenal that abides the whole history of philosophy, as well as by ideas from the specific discipline known as phenomenology. The second generation of modern mythologists inherited an awareness of the role of human experience in relation to metaphysics through their engagement with a proto-phenomenological tradition that extends from Heraclitus's and Aristotle's concern for the particular, through the writings of thinkers like Plotinus and Vico, to the work of Immanuel Kant. The advent of phenomenology proper in the theories of G.W.F. Hegel and Edmund Husserl introduced them to the idea of reality as contingent upon experience, and, more broadly, bequeathed to them a branch of philosophy devoted specifically to studying the nature and structure of human consciousness. Central to this field of philosophy and, consequently, of considerable importance to these mythologists was Husserl's discovery of the *intentionality* of consciousness, the recognition that 'consciousness is always consciousness *of* something' (*Cartesian Meditations* 40–1). The idea that consciousness requires an object (an idea, emotion, or concrete thing, which is conventionally referred to, therefore, as an *intentional object*) allowed for the *reduction* or *bracketing* (to use the proper phenomenological terms) of inquiry from the criteria of other disciplines and approaches to the fundamental relations of consciousness itself and the phenomena that it manifests in the very act of thought. While this principle necessarily gave Husserl's phenomenology a somewhat anti-metaphysical bias, it nevertheless, through its emphasis on phenomena as primarily mental apprehensions, conceived of consciousness as 'transcendental subjectivity' (*Cartesian Meditations* 18–21).

The work of Husserl's student Martin Heidegger, however, grounded the concept of intentionality by factoring in the physical as well as the mental aspect of human experience, in an effort to push it beyond the Cartesian mind-body dualism that shores up, if only through analogy, traditional metaphysics. Early in his career, Heidegger thus conceived of consciousness as what he called *Dasein*, a state of 'Being-there' or of 'Being-in-the-world,' the root condition of human experience from which existence is constituted. The principle of *Dasein*, according to Heidegger, establishes that existence is a function of experience, a fact which necessitates the reduction of ontology, that branch of metaphysics concerned with absolute reality, to phenomenology; or as he explains in the introduction to his influential study *Being and Time*:

> Phenomenology is the way of access to, and the demonstrative manner of determination of, what is to become the theme of ontology. *Ontology is only possible as phenomenology* ... Essentially, nothing else stands 'behind' the phenomena of phenomenology. (*Basic Writings* 82)

Heidegger's later writings on phenomenology were also of great significance to second-generation mythography for the emphasis that they placed on the role of language in human perception and the construction of phenomena. As Heidegger writes in the oft-quoted opening to his 'Letter on Humanism':

> Language is the house of Being. In its home man dwells. Those who think and those who create with words are guardians of this home. Their guardianship accomplishes the manifestation of Being insofar as they bring the manifestation to language and maintain it in language ... (*Basic Writings* 217).

Language, in other words, is the primary means by which the phenomena of perceived reality or existence are brought into being by consciousness, in what Heidegger regarded as a philosophical extension or analogy of the primordial moment of divine creation. Accepting Aristotle's understanding of myth as *mythos*, as a 'story' or 'plot,' an essentially verbal reality, Heidegger emerges as a central figure, if not a founding one, of what we are calling the phenomenology of myth.

Following Heidegger, French philosopher Maurice Merleau-Ponty grounded phenomenology still further through his insistence on a radical interconnection of body and mind in consciousness, in what is a decidedly post-metaphysical definition of existent phenomena and a profoundly anti-abstractionist understanding of the role of language in its creation. In Merleau-Ponty's 'ontology of the flesh,' as it has been called, the human body is not just the location of consciousness in the world but rather 'a crucial moment in the genesis of the objective world.' As he puts it in his ground-breaking study *Phenomenology of Perception*:

> since the genesis of the objective body is only a moment in the constitution of the object, the body ... will carry with it the intentional threads linking it to its surroundings and finally reveal to us the perceiving subject as the perceived world. (*Phenomenology* 72)

In Merleau-Ponty's view, consciousness is not simply situated in the phenomenal world, as in Heidegger's *Dasein*: it is radically and indissolubly embodied in and with it, such that there is no aspect of consciousness that is not mediated by the experience of sensory perception and physical form. Language is necessarily implicated in this condition, too, for as the philosopher deduces:

> [W]e have the experience of ourselves, of that consciousness which we are, and it is on the basis of this experience that all linguistic connotations are assessed, and precisely through it that language comes to have any meaning at all for us. (*Phenomenology* xv)

Human consciousness, for Merleau-Ponty, is a fusion of sensory perception, thought, and language working simultaneously to bring the phenomenal world into existence. 'We take up this unfinished world in an effort to complete and conceive it,' he explains (*Phenomenology* xx). In terms even more theologically suggestive than Heidegger's, he concludes that 'the world is precisely that thing of which we form a representation, not as men or as empirical subjects, but in so far as we are all one light and participate in the One without destroying its unity' (*Phenomenology* xii). As we shall observe later, this embodied phenomenology of Merleau-Ponty provides the strongest philosophical underwriting of the true phenomenology of myth that the second-generation modern mythologists were attempting to theorize.

Four mythologists in particular typified this phenomenological shift in modern mythography, three of whom punctuated it with the publication of masterworks in the late 1940s, and a fourth (the aforementioned foundational theorist) who worked through it in the essays on myth he wrote between 1934 and 1954. This last, of course, was Jung, whose *Symbols of Transformation*, while remarkable for its mythographic breadth and its break from the psychoanalytic school, nevertheless registered and was limited by the influence of Freud's focus on pathology. But Jung's later essays on myth, specifically those compiled in *The Archetypes and the Collective Unconscious*, clarified the contents of the mythic unconscious and advanced his theory of individuation, exploring the lived experience of myth and assigning it a productive value in the process. As Jung was working through this revision, the works of three younger mythologists confirmed the new phenomenological focus of mythography.

Scholars seldom make as impressive an entrance to their field as Northrop Frye made to literary studies with *Fearful Symmetry* in 1947, but the advent two years later of Mircea Eliade in religious studies and Joseph Campbell in comparative mythology[7] had something of the same epochal feel about it. In neither case was the appearance quite as remarkable as Frye's, whose suddenly formidable reputation had a *wunderkind* aura to it. Both Eliade and Campbell had notable previous publications. Eliade had published extensively in his native Romania in the 1930s, and his doctoral thesis, *Yoga: Immortality and Freedom*, appeared in French in 1936. Likewise, Campbell had provided commentary for a study of Navaho ceremony called *Where the Two Came to Their Father* (1943), co-authored *A Skeleton Key to Finnegans Wake* (1944) with Henry Morton Robinson, and edited thc late Heinrich Zimmer's *The King and the Corpse* (1948). But for both Eliade and Campbell 1949 marked their *de facto* theoretical debut. Eliade made his with not one but two works which remain standards in his field: a comprehensive survey of mythic symbolism called *Patterns in Comparative Religion*[8] and a shorter theoretical work entitled *The Myth of the Eternal Return*. Campbell made his with the work that may be the most widely read study of myth in English after Frazer, *The Hero with a Thousand Faces*. If 1912 is the watershed date of the first wave of modern mythography, the high-water mark of the second can be identified as the already momentous year of 1945. This *annus mirabilis* finds Jung in Basel writing one of the last essays of *The Archetypes and the Collective Unconscious*, portentously entitled 'The Phenomenology of the Spirit in Fairytales,' Eliade in Paris writing *The Myth of the Eternal Return* and the lectures that became *Patterns in Comparative Religion*, Campbell in New York working at *The Hero with a Thousand Faces*, and Frye in Toronto editing *Fearful Symmetry*.

Chief among the many similarities of these thinkers is their common theorizing of myth as, in Eliade's words, a 'valorization of human existence' and 'a complex system of coherent affirmations about the ultimate reality of things' (*Eternal Return* 3, ix). All these mythologists, and many of their commentators, recognized the phenomenological posture of their writings, with both groups invoking the term, and the terminology of, phenomenology. Despite his stature in the field commonly called the 'history of religions,' for instance, Eliade is often referred to as a 'Phenomenologist of Religion' (see Allen, and Rennie, *Changing*, for example). Eliade saw himself, in fact, as a scholar of both 'religious phenomenology and the history of religions' (*Patterns* 425). For his part, Jung likewise declared that 'my standpoint is exclusively phenomenological, that is, it is concerned with occurrences, events [and] experiences' (*CW 11* 6). Jung scholar J.J. Clarke, furthermore, observes that 'the term [phenomenology] ... began to enter [Jung's] vocabulary in the 1930's,' which is consistent with the period in question (Clarke 35). The term does not appear in the more 'middlebrow' vocabulary of Campbell's writings, or in critical commentaries on them, but his lifelong focus on the existential importance of finding what he called 'myths to live by' (the title of a collection of his essays published in 1971) could hardly be more explicitly phenomenological. Similarly, the central concern of Northrop Frye, according to Domenico Pietropaolo, is with 'the phenomenological status of the literary work' (Pietropaolo 89). 'My own approach has always been what is now being called phenomenological,' Frye once confirmed: 'That is, I am concerned not with intention but with intentionality.'[9] He also wrote, in an entry in his late notebooks, that his theories are primarily a 'Phenomenology of the Imagination' (*LN* 20), a phrase that could readily constitute an alternative title for the present study.

All four of these mythologists experienced remarkable fame in the wake of their publications. Jung's contribution to psychology was confirmed as second only to Freud's, and his influence extended beyond that field through the world of art and literature and into modern occultism. Eliade's academic prestige allowed him to relocate from Paris to the University of Chicago, and establish in the United States the branch of religious studies called (ironically, some have suggested) the 'history of religions.'[10] Campbell's book exercised a huge and unexpected influence over a generation of artists, inspiring such diverse creations as the novels of Richard Adams, the films of George Lucas, and the music of 'The Grateful Dead.' Frye's study almost single-handedly retrieved Blake in particular, and Romanticism in general, from the literary lunatic fringe to which they had been relegated by the New Criticism, and fertilized Canadian literature with a strong interest in mythic themes. Above all, these works fostered the dominant theories for understanding myth and the mythic dimensions of literature, as any major survey or anthology of literary and cultural theory will indicate.[11] They collectively recovered the idea of the 'archetype' (Greek, *arche*, 'first' or 'original' + *typos*, 'form' or 'type'), a term each used in different ways to refer to the recurrent units of myth, from Neoplatonic and Gnostic obscurity and ensconced it in the vocabulary of the humanities. For over fifty years the notion has served, with varying degrees of effectiveness and critical acceptance, as a fulcrum for building insight into the deeper orders of thought and culture.

For all of this, it would be highly misleading to imply that the work of these four mythologists constituted a single school or movement, and even more so to suggest that Northrop Frye was a part of any such grouping. No sooner do we observe that *Fearful Symmetry* seems to fit comfortably into the same phase of mythography as the works of Jung, Eliade, and Campbell than we also notice the important ways in which it stands apart. While all four mythologists eventually found a capable publisher in Princeton University Press,[12] Jung, Eliade, and Campbell were published through the controversial Bollingen Foundation,[13] whereas Frye's work emerged through the main academic press. Frye did not object to his work being generally associated with theirs by virtue of their mutual focus on myth: the Harvard conference on myth he shared with Eliade and Campbell in 1960, and the footnote in *Anatomy of Criticism* that puts *Fearful Symmetry* beside the works of Campbell and Jung,[14] are indications of this (Ayre 277, *AC* 361n). But he never appeared at the infamous Eranos conferences at which the other three mythologists routinely gathered. Not only did the *Jahrbücher* editors have to rely on less original and avowedly Jungian critics to elucidate the relationship of myth to literature, but Frye reviewed the conference proceedings in tones that hinted at both mockery and suspicion. After lightly remarking that 'it must be great fun to attend these Eranos conferences,' Frye worries that they appear to be 'produced by what might be called Jungian commissars' (*NFCL* 95–6). While Frye recognized that 'no one can reasonably deny that Jung is one of the seminal thinkers of our time,' he seldom missed an opportunity to differentiate his theories from Jung's (*NFCL* 95): 'I am continually asked ... about my relation to Jung, and especially about the relation of my use of the word "archetype" to his,' he later wrote; 'I have tended to resist the association, because in my experience whenever anyone mentions it his next sentence is almost certain to be nonsense' (*SM* 117; cf. *CP* 16). Indeed, much is implied by the fact that Frye critically reviewed the works of the other three mythologists, quietly confident of both his understanding and his over-standing of them.[15] This was not ego or hubris, but a clear recognition of the importance and implications of each theorist's work, including his own. While Frye's work shared a specific historical context and a set of methodological assumptions with the other mythologists, there are problematic philosophical and ideological positions taken by their works in which his is implicated only marginally, or not at all. It is in this observation that we may begin to consider *Fearful Symmetry* as a unique contribution to the study of myth, the significance of which has been overshadowed by the eminence of the other mythologists, and the ideas of which have been hampered by the assumption that its share in these contexts and assumptions necessitates involvement in positions of a problematic nature.

The development in the 1970s and 1980s of postmodern literary theory, particularly poststructuralism and cultural materialism, has brought about a marked devaluation of the theories of Eliade, Jung, and Campbell. The consensus of these critical schools is that their theories reify traditional logocentric ontologies, and 'essentialize' various contingent principles about human agency and the formation of mythic discourse. Although similar charges have been extensively levelled at Frye's second book, the famous *Anatomy of Criticism*, *Fearful Symmetry* has remained remarkably clear of such disapprobation. This is partly because of the narrower critical reception that comes with its being a study of a single poet's work, and the fact that critiques of it have risked contending with its reputation as 'the most comprehensive, learned, illuminating, and profound book on Blake of this or any other era' (Bentley 45). But insofar as *Fearful Symmetry* offers a comprehensive theory of myth, one which did as much as any to popularize and legitimize it in literary and cultural studies, it has tended not to draw the critiques faced by the work of the other three mythologists. Frye's early theories have not proved as susceptible to dismantling through the principles of poststructuralism as Eliade's have at the hands of Robert Baird, Jung's at those of Eric Gould, or Campbell's at those of William Kerrigan. Baird's observation that Eliade 'proceeds under the essential-intuitional approach' because he just 'assume[s] that there is something out there that corresponds to the term "religion" or "the sacred," and that [we] can identify it intuitively,' is naming a procedure and observing a conceptual problem more basic than any to be found in *Fearful Symmetry* (Baird 74). Gould's insistence that Jung's theory of mythic consciousness 'depends on some arbitrarily present "other" beyond nature, language, the socio-political context, or sensory evidence' (in other words, on 'the *a priori* status' of the archetype) is citing a premise more vulnerable than any upon which Frye's theories rest (Gould 22–3). Kerrigan's criticism, that Campbell's mythic structure 'metamorphoses into a crude collage done with scissors and paste ... as if a spell had been lifted' once one recognizes that it has 'no respect for locality,' is not one that may reasonably be levelled at Frye's theory of myth, derived as it is from the meticulous study of the particulars of Blake's poetry (Kerrigan 651–5). Indeed, if a name is needed for Frye's theory of myth in *Fearful Symmetry* (and afterward) the most appropriate is certainly 'apocalyptic humanism,' a term he himself applies to Blake's poetic project, for it is from that project that his theory is derived and in it that his theory is embodied (*FS* 188). More genuinely phenomenological in his presentation, myth for Frye is, as Murray Krieger has recognized, a 'humanistic construct' that requires 'no metaphysical sanction' (Krieger 21).

Northrop Frye and *Fearful Symmetry* have also not incurred as much suspicion from the inheritors of the poststructuralist legacy, the proponents of cultural materialism. Adept as they are at discerning the political imperatives behind the theorizing of universal cultural discourses such as myth, cultural materialists have nevertheless seldom found Frye and his early work tempting targets for their theoretical and often *ad hominem* ideological unmaskings. A rare example, the criticism levelled by Daniel O'Hara in *The Romance of Interpretation: Visionary Criticism from Pater to de Man* – that *Fearful Symmetry* espouses a hostility toward nature – has already been well answered by Caterina Nella Cotrupi (and will be discussed further in chapter 4). But never has Frye's work suffered inclusion in a study like Ivan Strenski's *Four Theories of Myth in Twentieth-Century History*, for instance, which holds Eliade to be a trafficker of absence, a purveyor of the 'illusion' of myth[16] whose project is further tainted by his early nationalist affiliations (Strenski 70–128). Nor has Frye drawn the attention of a critic like Robert Ellwood, whose book *The Politics of Myth* examines the conservative and even fascist political entanglements of the 'midcentury mythic trinity' of Jung, Eliade, and Campbell (Ellwood 1). While Ellwood's text is instrumental in putting various damaging charges against these mythologists into perspective, the need for such a study is itself instructive. The simple fact that Jung's idealist roots and rhetoric need to be differentiated from those of German National Socialism, that Eliade's mythography needs to be separated from his involvement in Romanian fascism, and that Campbell's work needs to be rescued from the stigma of his being an anti-Semitic and anti-communist Republican suggests that these three are markedly different from Northrop Frye. Whatever politics the mild Canadian had are innocuous in comparison, if not grounds for commendation. Frye's support of a liberal-left political party (the CCF, later NDP),[17] his recognition of the interpenetration of regional, national, and global identities, and his consistent if qualified sympathy with Marx[18] suggest his thought is thoroughly conversant with the broad political and social agenda of cultural materialism (something our study will substantiate). The most troublesome biographical detail that critics have observed about Northrop Frye, that he was an ordained minister in the United Church of Canada, is only occasionally cited. When it is, the fact that this is one of the most liberal churches in the world, or that Frye never actually held a clerical post in it, or that he had reservations about being ordained in the first place[19] is usually omitted in order to create an aura of conservatism that inevitably dissolves upon a closer examination of his life and work.

But the most significant ways in which Frye's work stands outside and apart from the theoretical assumptions and latent conservatism of the Eranos theorists are revealed through his comments on their work. While Frye acknowledges that Eliade's *Patterns in Comparative Religion* is 'a remarkable introduction to the grammar of comparative symbolism,' he is uncomfortable with its implied project of trying to revive the notion that 'in fact there is such a thing as a universal natural theology' (*NFCL* 100–1). For Frye, such a position is suspiciously retrograde: 'The difference between superstition and religion, which seems to disappear in Mr. Eliade's argument,' writes Frye, 'is that in religion ... feelings are transferred from the physical to the spiritual world, from outer time and space to inner experience' (*NFCL* 106). Frye resists Eliade's principle that the forms of religion are derived from the forms of the external or conceptual world because, in his view, this involves an implicitly conservative estimation of the powers of human consciousness, which in turn places intolerable limits on a theory of myth. If Eliade's theory locates the roots of myth and religion too much outside and beyond human consciousness, then Frye sees Jung as making the same mistake in the other direction, that is, locating myth too much beneath consciousness. Frye thus finds Jung's sense of mythic consciousness to be equally conservative, by virtue of his distant rooting of myth in the collective unconscious, and his mitigation of it by a stubborn individualism:

> There is, to use his own term, a complex in Jung's mind that makes him balk like a mule in front of the final acceptance of the totality of the self, the doctrine that everybody is involved in the fate of everybody else, which the uncompromising charity of the great religions invariably insists on. His 'collective unconscious' is actually the total mythopoeic power of humanity and has nothing to do with ancestor cults of 'racial differentiation,' or groping around in the windy bowels of Teutonic exclusivism. But the explicit affirmation of this obvious fact seems to stick in his throat. (*NFCL* 121)

This limitation of Jung's, which we can observe Campbell chafing against in his notion of a universal mythic hero, stands in marked contrast to the unabashed emphasis that Frye's theory places on a single unified and redeemed humanity, 'the eternal reality of Everyman's existence, the spiritual form of Everyman' (*FS* 248). If there is a structure and limit to human mythic consciousness, Frye would argue, it can only be the totality of human mythic consciousness, and thus this is the only structure and limit his phenomenology of myth recognizes: Christ's last prayer before the crucifixion is *ut unum sint*, 'That they may be one' (John 17:11), or as Blake writes, 'More! Is the cry of the mistaken soul, less than All cannot satisfy Man' (Blake 2).

All of this begins to suggest that we have in *Fearful Symmetry* the first work of the most liberal and radically humanistic mythologist of the twentieth century. More importantly, we have in it a theory of myth that is potentially revolutionary for its being genuinely phenomenological and not contingent upon an abstract or abstracted source or authority (what in postmodern theories of signification is called a 'transcendental signified'). That this assessment is not congruent with the reputation of conservatism and distinguished obsolescence *Fearful Symmetry* shares with the works of the Eranos mythologists means that it must be verified by testing Frye's mythography against those with which it has been associated (and, if one subscribes to the ideological critiques, rendered complicitous). This can only be done by proceeding with a comparative study of the theories of Jung, Eliade, Campbell, and Frye which examines their respective hypotheses about myth, while considering the implications of each for human consciousness and agency, and their relationship to what has been called the metaphysics of presence. Such a comparison, especially if it inclines in the direction of differentiation, is much needed and long overdue. The misconception in question has built up considerable inertia through the sheer number of anthologies, articles, surveys, and critical histories that associate Frye's thought with that of Jung, Eliade, and Campbell because of their common historical context and general subject. It will not be corrected unless a study is undertaken which compares and contrasts their mythographies as individual theories.

Four elements in the various theories of myth are ripe for comparison, all of which have already been alluded to or implied. First, there are the respective *definitions* of myth to be considered: What is 'myth' for each mythologist? Where in culture is it to be located? What is it that is being studied and theorized? What is the definition and status of the individual unit of myth that each conventionally calls an 'archetype'? Secondly, the hypothesis of each about the source and origin of myth, whether presented implicitly or explicitly, must be examined: What explanation is offered to account for *mythogenesis*, the generation of myth? By implication, this question takes us toward the most critical issues from a phenomenological point of view: How does myth emerge from and/or act upon human consciousness? How is it experienced? What sort of human subject does each theory of myth postulate or assume? Third, there is the question of myth's *structure*: What form does myth take in consciousness and/or culture? Can and do the archetypes of myth form a whole? And last, the *function* of myth that each mythologist demonstrates or assumes must be discerned: What is myth's role or purpose? What are its effects? What can be made of myth? Does it have what in philosophical terms we would call a 'teleology,' or in more humanistic terms, a 'destiny'?

We cannot hope to answer all these questions adequately, only to consider them enough to develop an understanding of Frye's theory in relation to the major mythographies of its milieu, and allow us to explore those mythographies as potential models of consciousness. Having gestured toward such a consideration already, we can see that from the particular hypothesis under review with regard to *Fearful Symmetry* unfold the following distinctions, which will be substantiated in the subsequent chapters of this study: Mircea Eliade's theory attempts a phenomenological presentation of the traditional Platonic conception of myth as descendant of ideal or transcendent forms. C.G. Jung's theory involves the overturning of this traditional structure, consistent with the Romantic tendency to invert traditional philosophical systems, and thus theorizes myth as ascendant from a similarly abstracted repository of forms located beneath consciousness. Joseph Campbell's theory attempts to see myth as both of these things simultaneously, mirroring each other in the human subject in what at times appears to be a fusion of traditional and Jungian perspectives. In contrast to these, Northrop Frye's Blakean theory of myth presents it as truly phenomenological, a genuinely creative act of human consciousness which opposes or augments historical and material consciousness not by speculating on what might lie beyond it, but by generating something that does.

one

De Caelis: The Platonic Patterns of Mircea Eliade

Reality is a function of the imitation of a celestial archetype.

Mircea Eliade, *The Myth of the Eternal Return* (5)

At first glance, Mircea Eliade's two texts of 1949, *Patterns in Comparative Religion* and *The Myth of the Eternal Return,* appear to be separate studies of myth that happen to have been published by the same author in the same year. Upon closer examination, however, one begins to suspect that the two works have been contrived to approach the subject of myth and mythic experience from opposite directions in order to provide a complete theory. While *Patterns* is broad, encyclopedic, and concerned with the arrangement of mythic space, *Eternal Return* is focused, theoretical, and presented as a discussion of the nature of mythic time. Together they constitute the backbone of Eliade's canon, and work in concert to present his theory of myth.

The central concept of that theory is the binary opposition that Eliade sets up between the *sacred* and the *profane,* which he presents as opposing ontological, perceptual, and cultural categories. A theory of myth typically requires a distinction to be drawn between a realm of experience and a discourse that is potentially mythic from one that is not, and much depends, we shall discover, on whether this distinction is deductively presumed or inductively established. In both of Eliade's texts of 1949 (and in most of his books in fact), the discussion proceeds from an explicit delineation of thesc categories. Eliade's terms themselves are adapted from the work of Emile Durkheim, but the distinction he draws between them is more essential than any that those in the French school of sociology would find it necessary to make. First and foremost, he maintains that the sacred is best understood simply as 'the opposite of the profane' (*Patterns* xviii), but his discussion thoroughly clarifies the axes of that opposition. While the sacred is the realm of the spiritual, the eternal, the 'real,' the centred and the ordered, the transcendent and the absolute, the profane is the field of the material, the temporal and historical, the illusory, the chaotic, the contingent, and the relative. Most human experience occurs within the sphere of the profane, taking place as it does in historical time and material space. The rarer substance of mythic experience, and the subject of myth as a discourse, is the sacred, which becomes accessible and perceptible when it manifests itself amidst the profane. The divinities of religion, or the feelings of numinosity that accompany psychological realizations or intense aesthetic experience, are manifestations of the sacred.

Eliade calls a manifestation of the sacred a *hierophany* (Greek, *hiero,* sacred + *phainein,* to show), literally 'a showing of the sacred.' As he formulates it in his *Encyclopedia of Religion,* a hierophany occurs when 'a reality of an entirely different order than those of this world becomes manifest in an object that is part of the natural or profane sphere' (*Encyclopedia* 313). A 'paradoxical coming-together of sacred and profane, being and non-being, absolute and relative, the eternal and the becoming, is what every hierophany, even the most elementary, reveals' (*Patterns* 29). Functionally, however, a hierophany signals 'a more or less clear choice, a singling-out' because 'A thing becomes sacred in so far as it embodies (that is, reveals) something other than itself': something which other things of its kind do not (*Patterns* 13). There are several kinds of hierophany, Eliade specifies, such as the *kratophany* (a showing of power or force), the *theophany* (a showing of a god), and the vague *ontophany* (the showing forth of 'being' or 'reality'). An example of a kratophany might be the attribution of lightning bolts to a thunder or storm god, or the parting of the Red Sea to the power of Yahweh. An obvious example of a theophany would be divine incarnation. Insofar as the sacred for Eliade is by definition 'the real,' the notion of the ontophany seems oddly redundant, as any hierophany is a revelation of sacred reality. It seems to serve only an emphatic purpose.

That the hierophany is conceived by Eliade as a 'breakthrough in various levels of existence' and a sudden 'coexistence of contrary essences' is conveyed in the word he often substitutes for 'manifestation' in his discussions: 'irruption.' The ongoing irruption of the sacred within the realm of the profane is what Eliade calls 'the dialectic of the sacred,' 'the dialectic of hierophany,' or simply the 'hierophanization.'

According to Eliade, an awareness of this process is what mythic experience registers, particularly as it takes place under the auspices of religion: 'the dialectic of the sacred belongs to all religions,' he maintains, 'not only to the supposedly "primitive" forms. It is expressed as much in the worship of stones and trees, as in the Indian avatars, or the supreme mystery of the Incarnation' (*Patterns* 30). The sacred is the universal name for which the Melanesian word *mana*, the Sioux *wakan*, the Iroquois *orenda*, the West Indian *zemi*, the pygmy *megbe*, the Hindu *brahman*, and the Christian *holy spirit* are particulars (*Patterns* 20). From the perspective provided by mythic experience,

> neither the objects of the external world nor human acts, properly speaking, have any autonomous intrinsic value. Objects or acts acquire a value, and in doing so become real, because they participate, after one fashion or another, in a reality that transcends them. (*Eternal Return* 3–4)

This reality, the sacred, 'is a force different in quality from physical forces,' Eliade writes, 'a force that can make things powerful, *real* in the fullest sense' (*Patterns* 19–20, 21).

For Eliade, myth as a discourse and a system of rituals develops out of mythic experience by virtue of the human tendency to try to commemorate or repeat the experience of hierophany. This process involves an adoption of the object or action of the hierophany as a symbol, which is then repeated in culture as a significant image or ritual behaviour. Such repetitions often begin with, and occur most notably in, the traditional oral and written narratives we call myths, which in turn become the basis of other cultural practices that engage the sacred, such as religion and the arts.[1] Functioning symbolically, the recurrent object or behaviour is understood to perpetuate or repeat the hierophany, or even be a new and different hierophany unto itself: 'It is not only because it continues a hierophany or takes its place that a symbol is important,' Eliade writes: 'it is primarily because it is able to carry on the process of hierophanization and particularly because, on occasions, it is *itself* a hierophany' (*Patterns* 447). Eliade thus speaks of religious symbols as being 'a prolongation of hierophanies and an autonomous form of revelation' (*Patterns* 448). The purpose of such symbols is to

> carr[y] further the dialectic of hierophanies by transforming things into *something other* than what they appear to profane experience to be: a stone becomes a symbol for the centre of the world, and so on; and then, by

> becoming symbols, signs of a transcendent reality, those things abolish their material limits. (*Patterns* 452)

When Eliade uses the term *archetype*, as he frequently does in these two texts, this is what he means by it: a repeated symbol or ritual action that incarnates or otherwise partakes of the sacred. In the introduction to the 1959 reprinting of *The Myth of the Eternal Return*, Eliade clarifies his definition of the word as he distances his usage of it from Jung's:

> I have used the terms 'exemplary models,' 'paradigms,' and 'archetypes' in order to emphasize a particular fact – namely, that for the man of the traditional or archaic societies, the models for his institutions and the norms for his various categories of behaviour are believed to have been 'revealed' at the beginning of time, that, consequently, they are regarded as having a superhuman or 'transcendent' origin. In using the term 'archetype,' I neglected to specify that I was not referring to the archetypes described by Professor C.G. Jung ... [F]or Professor Jung, the archetypes are structures of the collective unconscious. But in my book I nowhere touch upon the problems of depth psychology nor do I use the concept of the collective unconscious. As I have said, I use the term 'archetype' ... as a synonym for 'exemplary model' or 'paradigm,' that is, in the last analysis, in the Augustinian sense. (*Eternal Return* xiv–xv).

We will return to the question of what is implied by Eliade's use of the appellation 'Augustinian' and the ambiguity created by the phrase 'believed to have been "revealed."' The more immediate question has to do with the role of the Eliadean archetype as an 'exemplary model': what exactly is accomplished by the repetition of hierophanies in culture through archetypes? Eliade provides an answer to this question further in *The Myth of the Eternal Return*, when he discusses 'the abolition of time through the imitation of archetypes and the repetition of paradigmatic gestures' (*Eternal Return* 35):

> A sacrifice, for example, not only exactly reproduces the initial sacrifice revealed by a god *ab origine*, at the beginning of time, it also takes place at that same primordial mythic moment; in other words, every sacrifice repeats the initial sacrifice and coincides with it. All sacrifices are performed at the same mythical instant of the beginning; through the paradox of rite, profane time and duration are suspended. And the same holds true for all repetitions, i.e., all imitations of archetypes; through such imitation, man is

> projected into the mythical epoch in which the archetypes were first revealed ... [I]nsofar as an act (or an object) acquires a certain reality through the repetition of certain paradigmatic gestures, and acquires it through that alone, there is an implicit abolition of profane time, of duration, of 'history'; and he who reproduces the exemplary gesture thus finds himself transported into the mythical epoch in which its revelation took place. (*Eternal Return* 35)

The purpose of the Eliadean archetype, in other words, is to project its perceiver or ritual adherent back to the occasion and source of its original hierophany, i.e., into the realm of the sacred. Myth is thus, for Eliade, a cultural practice whose primary aim is the recovery of origins through the maintenance of the initial revelations of the sacred. This principle requires him to replace the traditional Greek meaning of the word 'myth' with his own particular definition: 'We must get used to dissociating the idea of "myth" from "word" or "fable" (cf. the Homeric use of *mythos*: "word," "discourse") and connecting it with "sacred action," "significant gesture," and "primeval event"' (*Patterns* 416). Religion, on the other hand, as a ritualization of myth, remains quite faithful to its etymology in Eliade's view, as it is derived from the Latin *re* + *ligio* ('to link back'). What myth and religion strive to link us back to is an awareness of what Eliade sometimes calls 'hierophantic time,' or, more frequently, *illud tempus* ('that time'):[2] the age of origins and sacred experience narrated in myth, which exists prior to and apart from linear historical time (connoting therefore what religion usually calls 'eternity'). As sacred time unfolds in sacred space, the phrase has a spatial referent as well. Eliade's principle that myth is devoted to the recovery of origins compels him to regard creation or *cosmogonic* myths as having primary cultural importance. *The Myth of the Eternal Return,* in particular, outlines how a startling array of rituals, from birth and wedding rituals to healing and funeral rites, involve a recitation of or an allusion to a creation myth as a means of reconnecting ritual participants with sacred reality and rescuing them from the depredations of historical time.[3]

It is in this aspect of his theory, the recovery of mythic experience in human life and culture through archetypes, that we would expect Eliade to begin detailing a phenomenology of myth. His discussion is both vague and problematic, however, and his account of the process is hindered by assumptions he has made about the sacred that precede his phenomenological considerations, and which are in need of qualification. In particular, there is the question of what Eliade means when he says that he is using the word archetype 'in the Augustinian sense' to refer to mythic models that are '*believed* to have been "revealed" at the beginning of time' (as opposed to simply 'revealed'). The provision seems to be connected to a phenomenological focus and his apparent project of attempting to provide 'an epistemological account of the subjective experience of the sacred' (Dudley 55). The label 'Augustinian' is the more significant description, however, having to do with his central presumptions about the nature and structure of the sacred itself. Eliade is almost certainly alluding to Augustine's discussion of *de ideis* in his *De diversis quaestionibus octoginta tribus.* There the Bishop of Hippo speaks of *ideae principales* which are *ipsae formatae non sunt ac per hoc aeternae ac semper eodem modo sese habentes, quae Divina Intellegentia continentur:* 'principal ideas' or 'first forms' which are 'not themselves formed, and thus being eternal and existing always in the same state, are contained in the Divine Understanding' (46.2). *Idea principalis* is essentially a Latin equivalent of the Greek *archetypos,* for it carries the same denotative meaning. As a concept, it is central to Augustine's theory of religious knowledge, which, as he intends, is Platonic in nature and derivation.[4] Eliade's positing of the sacred as a transcendent and eternal source and reality, with a concomitant conceptual status as both *a priori* and *sui generis,* has already suggested this philosophical orientation to us, but numerous other remarks in his discussions confirm it: Eliade maintains, for instance, that 'for archaic man, reality is a function of the imitation of the celestial archetype,' which seems to be a clear allusion to the Platonic doctrine of eternal transcendent forms (*Eternal Return* 5).[5] We have also Eliade's frequent references to myth as an 'archaic' or 'primitive ontology,' by which he means a traditional means of trying to discern absolute reality and existence. One such reference explicitly acknowledges the philosophical tradition in question (*Eternal Return* 44):

> [A]n object or act becomes real only insofar as it imitates or repeats an archetype. Thus, reality is acquired solely through repetition or participation; everything which lacks an exemplary model is 'meaningless' ... Hence it could be said that this 'primitive' ontology has a Platonic structure; and in that case Plato could be regarded as the outstanding philosopher of 'primitive mentality,' that is, as the thinker who succeeded in giving philosophic currency and validity to the modes of life and behavior of archaic humanity. Obviously, this in no way lessens the originality of his philosophic genius; for his great title to our admiration remains his effort to justify this vision of

archaic humanity theoretically, through the dialectic means which the spirituality of his age made available to him. (*Eternal Return* 34–5)

What proceeds from an ontological premise necessarily becomes an entire metaphysical system, and this too Eliade acknowledges: 'Myth expresses in action and drama what metaphysics and theology define dialectically,' he writes; 'only its limited means of expression ... distinguish it from the developed and coherent systems of theology and metaphysics' (*Patterns* 418, 384). 'If one goes to the trouble of penetrating the authentic meaning of an archaic myth or symbol, one cannot but observe that this meaning ... implies a metaphysical position' (*Eternal Return* 3). We must take special note of the clause that follows Eliade's important definition of myth quoted earlier: 'a complex system of coherent affirmations about the ultimate reality of things, *a system that can be regarded as constituting a metaphysics*' (*Eternal Return* 3, italics added).

That Eliade's notion of the sacred has a Platonic ancestry should not come as a surprise to anyone acquainted with his academic background. While accounts of Eliade's early intellectual development are often dominated by discussion of the time he spent studying Eastern philosophy under the sage Surendranath Dasgupta at the University of Calcutta (1928–31), his studies prior to this at the University of Bucharest (1925–8) were equally formative.[6] It was during this time that Eliade produced an MA thesis on Renaissance philosophy from Marsilio Ficino to Giordano Bruno, a period of Italian intellectual history dominated by the revival of Platonic philosophy. Eliade's study appears to have suffused his thought with the principles of mystical Platonism, which evidently became the philosophical foundation of his mature work.

The Platonic basis of Eliade's theory of myth presents a number of problems, however, owing to the fact that it assumes the sacred has *a priori*, objective and transcendent reality. As Robert Baird observes, '[n]ot only are the hierophanies which he describes hierophanies for those involved, but they are *in fact* hierophanies ... an ontology has been posited from the start' (Baird 87). This generally places more emphasis in his theory on pure metaphysics and less on phenomenology and the human experience of myth and, in particular, makes the true locus of reality a transcendent realm inaccessible to human consciousness as such. The first effect of this is that it renders his notion of the sacred terminally hypothetical and speculative: the source of hierophanies and the sanction and destination of archetypes remain perpetually unknowable and unrealizable, as the transcendent reality behind particular manifestations of the sacred is never in evidence to human experience. For a human thinker, ensconced in space and time, to insist that a phenomenal event is a hierophany and therefore evidence of an *a priori*, noumenal sacred realm is like a land-dweller who cannot swim insisting that waves on the surface of a murky lake are caused by an enormous fish: it is a hypothesis of questionable plausibility which he has no means of verifying, and may well be a mistaken attribution of his own influence to an external source. It may be objected, of course, that things such as faith and mystery must have a place in a theory of myth and religion like Eliade's. This may be true, but if such a theory is not immediately to devalue our embodied human existence as well as our higher faculties (creativity, rational thought), that place must be nearer the destination of the theory and not its point of departure. The second effect of Eliade's Platonism is that it also attributes agency to the sacred: Eliade's theory, as Guilford Dudley recognizes, 'holds that the sacred manifests itself ... by a self-initiated act' (Dudley 54–5). With reality and agency consolidated in the transcendent realm, human mythic experience is reduced to the simple matter of registering the residual comings and goings of the sacred, presumed through the veil of material existence, and preserving them as effectively as possible.

This ancillary action is presented repeatedly in Eliade's discussions of the experience of his mythic subject, what he calls in his texts of 1949 'archaic' or 'primitive man,' but would later famously dub *homo religiosus* in *The Sacred and the Profane* (1957). Despite the connotations of the adjectives 'archaic' and 'primitive,' it is not Eliade's intention to anteriorly position his mythic subject in history so much as to stress that that mythic experience seems to occur more fully and more frequently in so-called 'primitive' cultures and states of mind. As John Cave observes, Eliade means his terms 'to refer to all humans,' because they 'designate a quality of the human condition' (Cave 92). '*Homo religiosus* is not a historical but an archetypal religious man,' Baird echoes, as '[h]istorical persons participate in this archetype to various degrees' (Baird 86). What we notice immediately about the mythic experience of Eliade's 'archaic man' is that it is presented as coming simply as a result of his *contemplatio mundi*, his contemplation of the natural, external world and his reception of sense stimuli from it. Eliade does not use this Latin expression for the act, but it is suitable insofar as it encompasses both the act of passively perceiving and the act of reflecting upon the physical universe.

We notice this particularly in *Patterns in Comparative Religion* as Eliade outlines the hierophanies that establish the various structures of natural symbolism. His description of the hierophany of the sky, for instance, leaves little doubt that he regards mythic (metaphysical) experience as something that presents itself to *homo religiosus,* who plays only a limited role in its becoming mythic in the form of a 'heaven' or a 'sky god':

> There is no need to look into the teachings of myth to see that the sky itself directly reveals a transcendence, a power and a holiness. Merely contemplating the vault of heaven produces a religious experience in the primitive mind ... Such contemplation is the same as revelation. The sky shows itself as it really is: infinite, transcendent. The vault of heaven is, more than anything else, 'something quite apart' from the tiny thing that is man and his span of life. The symbolism of transcendence derives from the simple realization of its infinite height. 'Most High' becomes quite naturally an attribute of the divinity. The regions above man's reach, the starry places, are invested with the divine majesty of the transcendent, of absolute reality, of everlastingness ... The 'high' is something inaccessible to man as such; it belongs by right to superhuman powers and beings ... All this derives from simply contemplating the sky ... [E]ven before any religious values have been set upon the sky it reveals its transcendence. The sky 'symbolizes' transcendence, power and changelessness simply by being there ... The transcendence of God is directly revealed in the inaccessibility, infinity, eternity and creative power (rain) of the sky. The whole nature of the sky is an inexhaustible hierophany. (*Patterns* 39–40)

The subordination, if not a relative abjection, of the human subject is well in evidence here. The most that is afforded *homo religiosus* is that his 'contemplation is the same as revelation,' which, despite the evocative parallelism, is saying that mythic experience is a simple matter of passively receiving sense data from the objective universe. Indeed, Eliade is careful to stress that any other human faculties, beyond the merely perceptive, are not required in the incurring of mythic experience: 'The sky,' he writes, 'needs no aid from mythological imagination or conceptual elaboration to be seen as *the* divine sphere' (*Patterns* 54). What Eliade is overlooking here is that for something to be seen as anything whatsoever, and particularly as something relevant to human life and experience, requires some sort of imagination, elaboration, or interpretation. We shall encounter this crucial principle when we turn to the mythic theory of Frye's *Fearful Symmetry.*

Other discussions of the natural hierophanies in Eliade's *Patterns* suggest that his mythic subject is essentially a primitive Platonic or Neoplatonic philosopher. A passage in which this is particularly discernible is his account of archaic man's perception of the potential sacredness of rocks and stones:

> The hardness, ruggedness, and permanence of matter was in itself a hierophany in the religious consciousness of the primitive. And nothing was more direct and autonomous in the completeness of its strength, nothing more noble or more awe-inspiring, than a majestic rock, or a boldly standing block of granite. Above all, stone *is*. It always remains itself, and exists of itself ... Rock shows him something that transcends the precariousness of his humanity: an absolute mode of being. Its strength, its motionlessness, its size and its strange outlines are none of them human: they indicate the presence of something that fascinates, terrifies, attracts and threatens, all at once. In its grandeur, its hardness, its shape and its color, man is faced with a reality and a force that belong to some world other than the profane world of which he is himself a part. (*Patterns* 216)

In his insistence that the mythic experience of *homo religiosus* stems from his recognition that a stone 'always remains itself,' Eliade is not even affording him the awareness of elemental flux and change that is an attribute of Heraclitean philosophy. What Eliade's mythic subject is apparently experiencing is, as Bryan Rennie observes, that which exists '*beyond* the actual existence of the stone ... the *quality* of strength of hardness, the *concept* of absoluteness, the *implications* of motionlessness, the *otherness* of inhumanity. All abstract, notional, conceptual ideas' (Rennie, *Reconstructing* 18): ideas, in other words, which correspond more to the Platonic *eidos* than anything else. Similar contentions of Eliade, such as that 'water implies regeneration,' or that 'the mere existence of the soil' inspires the hierophany of the Earth, also suggest that he subscribes to a Platonic model of metaphysical awareness (*Patterns* 189, 242).

We must recognize, however, that it is not solely Eliade's Platonism that is responsible for his painting this diminutive picture of humanity with regard to mythic experience, for it is only by way of implication that Platonic principles can be seen as inclined against humanist ones. When Eliade emphasizes the otherness of the sacred, speaks of it as something 'that fascinates, terrifies, attracts and threatens,' or refers to 'the tiny thing that is man and his span of life,' he is revealing the influence of a thinker more convinced of the subordination of humanity before the transcendent than Plato. The abjection of *homo religiosus* in relation to the sacred as articulated by Eliade bears close resemblance to the poor standing of humanity before *Das Heilige* (German, 'The Holy'),[7] as outlined in Rudolf Otto's *The Idea of the Holy* (1917). Although it was not until *The Sacred and the Profane* that Eliade explicitly acknowledged the influence of Otto, that influence can be felt just as readily in Eliade's discussion of the experience of 'archaic man' in his texts of 1949 (*The Sacred* 8). His notion of the sacred itself is a Platonic inheritance, but 'there is no doubt that Eliade accepts as his starting point Otto's concept' when it comes to discussing the relation of *homo religiosus* to it (Rennie, *Reconstructing* 27). Eliade's 'archaic man' regards the sacred as what Otto calls the *mysterium tremendum et fascinans*, the 'terrible and fascinating mystery.' The sacred is existentially to him something *ganz andere* ('wholly other'), which possesses 'an overwhelming superiority of power' over him (*The Sacred* 9). Eliade's adoption of this perspective not only results in his mythic subject being resigned to the abject position outlined in the passages quoted above, but also reveals to his reader the troubling contradiction upon which his theory of myth is built: it is, as Hans Penner writes, 'the problem of a phenomenology of religion without a defined object, for the object is, and remains, "wholly other"' (Penner 127).[8]

Homo religiosus is no more formidable a figure when it comes time to proceed from the recognition of hierophanies to the repetition of them in culture as archetypes. That a hierophany is, apparently, the presentation of a pre-existent abstract concept or transcendent category means that the human faculties employed in the adoption and repetition of its object are imitative, and not creative. Eliade argues contrariwise in *The Myth of the Eternal Return*, that having an awareness of hierophanies and the ability to repeat them in his own life affords his mythic subject a degree of agency and creativity, as he possesses the ability to renew time and reality archetypally (*Eternal Return* 154–9): 'The man of archaic civilizations can be proud of his mode of existence, which allows him to be free and to create,' he insists: 'He is free ... to annul his history through the periodic abolition of time and collective regeneration' (*Eternal Return* 157). Insofar as Eliade is here comparing the agency and creativity of *homo religiosus* to that of profane man (who has no such perception of or influence over his history and reality), he is correct. But as will become evident when we turn our attention to the manifold structure of Eliade's archetypes, the reality that is mythically recognized and renewed through those archetypes is more natural than human, one that is thrust upon humanity rather than one of its own creation: Eliadean archetypes are 'extrahuman models' (*Eternal Return* 95). An awareness of the implications of this fact seems to be behind several surprisingly negative concessions Eliade makes in *Eternal Return*. He allows, for instance, that, 'viewed in its proper perspective, the life of archaic man' is 'a life reduced to the repetition of archetypal acts,' a life devoted to 'the unceasing rehearsal of the same primordial myths,' a life 'imprisoned within the mythical horizon of archetypes and repetition' (*Eternal Return* 86, 156)

A final theoretical problem arises when we note that Eliade says next to nothing about the experience of archetypal repetition itself, its actual phenomenology, as he does not (and indeed cannot) articulate in detail the process by which it occurs. Unconcerned with and unsupported by such specifics as the operations of psychology or the subject matter of literary criticism, Eliade is less compelled to articulate the immediate experience of archetypal participation. To observe this is not to advocate deferral to another subject field, for such an articulation would not necessarily require him to attend to anything other than 'religious experience' as compiled by William James, for example. The real problem is the one of lack which we have already cited as resulting from the metaphysical basis of Eliade's theory. From a poststructuralist point of view, *homo religiosus* is saddled with the dilemma of 'absence,' for one cannot experience an abstraction or transcendental category as such, or evince the efficacy of such things beyond setting up *a priori* the conceptual necessity of it. From a phenomenological point of view, there is the apparent lack of what that philosophical discipline refers to as the intentional object, the thing by which or through which consciousness occurs, constituting actual experience to the subject. It appears that *homo religiosus* has no such object (and hence no real consciousness), not only because, as Penner observes, his presumed object is wholly other and unknowable, but also because that object has always already made an object out of him. Recall that, for Eliade, the sacred is a force of 'overwhelming superiority' whose archetypes are 'autonomous form[s] of revelation.' Their efficacy is apparently *a priori* and largely independent of archaic man's ability to receive and repeat them. There is little more that needs to be said about that process, in other words, than to observe its occurrence and its presumed result. The only accounts Eliade provides of the archetypal experience, therefore, are bald descriptions like 'ritual projects [archaic man] into the mythical epoch,' or 'an archetypal model is a reactualization of the mythical moment' (*Eternal Return* 22, 75). The verbs 'project' and 'reactualize' are in fact the only words he uses to describe the archetypal process, and it is crucial to note that they are actions that originate with the archetype itself, as symbol or ritual, and not *homo religiosus.* Each term occurs several times in *The Myth of the Eternal Return* and *Patterns in Comparative Religion,* with the result of providing little more than labels for a process which Eliade is ultimately compelled, by virtue of his metaphysical assumptions, to regard as beyond human influence, understanding, or experience. In what should be the most phenomenological part of his theory of myth, Eliade does not provide anything resembling a phenomenology. No real insight into human mythic consciousness is given, or even possible.

Everything that we have observed about Eliade's metaphysical theory of myth comes to bear, in one way or another, on his overall archetypal structure. As his primary aim (particularly in *Patterns in Comparative Religion*) is to catalogue hierophanies and archetypes, Eliade is more intent upon classifying them than arranging them in a structure. A structure is nevertheless discernible, and it is fair to assume that the theorist expects his readers to intuit its shape, especially since it follows from his theoretical assumptions. Two general principles govern the structure of Eliade's world of hierophanies and archetypes, and determine their priority (both in the sense of their relative importance and the order in which they tend to appear to *homo religiosus*). They are exactly the principles one would expect to govern the revelation of a cosmos of Platonic forms. The first is a conceptual movement from the upper to the lower, and the second is a conceptual movement from the general to the specific. Upon consideration, we recognize that the two principles are really one, the conceptual movement from transcendent to immanent form.

All things apparently proceed from the celestial or 'ouranic' hierophany, the hierophany of the sky, which sets off a mythic chain reaction of sorts by presenting to *homo religiosus* the principle of transcendence itself and presumed existence of the realm of the sacred. 'Height, "being on high," infinite space – all these are hierophanies of what is transcendent, what is supremely sacred,' writes Eliade (*Patterns* 109). Furthermore,

> The symbolism of the sky has held its position in every religious framework, simply because its mode of being is outside time; in fact, this symbolism gives meaning and support to all religious 'forms,' and yet never loses anything itself by doing so. (*Patterns* 111)

The 'celestial and atmospheric hierophanies very early became the centre of those religious experiences which made later revelations possible' (*Patterns* 94). Functionally, then,

> [T]he supreme sky god everywhere gives place to other religious forms. The morphology of this substitution may vary; but its meaning is in each case partly the same: it is a movement away from the transcendence and passivity of sky beings towards more dynamic, active and easily accessible forms. One might say that we are observing a 'progressive descent of the sacred into the concrete.' (*Patterns* 52)

A host of other archetypal specifications thus typically follow the prime ouranic hierophany, extensions or centrings of the revelation of transcendence and eternality. These include sun gods, storm gods, and other celestial entities,[9] the mythic valuation of mountains and other high places, and any ritual action involving ascension or upward movement. All other archetypal regions and figures are assumed to have as their metaphysical guarantor the celestial or ouranic realm.

Next come the *chthonic* and lunar hierophanies, the hierophanies of the earth and the moon. Eliade is not specific as to which type of hierophany comes first, but he makes it clear that they are connected by virtue of their shared governance over all the mythic rhythms and cycles of life and time: the totality of the earth upholds all forms of life and cycles of time, of which the moon's phases dictate or register the progression. The 'sub-lunar world is not only the world of change but also the world of suffering and of "history,"' Eliade writes: 'Nothing that happens in this world under the moon can be "eternal," for its law is the law of becoming, and no change is final; every change is merely part of a cyclic pattern' (*Patterns* 183). In terms of its reception by *homo religiosus*, however, this is an overstatement, as it is their eternal recurrence that lends the cycles of life their mythic resonance: the earth is 'a womb which never wearies of procreating,' embodying 'the inexhaustible power of creation' (*Patterns* 261). Likewise, the moon

> shows man his true human condition; that in a sense man looks at himself, and finds himself anew in the life of the moon. That is why the symbolism and mythology of the moon have an element of *pathos* and at the same time of consolation, for the moon governs both death and fertility, both drama and initiation. Though the modality of the moon is supremely one of change, of rhythm, it is equally one of periodic returning; and this pattern

> of existence is both disturbing and consoling at the same time – for though the manifestations of life are so frail that they can suddenly disappear altogether, they are restored in the 'eternal returning' regulated by the moon. (*Patterns* 184)

It is the eternality of the rhythms and cycles of life that gives all the archetypal specifications of the chthonic and lunar hierophanies their value. These specifications include sacred stones, trees, and plants, and the gods, goddesses, and rituals of harvesting and agriculture. Sacred stones and trees take on particular value within the realm of the lunar-chthonic because of their apparent conjuring of the eternal and transcendent within the cycles of time, the former because of their presumed permanence and the latter because of their status as a constantly regenerating central ligature that reaches into the archetypal realms above and below. 'Trees are suitable symbols of *axis mundis* by virtue of the fact that they at once inhabit subterranean, surface and atmospheric spaces' (*Patterns* xiv). 'Stone stood supremely for reality; indestructability and lastingness,' Eliade writes: 'the tree, with its periodic regeneration, manifested the power of the sacred in the order of life' (*Patterns* 271).

Lastly, there are the aquatic hierophanies, of which the seas and oceans are the primary embodiment. Like the ouranic hierophany, the archetypal power of the aquatic hierophany resides in its representation of eternal factors beyond human comprehension and beyond the cycles of life: but it is subordinate to the ouranic, in that it is pre-formal and has no concrete structure. The aquatic hierophanies invest and divest the forms that manifest themselves in the chthonic realm, in fact, which are in turn presumed to be those dictated by or through the celestial regions. Eliade provides a complete and yet succinct presentation of this complex relationship:

> In whatever religious framework it appears, the function of water is shown to be the same; it disintegrates, abolishes forms, 'washes away sins' – at once purifying and giving new life. Its work is to precede creation and take it again to itself; it can never get beyond its own mode of existence – can never express itself *in forms.* Water can never pass beyond the condition of the potential, of seeds and hidden powers. Everything that has form is manifested above the waters, is separate from them. On the other hand, as soon as it has separated from water, every 'form' loses its potentiality, falls under the law of time and of life; it is limited, enters history, shares in the universal law of change, decays, and would cease to be itself altogether were it not

> regenerated by being periodically immersed in waters again, did it not again go through the 'flood' followed by the 'creation of the universe.' Ritual lustrations and purifications with water are performed with the purpose of bringing into the present for a fleeting instant 'that time', that *illud tempus*, when the creation took place. They are a symbolic re-enactment of the birth of the world or of the 'new man.' (*Patterns* 212)

The specifications of the aquatic hierophany are among the best-known archetypes in myth and ritual. In addition to the gods of the sea, they include features and locales like sacred rivers, fountains, caves, and wells, lesser divinities like sirens, mermaids, and nymphs, sacred creatures such as fish, dragons, and serpents, and, of course, the ablutions and rituals of baptism. 'All things ascend to life through water,' Eliade writes, 'and are dissolved again in it after death, from living individuals to the world itself' (*Patterns* 190).

It is difficult not to notice that this mythic cosmology resembles models of the 'great chain of being' produced by Renaissance philosophers and cosmologists (most of whom were Neoplatonists), which placed form without matter above, matter without form below, and a mingling of them at points between. Eliade does not allude to this specific cosmological model, but he does point out that many mythic traditions provide diagrams or visions of the universe as a whole which seem to represent his conceptual cosmos in pictorial form. He refers us in particular to an ancient symbol which, as we shall discover, our other mythologists also interpret as reflecting their respective theories about the total structure of archetypal symbolism (and which therefore constitutes a crucial touchstone of comparison). This is, of course, the *mandala* of Indo-Tibetan Buddhism. A 'sense of a cosmology is ... apparent in the construction of the *mandala* as practiced in the Tantric schools,' writes Eliade (*Patterns* 372). The intricate and carefully ordered symbol of the mandala, Eliade insists, is structured along the same axes of descent and centring as his cosmology. 'The *mandala* is both an *imago mundi* and a symbolic pantheon,' he states: 'these sacred constructions represent the whole universe in symbol: their various floors or terraces are identified with the "heavens" or levels of the cosmos' (*Patterns* 373).

Eliade's archetypal universe is an impressive structure, to be sure. But as it follows consistently from his problematic theoretical premises, it too has its problems. We must note, for example, the absence of any sort of infernal region in Eliade's mythic cosmos. This is surely a crippling omission given the prominence of hells and underworlds in myth and religion. A stock criticism of Eliade's fiction is that it does not allow for any sense of 'evil,' and it seems the same may be said of his archetypology (Rennie, *Reconstructing* 15). The sacred, as he defines it, never projects anything demonic or destructive. This seems to be a consequence of the principle embodied in such perennial Platonic insolvables as 'What is the ideal form of pain or punishment, or revolution, or chaos?' There can be none, obviously, and thus there is nothing in Eliade's understanding of the objective universe which conceptually evinces a mythic 'hell,' or a state of indeterminacy or abjection. There can be no accounting in Eliade's theory of myth, therefore, for the Hells of the monotheistic traditions, the Hades of Greek mythology, the Inferno of Dante, and even the Bardo state of Buddhism. As these mythic states and locales cannot be inspired by a transcendent sacred, they must be generated by aspects of the material, temporal realm. Whatever sense of the demonic there is in Eliade's thought is thus associated with the profane world, the human world of time and space, which constitutes the zone of chaos and suffering that archetypal transcendence remedies. Leaving aside for the moment the social implications of conflating the profane human world with 'hell,' we must acknowledge that, because demonic experiences and locales seem to be perennial aspects of myth and yet cannot be the result of a conceptual ideal or the presumed presence of a transcendental signified, some archetypes must therefore extend instead from the experience of humanity in its material and cultural context.

Related to this is the fact that Eliade's theory is hard pressed to account for the prominence of myths that promote human values and existence, and aspects of the profane world, before or above those of the gods, spiritual realities, and other manifestations of the sacred. A theory that holds myth to be the intimations of the sacred can have little to say about the obvious prominence of myths that depict human beings contending favourably with or against the gods and other transcendent powers. *The Epic of Gilgamesh,* the *Odyssey,* and the Christian traditions that emphasize the importance of the humanity of Christ are but a few examples of mythic valuations of the profane in the face of the sacred. Such myths present profane human existence as constituting a necessary precondition or result of the experience of the sacred, and even a dimension of existence to be valued in and of itself. As the introduction to a recent translation of the Gilgamesh epic emphasizes, 'Gilgamesh is celebrated more for his human achievement than for his relationship with the divine' (George xxxii). Similarly, the *Odyssey* opens with Odysseus' refusal of Calypso's offer of immortality, his repudiation of an existence outside time and beyond suffering. As Julian Jaynes remarks, Odysseus 'is the hero of the new mentality of how to get along in a ruined and god-weakened world' (Jaynes 273). When Eliade writes that 'the sufferings and trials undergone by [Odysseus] were fabulous, and yet any man's return home has the value of [Odysseus'] return to Ithaca,' he does so without realizing that this constitutes the archetypalization of journeying through profane space to a home that is a practical human social model and not an abstraction or transcendent principle (*Patterns* 382).

Both failings confirm for us yet again that the equation of myth and mythic experience with the sacred, as Eliade defines it, is both inadequate and problematic. Eliade himself seems to sense this in a qualification he makes early in *Patterns in Comparative Religion,* in which he admits to being uncertain about how some basic human activities become mythic and religious. There are, he writes,

> a mass of symbols, cosmic, biological or social occurrences, ideograms and ideas, which are of great importance on the religious plane, though their connection with actual religious experience may not always be clear to us moderns. We can understand, for instance, how the phases of the moon, the seasons ... or space symbolism, might have come to have religious value for early mankind, might have become hierophanies; but it is much harder to see how the same would apply to physiological actions such as nutrition or sexual intercourse ... We face in fact a double difficulty; first that of accepting that there is something sacred about all physiological life and, secondly, that of looking at certain patterns of thought ... as hierophanies. (*Patterns* 31)

Eliade is confident, in other words, that his theory can demonstrate how the perception of the sky or the sea might intimate to *homo religiosus* the existence of a transcendent realm, but suspects it may not shed much light on how archaic man's own functions and creations become mythic. To be fair, we must concede that Eliade does try to shed what light he can on that question. Acknowledging that the panorama of myth 'cannot be reduced to elementary hierophanies' such as the ones he discusses in *Patterns in Comparative Religion,* he chooses to focus more on cultural archetypes in *The Myth of the Eternal Return* (*Patterns* 30). But while it requires only a simple extension of his theory to show how a temple or pyramid is an imitation of a mountain and incarnates transcendent height or perfect geometry, or how a public orgy imitates or perpetuates natural fertility (both participating in the mythic 'eternal return'), his theory can provide little account of how exclusively human activities like communal feasting, marriage, 'scapegoating,' or war take on mythic and ritual significance, or how culturally generated things like a city or a sword become archetypal. Such archetypes cannot be evinced by the sacred through any natural or elemental form. Their value is not generated through their embodiment of some transcendent principle, but through an awareness of their practical and existential function in human life in the profane world. Thus, while Eliade discusses these rituals and archetypes in *Eternal Return* as militations against time and history, he does not and cannot situate them in his archetypal structure or account for their origin. He recognizes, however, that it is precisely this inability to see existential or material concerns as having a mythic or religious role that separates profane man from *homo religiosus*:

> [O]ne of the major differences separating the people of the early cultures from people to-day is precisely the utter incapacity of the latter to live their organic life (particularly as regards sex and nutrition) as a sacrament ... For the modern they are simply physiological acts, whereas for primitive man they were sacraments, ceremonies by means of which he communicated with the force that stood for Life itself. (*Patterns* 31)

A major aspect of the recovery of mythic consciousness by modern man, therefore, must be a restored sense of how the archetypalization of the objects, rituals and locales of his own 'physiological acts' and 'organic life' occurs. As we have shown, Eliade's theories do not provide us with much help in this regard, which is to say, in providing an actual phenomenology of myth. They fare particularly poorly in comparison to the humanistic theory of myth in Frye's *Fearful Symmetry*, as will become clear later in the fourth chapter. In our conclusion, furthermore, we shall discover that with the development of his theory of primary concern, Frye becomes the first mythologist to establish a precise phenomenological connection between embodied human existence and mythic consciousness. For the moment, however, we can find a strong register of Eliade's inability to provide this in the fact that, through he properly understands the word *sacrament* in the passage above, that understanding is absent in his overall theory: the word is not to be understood in its substantive sense, as referring to a sacred ritual or object, but in its verbal sense, the human action of making a ritual or object sacred.

Having discovered several problematic aspects of Eliade's theory of mythic experience and mythic structure, we are in a position where we must approach his statements about the overall potential or function of myth with suspicion. It is difficult not to find his oft-repeated point that archetypes 'destroy' or 'abolish' historical time and material space somewhat disturbing (*Patterns* 398, 407, *Eternal Return* 81). Indeed, there are overtones of religious militancy and fundamentalism in such conclusive remarks as 'the more religious a man is the more real he is, and the more he gets away from the unreality of meaningless change,' or that 'the dialectic of hierophanies tends to endlessly reduce the spheres that are profane and eventually to abolish them,' that they 'consecrate the universe' (*Patterns* 459). The problem is not Eliade's position that myth and the sacred function oppositionally or dialectically with regard to history and a profane world, for as we shall see that is a trait shared by all our mythologists. It is rather the implication that history and the profane world exist primarily to be destroyed and abolished by the hierophanies. Eliade's 'dialectic of the sacred' is a dialectic only in the crudest sense, in the sense of Derrida's binary that hides hierarchy, or the Manichean binary of postcolonial theory.[10] As we shall see, it is a far cry from the more complex dialectics of Jung and Frye, where history and the profane world play a role in or are redeemed by the revelation of eternity in myth.

Indeed, from the perspective of human life in time, there seems to be something very like a death drive at work in Eliade's teleology of myth, which results from its proceeding from a purely ontological (instead of a phenomenological) basis. In *The Myth of the Eternal Return,* for instance, Eliade writes that myth

> reveals an ontology uncontaminated by time and becoming. Just as the Greeks, in their myth of eternal return, sought to satisfy their metaphysical thirst for the 'ontic' and the static (for, from the point of view of the infinite, the becoming of things that perpetually revert to the same state is, as a result, implicitly annulled and it can be affirmed that 'the world stands still'), even so the primitive, by conferring a cyclic direction upon time, annuls its irreversibility. Everything begins over again at its commencement every instant ... [I]t is even possible to say that nothing new happens in the world, for everything is but the repetition of the same primordial archetypes; this repetition, by actualizing the mythical moment when the archetypal gesture was revealed, constantly maintains the world in the same auroral instant of the beginnings. (*Eternal Return* 89–90)

The best that the Eliadean theory of myth has to offer, in other words, is the stillborn world of pure form, the cold sterility of metaphysics, and what might be described as an archetypal Möbius loop or closed circuit. Any process, progression, or development is negated. Experience itself is obviated.

Despite the contradictions in his approach, Eliade nevertheless proceeds to give a name to the peak experience of myth in which his theory culminates. He has at least two terms for it, in fact, both of which carry connotations of supreme transcendence (or as he puts it, 'the metaphysics of ascent') while attempting to borrow from the language and empirical authority of psychology (*Patterns* 454). In *Patterns in Comparative Religion*, he speculates about the possibility of 'transconsciousness,' by which he means the attainment of a consciousness consisting of or containing all hierophanies, a consciousness of the totality of the sacred (*Patterns* 454). Mac Linscott Ricketts provides a better summary of the idea than Eliade himself does, but one which is equally revealing of the suspiciously anti-humanist metaphysics from which it is distilled:

> The transconscious, like the High God, is from above ... Eliade speaks of transcending of both conscious and unconscious planes and attaining something *beyond* Time and even the *near* eternity of nature. Eliade names this the 'transconsciousness,' a higher *logos* which is encountered in genuine mystic experience, the condition of the 'fully-awakened' man who is emptied of historical existence, time, sin, self, etc. and is established on the basis of the hierophany of the Unity of the Absolute, in a state of Being, supreme knowledge and absolute freedom. (Ricketts 26)

As to whether such a state is possible given what we have thus far discovered about the place of human experience in Eliade's thought, we have only to notice the erasures that occur in the few attempts of Eliade's commentators to engage the notion of transconsciousness. Dudley's remark, for instance, that 'consciousness of total being transcends that which can be contemplated by consciousness' (Dudley 64) is not an instructive or enlightened paradox, but the terminal example of the contradiction we have been orbiting all along: that phenomenological human experience and the notion of an *a priori* transcendent divine are mutually exclusive. We must arrive at the same conclusion, too, in considering the term Eliade uses several years later in his *Images and Symbols: Studies in Religious Symbolism* (1952) for this total archetypal transcendence: *metapsychoanalysis*. This he describes as 'an awakening, a renewal of consciousness,' a 'spiritual technique' of 'elucidating the theoretical content of the symbols and archetypes' which gives 'transparency and coherence to what is ... fragmentary' and 'fossilised in the religious traditions of all mankind' (*Images and Symbols* 35). The forced superlativity of this term, as well as Eliade's description of it, show it to be a manifestation of the human dream of acquainting ourselves with the contents of the mind of God, Augustine's *Divina Intellegentia*: a dream made impossible by the insurmountable gulf presented by Eliade's metaphysics and the relative insignificance he affords humanity in the face of the *ganz andere*.

Once a thorough perusal of Eliade's theory of myth is complete, it is difficult to ignore the crypto-fascist implications that seem to adhere to many aspects of it. They are all fruit from the poison tree of his sacred-profane ontological binary, a division which gives supreme value and yet supreme mystery to the former while confining human experience to the latter. The militant and colonialist rhetoric that peeks out from behind Eliade's description of the action of the archetypes of the sacred seems to endorse the notion than humanity ought to seek a transcendence of its perceived world, the most 'real' dimensions of its own life, for the sake of some imperceptible mystery. It is a relatively simple matter, in fact, to see how the disturbed mind of a dictator or terrorist, given the implication that the profane aspects of human life are demonic and dispensable on the one hand and the hermeneutic blank of an unknowable God on the other, might attempt to justify racial genocide or the targeting of innocent civilians. No one could rationally claim that Eliade's writings, specifically, have inspired such actions. Nevertheless, in Eliade we are in the presence of a tradition of religious metaphysics and mythic thought that is susceptible to being warped into a perverse rationalization and apology for such crimes against humanity. For our more immediate purposes, we must recognize that the flawed basis and the discomforting implications of Eliade's theory, as well as its simple inability to account for many essential aspects of mythic discourse, limit its usefulness to literary and cultural criticism. As Robert Baird writes, 'without its implied ontology, Eliade's method falls to the ground and becomes at best a means of classifying data' (Baird 89). We may salvage from Eliade a partial taxonomy of archetypes, in other words, but his theories on the generation and function of myth must be rejected. This should be the extent of our critical evaluation of Eliade, and the rest should be left to tend to itself. For our immediate purposes, as we well know, are not at all removed from the broader existential concerns of living in a world where catastrophes of the kind alluded to above actually occur, but ramify into them. Thus, just as a misunderstanding of myth may resonate in culture and fuel such tragedies, so the recognition of that misunderstanding as such prompts us to relocate it to its proper context in the apocrypha of mythography, and search instead for a humane phenomenology of myth that may actually be of benefit.

two

De Profundis: C.G. Jung and the Archetypes of the Collective Unconscious

Mythological ideas with their extraordinary symbolism evidently reach far into the human psyche ... where reason, will and good intentions never penetrate.

C.G. Jung, *The Practice of Psychotherapy* (*CW 16* 15)

The most influential mythologist of the twentieth century is, without question, Carl Gustav Jung. Since emerging after ten years of discipleship from the shadow of Sigmund Freud in 1912, Jung has enjoyed varying degrees of critical acceptance, but has never been without a large number of readers and devotees. The period from 1933 (when the Eranos conferences first began) to 1961 (the year of his death) can in retrospect be identified as the term of his greatest influence and, while his reputation has increasingly suffered since then, a strong core interest in his work persists. Virtually every major city in North America and Europe boasts a Jungian institute, society, therapist, or thinker of some kind, and commentary on his writings is nothing short of voluminous.

Jung's break with Freud was over myth itself and its relationship to psychology. Freud had always conceded the significance of myth, but only as a consequence of his 'sexual theory,' his general principle that the sexual instinct (the *libido*) is the prime determinant of human behaviour. Jung, on the other hand, had been considering whether mythic thought itself could be the prime motivator at least as early as 1909, when he had a dream that suggested to him that there was a common mythic foundation to all human psychic activity (*Memories* 158–62, Wilson 12). He later announced to Freud in a letter that 'mythology has got me in its grip' (Clarke 11). Freud's position was that myth and mythic thinking were cultural pathologies caused by the cluster of neurotic feelings and impulses he infamously dubbed the 'Oedipus complex,' after the famous plays of Sophocles. Freud saw religion, for instance, as a complex set of preventative and compensatory gestures aimed at curbing primal incestuous and parricidal urges and actions in culture (Freud 160–92). Jung, by contrast, had come to believe that myth and mythic thought were not effects, but root causes of human behaviour, and were to be understood as a system of psychological impulses coincident with a set of innate mythical images, rather than as pathologies arising from a single impulse named after a single mythological figure. Where Freud saw the libido as a specifically sexual impulse, Jung saw it more as a general 'life energy' which manifested itself in various psychological drives that were analogous to the diverse forms and images of myth. This substantial difference of opinion led to a personal and professional severance which was traumatic for both men, and left them rushing to print arguments defending their respective positions. Jung narrowly won the race to publication, when his *Wandlungen und Symbole der Libido* (later retitled *Symbols of Transformation* [*CW 5*]) appeared in 1912. Freud's *Totem and Taboo* followed fast on its heels later the same year.

While Freud was content to let his book stand as his major statement on myth, Jung was not. *Symbols of Transformation* was merely the first of many writings by Jung that related psychology to myth, such that myth came to be regarded as the central issue in his theory of psychology. Indeed, there is a continuing debate which is not likely to be settled any time soon (and which need not be) as to whether Jung is better seen as a psychologist or a mythologist. His ongoing interest in myth was due not only to the fact that he had through his break with Freud secured the freedom to pursue his true calling, but also had to do with the inadequacies of his first book on the subject. Despite its impressive breadth and its convincing suggestion that myth is constitutive of (rather than a consequence of) consciousness, *Symbols of Transformation* does not provide a complete or even an independent theory of myth. Its engagement with the themes of incest and schizophrenia[1] reveals the lingering influence of Freudian pathology, even as it fashions itself as groundbreaking by revealing these neuroses to be negative aspects of an ambivalent root myth-consciousness. While it is a provocative first presentation of Jung's psychology of mythic symbols, and gestures at the benefits of engagement with them, *Symbols of Transformation* is surprisingly narrow for such a weighty tome. Taking the fantasies of a single individual, the infamous 'Miss Miller,' as its test case, it focuses on only three mythic symbols, which are connected along an Oedipal axis: the hero, the mother, and the process of death and rebirth. The book is more concerned with exhaustively ramifying these symbols and relating them to as many mythic and religious traditions as possible than it is with providing an overall theory of myth. One Jungian commentator goes so far as to say that

> As an attempt to formulate a convincing alternative to Freud, *Symbols of Transformation* cannot be regarded as a success. With its long footnotes, its quotations from Greek and Latin, its discussions of Babylonian and Egyptian and Hindu mythology, it produces the impression that Jung is trying to bludgeon the reader into submission by sheer intellectual exhibitionism. (Wilson 64)

But in *Symbols of Transformation* Jung did succeed in demonstrating the need for and the possibility of 'depathologizing' the psychology of myth. If Jung's far-reaching allusions proved anything it was that something as universal, productive, and multivalent as myth could not reasonably be regarded as a cultural neurosis or the consequence of a single instinctual drive. The space for inquiry that Jung opened with the book was not something he could immediately exploit, however. The break with Freud and the rush to get *Symbols of Transformation* into print left him very near a nervous breakdown, and he still had to construct a life and a professional reputation apart from the burgeoning field of psychoanalysis. The fifteen years following the First World War were thus largely a period of recuperation, consolidation, and exploration for Jung, during which he appeared to be gathering the resources and preparing a platform for the presentation of a more complete mythic theory. In 1916, he began providing a vocabulary for his ideas: he named his field 'analytic psychology,' which came to signify his research as 'psychoanalysis' had come to signify Freud's. He dubbed the common mythic foundation of human psychology the 'collective unconscious' and adopted the term 'archetype' for its constituent elements. From 1916 to 1930, he sought to clarify his theories through the study of occult traditions and primitive societies, and he speculated on the utility of his ideas to literary criticism. His research interests included Christian Gnosticism, Eastern and Western alchemy, and Kundalini yoga. He made visits to the Pueblo Indians of New Mexico, the Elgonyi tribe of Kenya, and various other locations in Africa, particularly Egypt. In 1922, he wrote a paper entitled 'On the Relation of Analytical Psychology to Poetry,' and another in 1930 called

'Psychology and Literature.' As much of Europe began courting the politics of fascism as a prelude to a second great war, Jung was apparently ready to begin presenting his mature mythography. At the first Eranos conference in 1933, which was attended by such luminaries as Rudolf Otto, Martin Buber, and Heinrich Zimmer, Jung read a paper entitled 'A Study of the Process of Individuation' (the name he gave to the process of psychological growth through mythic awareness). At the second Eranos meeting in 1934, he offered 'Archetypes of the Collective Unconscious.' These two papers bookended the volume eventually entitled *The Archetypes and the Collective Unconscious* (*CW 9i*), a collection of twelve essays written between 1933 and 1954 (mostly Eranos presentations), which, taken as a whole, constitute Jung's most complete theory of myth.

It was during this mature period that the term 'phenomenology' began to enter Jung's vocabulary (Clarke 35). This was not only an indication of the resurgent influence on his thinking of the phenomenological aspect of Romantic philosophy, which had figured prominently in his student readings prior to medical school. It also signalled his intention to move beyond a pathological and diagnostic perspective on myth into a positive, experientially based engagement with it. The fact that Jung's focus was psychological meant that the phenomena of human experience and the thought patterns connected with it were the subject matter of his research, and ensured that they would receive due consideration. But Jung wanted to generate a psychology of myth that went beyond the merely analytical and therapeutic, into the realm of existential empowerment and affirmation.[2] His thriving readership and enduring reputation suggest he had some success in this. But as we shall discover, these orientations and intentions did not prevent him from making certain metaphysical assertions that dilute the phenomenological basis from which he hoped his theories would derive their authority. Moreover, as we shall see, these assertions in concert with the specifics of his archetypology create for Jung's theory some disconcerting implications.

As Eliade begins by dividing reality and experience into a mythical sacred and a non-mythical profane, so Jung begins with a distinction between the unconscious and the conscious. With Jung, the mythic/non-mythic division from which most mythography proceeds begins a process of being internalized and humanized. Jung's division, however, is less binaristic and more complex than Eliade's. Jung largely accepts, for example, the Freudian theory of the unconscious as a psychic space which is created through neuroses and traumatic experiences, and which functions to contain them apart from the conscious mind. But while Freud sees this as the whole of the unconscious, Jung refers to it as merely the *personal unconscious,* as he regards it as a dimension of the psyche that is unique to each person and created through his or her personal experience. Beneath this, Jung maintains, is a *collective unconscious,* a deeper layer of the unconscious which is universal in that it is common to every human psyche, and pre-existent in that it is inherited and not created by individual experience. The existence of such things as instincts and intuitions had long troubled psychologists prior to Jung and had forced them to concede that there were certain psychological predispositions that human beings innately possessed, that not all thought and behaviour was acquired or learned. A similar problem faced anthropologists and social philosophers when they observed seemingly stable and recurrent dimensions of art and culture. Frazer himself was among the first to suggest that such similarities could be psychological in origin when he speculated in *The Golden Bough* that the recurrent myths he had noticed in disparate primitive societies might have something to do with 'the similar constitution of the human mind' (Frazer 448). Jung's notion of the collective unconscious is a hypothesis intended to account not only for such minute phenomena as instincts, but also for the fact that certain aspects of human behaviour and art seem to be present in all cultures at all times, and are therefore apparently universal. Some deeply buried or perennial aspect of the human mind which remains constant was the only reasonable explanation for these stable cultural structures, Jung argued, and one could only assume that they were external reflections of the structures of a hidden, inherited psychology. 'The universal similarity of the human brain leads to the universal possibility of a uniform mental functioning,' Jung writes, echoing Frazer in the more concrete language of psychology (*CW 7* 145): 'The collective unconscious is simply the psychic expression of the identity of brain structure irrespective of all racial differences' (*CW 13* 11).

But the fact that the collective unconscious was the source of universal forms made it (like Eliade's sacred) analogous to what religion knows as eternity. Thus Jung just as readily refers to the collective unconscious as 'a treasure house of eternal images,' a 'primitive wonder-world,' and a 'potential world outside time' (*CW 9i* 7, 32, *CW 14* 505). Like Eliade's profane, Jung's conscious mind has to do with the material, rational, historical, contingent contexts of human life, whereas the collective unconscious, like the sacred, is linked to the spiritual, the irrational, the universal, and the absolute. What Eliade regards as forms descended from a transcendent source are seen by Jung as ascended from a concealed, universal unconscious. As we shall soon see, the fact that the collective unconscious precedes the conscious in the unfolding order of Jungian mythography creates some of the same difficulties caused by Eliade's conception of the sacred as *a priori* to the profane.

As we have noted, an 'archetype' is what Jung eventually came to call any one of these structures of the collective unconscious (after toying with the terms 'primordial image' and 'mythologem'). The prominence of Jung's theories in mythography and psychology has given rise to the mistaken assumption that the word 'archetype' by definition refers to an aspect or element of the collective unconscious. There are other conceptions of the word and its etymology lies along other lines, as we have shown. But for Jung himself, the two concepts are inseparable as part and whole. Jung sees archetypes as rooted in the same deep psychological ground as instincts, and he often ties the two together. Instincts 'form very close analogies to the archetypes,' Jung writes, 'so close, in fact, that there is good reason for supposing that the archetypes are the unconscious images of the instincts themselves, in other words, that they are *patterns of instinctual behaviour*' (*CW 9i* 43–4). But tethering the archetype to the predisposition of human instinct cannot account for those aspects of culture and behaviour that are not merely reactive but productive. Thus Jung has to consider the relation of his notion of the archetype to the *idea*, which takes him into the perilous field of metaphysics which, as our discussion of Eliade revealed, haunts the history of both words. Here Jung treads lightly, simultaneously invoking and eschewing the tradition of Platonic metaphysics from which the idea is derived:

> In former times, despite some dissenting opinion and the influence of Aristotle, it was not too difficult to understand Plato's conception of the Idea as supraordinate and pre-existent to all phenomena. 'Archetype,' far from being a modern term, was already in use before the time of St. Augustine, and was synonymous with 'Idea' in the Platonic usage ... Were I a philosopher, I should continue in this Platonic strain and say: Somewhere, in 'a place beyond the skies,' there is a prototype or primordial image ... that is pre-existent and supraordinate to all phenomena ... But I am an empiricist, not a philosopher. (*CW 9i* 75)

While this last assertion is questionable given the nature and scope of Jung's intentions, it prompts him to clarify that archetypes are not inherited ideas but merely 'inherited possibilities of ideas,' 'inherited *possibilities* of human imagination' which constitute 'potential existence only' (*CW 9i* 66, *CW 7* 64, *CW 9i* 179). His ultimate solution is to make a distinction between the *archetype* and the *archetypal image* which is its incarnation. The latter is the concrete, tangible image or action that constitutes the cultural structure or behaviour in question, which can be taken as an object of study by an analyst or critic. The former, however, is merely a kind of psychic hypothesis, the abiding potential for or possibility of that image or action, which is unknowable in itself but recognizable through its concrete manifestation. 'The term "archetype" thus applies only indirectly' Jung writes, as 'it designates only those psychic elements which have not yet been submitted to conscious elaboration ... In this sense, there is a considerable difference between the archetype and the historical formula that has evolved' (*CW 9i* 5). The archetype is made actual by the archetypal image, in other words, as form is made actual by the presence of content, a relationship Jung uses an unexpectedly effective analogy to illustrate:

> Again and again I encounter the mistaken notion that an archetype is determined in regard to its content ... that it is a kind of unconscious idea (if such an expression be admissible). It is necessary to point out once more that archetypes are not determined as regards to their content, but only as regards their form and then only to a very limited degree. A primordial image is determined as to its content only when it has become conscious and is therefore filled out with the material of conscious experience. Its form ... might perhaps be compared to the axial system of a crystal, which, as it were, preforms the crystalline structure in the mother liquid, although it has no material existence of its own ... The archetype in itself is empty and purely formal, nothing but a *facultas praeformandi*, a possibility of representation which is given *a priori*. (*CW 9i* 79)

It is a significant advancement upon or correction of traditional (Augustinian or Eliadean) archetypology for Jung to insist that the material aspect of the archetype is as essential as its form and not a mere shadowy reflection of it. In doing so he is recognizing that a phenomenology of myth must indeed be a study of the phenomena of myth, and turns sharply on the question of perceptible realities. While there remains, in Jung's distinction, an abstract or metaphysical component of the archetype (the consequences of which will meet us in due course), he does not entertain any illusions that the archetype's destiny involves simply returning to its origin. Where Eliade saw the archetype as pointing back to a noumenal sacred from whence it came, Jung studies the archetype as it is directed outward in a dialectical engagement with the material universe of human perception. The archetype emerges from the collective unconscious through the process Jung calls *constellation* or *projection*, in which it is externalized onto some object or situation of the conscious world, directing the perception of it for a human subject who therefore stands at the centre of the archetypal process.

Far from being connected with the neuroses and compulsions Freud found lurking in the unconscious, the archetypes of the collective unconscious are, Jung maintains, 'among the inalienable assets of every psyche' (*CW 9i* 84). Emanating as they do from that aspect of the mind that all human beings share, they are 'the "human quality" of the human being, the specifically human form his activities take' (*CW 9i* 78). Archetypes 'occur practically everywhere and not with the monstrous products of insanity,' and are hence better understood as 'primordial affirmations' (*CW 9i* 39–40, 116). Jung states that:

> An archetype is in no sense just an annoying prejudice; it becomes so only when it is in the wrong place. In themselves, archetypal images are among the highest values of the human psyche; they have peopled the heavens of all races from time immemorial. To discard them as valueless would be a distinct loss. (*CW 9i* 84)

Even if such a situation as this ever came about, Jung insists that one way or another the archetype would re-emerge as a factor:

> Even if all proofs of the existence of the archetypes were lacking, and all the clever people in the world succeeded in convincing us that such a thing could not possibly exist, we would have to invent them forthwith in order to keep our highest and most important values from disappearing into the unconscious. (*CW 9i* 93)

This point, according to Jungian analyst Sherry Salman, underscores the central achievement of Jung's research: that he '"depathologized" the archetypal and transpersonal layer of the psyche by verifying its function as the creative matrix' (Salman 68).

The most fundamental and recognizable values that the Jungian archetypes produce are, obviously, those embodied in the various structures of myth. As the patterns of imagery and action that are the oldest on record and yet continually recurring in culture, the symbols of myth can only be assumed to be cognate with the archetypes themselves. Jung presented the relationship between myth and the collective unconscious with subtle differences each time he discussed it, but largely held to the view that they are essentially equivalent to one another along an interior-exterior axis: 'The collective unconscious ... appears to consist of mythological motifs or primordial images, for which reason the myths of all nations are its real exponents,' Jung theorizes. 'In fact, the whole of the mythology could be taken as a sort of projection of the collective unconscious' (*CW 8* 152). '[M]yths and symbols ... arise autochthonously in every corner of the earth and yet are identical,' Jung writes, 'because they are fashioned out of the same worldwide human unconscious, whose contents are infinitely less variable than are races and individuals' (*CW 6* 120–1).

That myth is a projection of the collective *un*conscious means that human beings may or may not be aware that they are participating in the cultural activity of mythmaking. Archetypes 'are to be found in the myths and legends of all peoples and all times,' Jung writes, 'as well as in individuals who have not the slightest knowledge of mythology' (*CW 11* 573). But whether they are projected knowingly or unknowingly, Jung's research suggested to him that archetypes tend to emerge at those junctures where the 'anxiously-guarded supremacy of consciousness' (*CW 9i* 23) is least assured:

> Just as the archetypes occur on the ethnological level as myths, so also they are found in every individual, and their effect is always strongest, that is, they anthropomorphize reality most, where consciousness is weakest and most restricted, and where fantasy can overrun the facts of the outer world. (*CW 9i* 67)

In other words, potentially anywhere: the principle that the archetypes inform the essential human behaviours means that virtually any part of human life or culture may become archetypal, including those not conventionally associated with myth. The archetype of feminine divinity, for example, 'no longer crosses our path as a goddess,' Jung writes, but 'when a highly esteemed professor in his seventies abandons his family and runs off with a young red-headed actress, we know that the gods have claimed another victim' (*CW 9i* 30). While myth is the primary cultural manifestation of the collective unconscious, Jung suggests that fields affording opportunities for free expression are the next most likely outlets of archetypal activity. Dreams, religion, literature and the arts, speculative philosophy, politics, sex and romance, and even science are just some of the human activities that Jung sees as being strongly influenced by the collective unconscious: all of which, he maintains, might be better illuminated by our understanding of archetypes.

If Eliade's archetypes of the sacred are Neoplatonic and Augustinian, then Jung's archetypes of the collective unconscious are neo-Kantian, and this accounts for much of Jung's ambivalence on the question of metaphysics. Immanuel Kant's bedrock principle that the phenomenal is all that can be queried and that the noumenal is unknowable (*Prolegomena* 289),[3] one of the first and most influential phenomenological discoveries, is reflected in Jung's distinction between the archetype and the archetypal image. But so too is Kant's belief that a noumenal factor may nevertheless be responsible for the ordering of the phenomenal, and might well be a theoretical necessity for the discussion of it. Responding to the sceptical subjectivism of David Hume, Kant conceded that reality as it actually is cannot be known, but he maintained that this does not necessarily lead to the conclusion that we are all locked in our own private, solipsistic worlds. In *Critique of Pure Reason,* Kant argues rather that our impressions of the world are not individual or unique, but are structured by modes of perception and thinking that are universal and collective, that is, practised by everyone (*Critique* 37).[4] These modes of perception give us no access to absolute reality, of course, but they do give us a basis of acknowledging phenomena and determining what is 'real' from the perspective of human life. Such perceptions include the awareness that we exist in a world of material forces governed by various conceptual principles and bounded by the dimensions of time and space. These are not mere conventions or contingencies that we agree upon in order to function, Kant theorized, but are actually built into the minds of human beings as the necessary conditions of awareness and knowledge. Principles such as space, time, substance, necessity, and causality, which had previously been understood as pure transcendent ideas, are in fact perceptions that the mind is preconfigured to recognize, constituting what Kant called 'categories of understanding.' 'Platonic metaphysics had located the transcendent realm in eternity, beyond reach of the human mind,' Paul Kugler summarizes. 'Kant, struggling with the arbitrary fictionalism resulting from dispensing with all transcendental foundations, established a new ground within the human mind, but transcendent to the knowing subject' (Kugler 78). This 'new ground,' which Kant (and Husserl after him) called 'the transcendent subject,' is as much the inspiration for Jung's collective unconscious as any notion he adapted from the field of depth psychology, and his archetypes are largely mythic specifications of Kant's 'categories of understanding.' 'Epistemologically I take my stand on Kant,' Jung writes (*Letters* 294, cf. *CW 9i* 84), and his taking of the 'transcendent subject' as the source of myth amounts to a transplantation of the metaphysical into an equally unknowable region of the mind, something he acknowledges when he presents the collective unconscious as an internal analogue or inversion of the Platonic realm:

> [I]t is Kant's doctrine of categories, more than anything else, that destroys in embryo every attempt to revive metaphysics in the old sense of the word, but at the same time paves the way for a rebirth of the Platonic spirit. If it be true that there can be no metaphysics transcending human reason, it can be no less true that there can be no empirical knowledge that is not already caught and limited by the *a priori* structure of cognition. (*CW 9i* 76)

In accepting Kant's major tenets, Jung takes up the task of offering an actual phenomenology of myth such as would be impossible through Augustinian and Ottonian principles. But insofar as this still means accepting the existence of a set of abstract metaphysical preconditions to mythic consciousness, Jung's theory tends to become mired in some of the same contradictions and limitations that hindered Eliade's theory of myth.

This is evident when Jung turns to the question of mythogenesis and the status of his mythic subject. On the one hand, he wants to provide a phenomenological account of the origins of mythic consciousness, and yet on the other he must concede the metaphysical basis of the archetypes and the collective unconscious. It is not uncommon, in fact, to find Jung attempting to provide a phenomenology of mythic origins, only to have it run aground of the metaphysical assumptions from which he is proceeding. Jung writes, for example,

> I have often been asked where archetypes or primordial images come from. It seems to me that their origin can only be explained by assuming them to be deposits of the constantly repeated experiences of humanity. One of the commonest and at the same time most impressive experiences is the apparent movement of the sun every day. We certainly cannot discover anything of the kind in the unconscious, so far as the known physical process is concerned. What we do find on the other hand, is the myth of the sun-hero in all its countless variations. It is this myth, and not the physical process,

> that forms the sun archetype. The same can be said of the phases of the moon. The archetype is a kind of readiness to produce over and over again the same or similar mythical ideas. Hence it seems as though what is impressed upon the unconscious were exclusively the subjective fantasy-ideas aroused by the physical process. We may therefore assume that the archetypes are recurrent impressions made by subjective reactions. Naturally this assumption only pushes the problem further back without solving it ... [T]hey are grounded in the peculiarities of the living organism itself and are therefore direct expressions of life whose nature cannot be further explained. (*CW 7* 68–9)

Here Jung is speculating that the archetype, as he elsewhere phrases it, is 'a mnemic deposit, an imprint or engram ... which has arisen through the condensation of countless processes of a similar kind,' a 'psychic expression of thc physiological and anatomical disposition' of the brain (*CW 6* 443–4). But these are remarks out of which no tenable phenomenological theory of mythic origins emerges, as he cannot say what those processes are or what that disposition is. What he is in fact suggesting is that the collective unconscious, as the basis of human thought, has developed separately from its material context, and is in every way prior to it: The 'peculiarities of the living organism' in which Jung sees the archetypes as being grounded are the pure functions of a mind that is fundamentally separate from and *a priori* to its physical world and the conditions of its embodiment. It is little wonder, then, that he claims that these factors 'cannot be further explained,' for as with all metaphysical claims, they are posed as self-affirming and indubitable facts. A clue to Jung's actual position is found in his statement that the deeper layers of the human psyche become 'increasingly collective until they are universalized and extinguished by the body's materiality' (*CW 9i* 173), which is to say that mythic consciousness functions apart from the physical contexts of the human life, the body, and the material world. Jung eventually came to concede that the collective unconscious

> is part of the inmost mystery of life, and it has its own peculiar structure and form ... Whether this psychic structure and its elements, the archetypes, ever 'originated' at all is a metaphysical question and therefore unanswerable. The structure is something given, the precondition that is found to be present in every case. (*CW 9i* 101)

Thus does Jung accept what is essentially a Cartesian principle, the notion that there is a fundamental fissure between mind and body, and that consciousness engages only its own self-generated contents (in the case of Descartes, the existence of its own doubt: in the case of Jung, of the archetypes). In such a model of consciousness, the mind either assumes a mantle of metaphysical supremacy over the phenomenal world, which it then perceives as reflecting its own abstract lineaments (as the so-called logocentric theories of signification operate), or it throws off that mantle and finds the phenomenal world to be full of sound and fury but signifying nothing (as poststructuralism claims). Jung's collective unconscious is recognizably a case of the former, to the extent that he makes its assumption of metaphysical authority inevitable and involuntary. For Jung, archetypes are the '*a priori* and formal conditions of apperception' whose function is 'to assimilate all outer sense experience to inner, psychic events' (*CW 9i* 66, 6). They 'do not proceed from physical facts' (*CW 9i* 154), but rather 'outweigh the influence of sensory stimuli' so as to 'mould [it] into conformity with the *pre-existing* image' (*CW 9i* 66). They are 'symbolic expressions of the inner unconscious drama of the psyche which become accessible to man's consciousness by way of projection – that is, mirrored in the events of nature' (*CW 9i* 6).

This process of projection is therefore not in itself a liberating or empowering one for Jung's mythic subject, which he often refers to simply as 'modern man' (apparently to stress the enduring primacy of primordial modes of thought in contemporary life). Even as the archetype may guide modern man into the creation of important cultural forms and greater self-awareness, the fact that it is metaphysically prior to his consciousness and that the projection of it 'is an unconscious, automatic process' (*CW 9i* 60) puts him in much the same anterior and abject position as Eliade's *homo religiosus*. Jung's mythic subject is similarly 'possessed by a supraordinate idea' (*CW 9i* 62). As we shall see when we discuss them in detail, Jung's archetypes are, admittedly, humanistic in nature, and he does concede that they can be consciously cultivated to a certain degree through the faculty he called the 'active imagination.' But even as they are 'ours' in the sense that they originate in a layer of our own psyche and can reflect our best interests, they are *other* in the ways that matter most, in that we cannot influence or take responsibility for them, and can only act secondarily to them, as consciousness is secondary to the collective unconscious. Benevolent or not, Jung's archetypes are alien factors in that they 'irrupt autonomously' (*CW 9i* 285) or 'arise autochthonously' (*CW 6* 120–1) into consciousness. Jung all but designates the collective unconscious an external authority, in fact, when he states that it often 'behaves so autocratically that it denies tangible reality' (*CW 9i* 154). Like *homo religiosus*, therefore, Jung's mythic subject is well objectified by the archetypal process, even as he supposedly stands at the centre of it: 'Modern man, in experiencing the archetype,' Jung insists, 'comes to know that most ancient form of thinking as an autonomous activity whose object he is' (*CW 9i* 37).

Eric Gould points up the unfortunate implications of Jung's archetypal theory for human agency in the scathing critique he delivers in the opening chapter of his *Mythical Intentions in Modern Literature*:

> [I]f we follow Jung, [we] discover that our conscious life is always condemned to be subservient to some kind of unattainable, superior fact. We are, that is, always on the defensive. Most troublesome is the fact that his archetypalist interpretation is entirely dependent on the *arbitrary* emergence of those primordial image-symbols ... We are in their grip, whether we like it or not, and yet never really know what we are in the grip of ... [N]o matter what we think we know, consciousness always depends on some arbitrarily present 'other' beyond nature, language, the socio-political context, or sensory evidence. Archetypes move hesitantly from the dimly lit world of unconscious figures, under mysterious conditions, to a tentative union with consciousness, constantly struggling, it would seem, to return from whence they came. (Gould 21–2)

The collective unconscious poses 'a potential danger to our equilibrium,' Gould insists. It is 'the mysterious origin of the instincts and intuitions, personified into a force which not only nurtures archetypes, but which is far more powerful in its intent to reveal them than man can possibility tolerate' (Gould 23). Gould recognizes that much of the immense popularity of Jung's theory of myth derives 'from [its] attempt to have one's metaphysical cake and eat it too,' by which he means its attempt to render the archetypal realm as both self and other, both phenomenal and metaphysical, both human experience and transcendent reality (Gould 22). In religious terms, the effort amounts to an attempt to moderate or domesticate Otto's *ganz andere* into the collective unconscious. But however effective the effort, it cannot alter the implications of the original premise. Jung's collective unconscious remains a *mysterium tremendum*, with all the potential subordination of conscious human life that this entails. The contents of the collective unconscious, Jung writes, 'may at any time burst in upon us with annihilating force' (*CW* 7 202).

Gould also identifies an additional problem with Jung's theory of myth that has to do with its applicability as literary theory. It is a problem that would also have arisen in Eliade's mythography had he shared Jung's aspiration to cleave from his thought a viable theory of literary creation. The distance between a metaphysically based theory of myth, which holds archetypal structures to be ontologically absolute, and the fact that myths and archetypes are narratives and metaphors created by human beings within their own linguistic systems is something that Jung, like Eliade, tends to ignore. While some of the discrepancy may be answered by Jung's Kantianism, Gould is nevertheless justified in observing that:

> Another real problem with [Jung's] theory ... is that it does not provide us with a transition in language from the supernatural to the natural, regardless of whether we believe the supernatural exists or not ... [A]s far as literary theory is concerned ... no reliable theory of language as both the interpretive medium and the very process of coming-into-consciousness accompanies the argument. (Gould 22–3)

Indeed, this issue does not come under adequate scrutiny until a mythologist who is also a literary theorist, Northrop Frye, advances a theory of myth that is also a theory of literature. As a specific problem in mythography, it remains unsolved, in fact, until the final phase of Frye's career (to be discussed in our concluding chapter), when he expanded his purview still further to provide a theory of language, and specifically a phenomenology of mythic language. Frye's theories involve a transition in language not from the supernatural to the natural, however, but from the natural to the supernatural.

In the wake of Gould's observations about the consequences of Jungian theory for human agency, the more immediate problem is the one posed to cultural theory at large: if archetypes are the pre-conscious determinants of perception and therefore of cultural and aesthetic form, and the projection of archetypes is an involuntary process, then human beings exercise no positive or productive control over the structure and development of art and culture. Agency can be exercised only in the degree to which human beings come to comprehend the structure and development of art and culture after the fact. This would be an intolerable situation, even if it did stand in accord with the majority of our cultural and aesthetic experience, which it does not. We need only to flip Jung's theory on its head or approach it from the other direction to see this: the suggestion that the intense concentration of conscious faculties inherent in the work of the artist, the politician, or the engineer, for example, has little bearing on the essential nature of art, policy, or technology, and therefore on the broader structure of culture, is not only implausible but dangerous. Nevertheless, Jung maintains:

> Archetypes are like river beds which dry up when the water deserts them, but which it can find again at any time. An archetype is like an old watercourse along which the water of life has flowed for centuries, digging a deep channel for itself. The longer it has flowed in this channel the more likely it is that sooner or later the water will return to its old bed. The life of the individual as a member of society and particularly as part of the State may be regulated like a canal, but the life of nations is a great rushing river which is utterly beyond human control, in the hands of One who has always been stronger than men ... Thus the life of nations rolls on unchecked, without guidance, unconscious of where it is going, like a rock crashing down the side of a hill, until it is stopped by an obstacle stronger than itself. (*CW 10* 189)

This passage, from Jung's essay 'Wotan' (1936), is often cited by his defenders as his warning that Nazism is a projection of the most destructive dimensions of the collective unconscious and represented an imminent threat. Having extracted the implications we have from Jung's theory, we can see that determining whether Jung was sufficiently wary of Nazism, or whether Nazism constitutes mythmaking (as opposed to an appalling perversion of myth) are important but ultimately secondary issues. The central problem, from a theoretical point of view, is that Jung's model of mythic (un)consciousness makes such dangerous and hateful movements, and the wars fought to dissolve them, seem like inevitable accidents of culture, titanic clashes of archetypal powers 'utterly beyond human control.' Worse still, Jung's theory forces the mythologist to become an apologist for such events and movements. 'It has always been terrible to fall into the hands of a living god,' Jung intones; 'We who stand outside judge the Germans far too much as if they were responsible agents, but perhaps it would be nearer the truth to regard them also as *victims*' (*CW 10* 393). If this is so, it is because the 'living god' of the collective unconscious, this 'One who has always been stronger than men,' is *other*, and therefore potentially fascistic and indifferent toward conscious human life and concerns. If we accept this living god as our own, then myth, as his creation, must also be considered thus.

The picture Jung paints of the overall structure of the collective unconscious is not as immediately threatening as this, but it is not without negative implications. In Jung's presentation of this overall structure, we can see evidence of the tension that exists in his thought between the metaphysical and the phenomenological, particularly where his methodology is concerned. 'I try to keep to first hand-experience and to leave metaphysical beliefs ... to look after themselves,' Jung insists. 'I am entrapped in the psyche and ... I cannot do anything except describe the experiences that befall me there' (*CW 16* 123–4). Yet when it comes time to enumerate the contents of the collective unconscious, he eschews this inductive methodology in favour of a deductive one that is intended to confirm his thesis that the collective unconscious is the hidden matrix of myth and projects its fundamental forms: 'Since archetypes are supposed to produce certain psychic forms,' he pronounces, 'we must discuss how and where to get hold of material demonstrating these forms' (*CW 9i* 48).

In whatever proportion Jung combined the results of his psychological analysis with his extensive cultural research, however, his collective unconscious contains many of mythology's most perennial figures and forms. His arrangement of these figures and forms is quite fluid, though, so that the collective unconscious may be said to display not so much a precise archetypal structure as a complex interweaving of archetypal clusters. Some archetypes are aspects or parts of other archetypes, or become so in certain contexts, and virtually any archetype may also stand for the whole of the collective unconscious. The task of elucidating Jungian archetypology is made more difficult by this fluidity, but insofar as the archetypes nevertheless tend to 'appear in regular succession,' it is possible, as noted Jungian analyst C.A. Meier observes, 'to outline a hierarchy of the figures' (Meier 90). Jung himself would resist the word 'hierarchy' if it were taken to mean that one archetype is inherently more important than another, but he clearly saw the collective unconscious in terms of deepening levels.

The first archetype that is usually encountered – the 'apprentice-piece' of archetypal analysis as Jung refers to it – is the figure he calls the *shadow* (*CW 9i* 29). The shadow typifies all the traits, attitudes and actions that consciousness disavows or does not recognize in itself, especially extreme emotions and irrationalities. A portion of the shadow archetype inhabits the personal or Freudian unconscious, Jung says, because individual consciousness tends to repress elements that run contrary to its sense of itself, producing a 'dark half of the personality' (*CW 11* 152). But this is a function of the shadow archetype as it is rooted in the collective unconscious, where it exemplifies the essential counter-valuations of humanity, particularly images and behaviours associated with evil, aggression, or cruelty (*CW 9i* 262). This fundamental moral contrariness is perhaps why the shadow archetype is the first to appear as the contents of the collective unconscious are engaged or projected, and why it so readily symbolizes the collective unconscious as a whole. The sense of conflict that abides in the relationship between consciousness and the collective unconscious is the result of the shadow's antithetical energy, and generates the villains of myth, literature, and psycho-drama. Insofar as myths, stories, and psychological crises usually involve a conflict between a given moral principle and its contrary, they also usually entail the expression or projection of the shadow in some form, and this serves as the catalyst for whatever developments follow. When the shadow's destructive behaviours or images can be recognized as having an ultimately productive or instructive effect, however, Jung suggests that a particular and beneficial aspect of the archetype called the *trickster* has been activated. This figure, which inspires such incarnations as the mischievous animal-gods of North American Indian mythology, the wise fools and tricky slaves of Roman and Shakespearean comedy, or the shape-shifters and fearsome shamans of the epic tradition, illustrates the paradox of 'the mythological truth that the wounded wounder is the agent of healing' (*CW 9i* 256). Whereas the shadow proper tends to produce a consistently antagonistic figure, the trickster tends rather to pass, like the wrathful God of the Old Testament, through a demonic persona *en route* to becoming an ultimately redemptive force:

> These mythological features extend even to the highest regions of man's spiritual development. If we consider, for example, the daemonic features exhibited by Yahweh in the Old Testament, we shall find in them not a few reminders of the unpredictable behaviour of the trickster, of his senseless orgies of destruction and his self-imposed sufferings, together with some gradual development into a saviour and his simultaneous humanization. (*CW 9i* 256)

In this observation it becomes clear that Jung sees the trickster as subtly blending into the next archetype that is typically encountered, the *wise old man.* Here the creative wisdom of the trickster assumes a more straightforward and sympathetic countenance, producing one of the most universal and recognizable figures in myth, the paternal mentor or guide:

> The figure of the wise old man can appear so plastically, not only in dreams but also in visionary meditation ... that, as is sometimes apparently the case in India, it takes over the role of a guru. The wise old man appears in dreams in the guise of a magician, doctor, priest, teacher, professor, grandfather, or any other person possessing authority. The archetype of the spirit in the shape of a man, hobgoblin or animal always appears in a situation where insight, understanding, good advice, determination, planning, etc., are needed but cannot be mustered on one's own resources. The archetype compensates this state of spiritual deficiency by contents designed to fill the gap. (*CW 9i* 215–16)

Religious figures such as Moses and the prophets of the Old Testament, or Utnapishtim of *The Epic of Gilgamesh,* are examples of the wise old man, as are mythopoetic figures like the wizard Merlin of Arthurian mythology or Gandalf of J.R.R. Tolkien's *The Lord of the Rings.* Jung seems to have hoped that the Wotan archetype which he saw as inspiring Nazism would morph from shadow into trickster and into the wise old man that is his primary personification in Germanic mythology, but needless to say this did not occur.[5] 'The old man knows what roads lead to the goal and points them out,' Jung characterizes. 'He warns of dangers to come and supplies the means of meeting them effectively,' which might be something as basic as a 'profound reflection or a lucky idea' (*CW 9i* 221, 217):

> Indeed the old man is himself this purposeful reflection and concentration of moral and physical forces that comes about spontaneously in the psychic space outside consciousness when conscious thought is not yet – or is no longer – possible. The concentration and tension of psychic forces have something about them that always looks like magic: they develop an unexpected power of endurance which is often superior to the conscious effort of will. (*CW 9i* 219)

This effect of the wise old man archetype, Jung says, 'tempts one to connect him somehow or other with God' (*CW 9i* 225), which is probably the prime example of the archetype and suggests that through it one enters the deepest layer of the unconscious.

What the wise old man is the guide or initiator to is the *anima* (Latin, 'spirit' or 'soul'). This broad and multivalent archetype represents 'the feminine and chthonic part of the soul,' and influences to one degree or another most of the representations or experiences of the feminine, the earthly, and the material (*CW 9i* 59). Just as the shadow may in its moral inversion typify the whole of the collective unconscious, so may the anima in its contrasexual otherness. The anima is usually recognizable for being a powerful and captivating female figure. This figure may be young and alluringly virginal, a goddess, maiden, or muse: or she may be older, fecund, and replete with maternal authority (or both simultaneously, as with Catholicism's Virgin Mary, or in duality as with the Greek myth of Demeter and Persephone). The deeper and more potent of the two manifestations is the anima's maternal aspect, however, which Jung refers to as the *great mother* or the *chthonic mother.* She often typifies the source and totality of the collective unconscious against which the conscious subject struggles but apart from which it is incomplete:

> She is not a shallow creation, for the breath of eternity lies over everything ... The anima lives beyond all categories ... Since the beginning of time, man ... has been engaged in combat with his soul and its daemonism. If the soul were uniformly dark it would be a simple matter. Unfortunately this is not so, for the anima can also appear as an angel of light, a psychopomp who points the way to the highest meaning ... If the encounter with the shadow is the 'apprentice-piece' of the individual's development, then that with the anima is the 'master-piece.' The relation with the anima is again a test of courage, an ordeal by fire for the spiritual and moral forces of man. (*CW 9i* 29)

If the conscious subject is female, then the archetypal equivalent that she encounters is the *animus,* the rational, masculine component of the collective unconscious. This archetype manifests itself as a powerful male figure, an idealized husband, warrior, prince, or father, or conversely, a seductive rogue or criminal. As the anima represents the principle of *eros* to the male, the animus represents the principle of *logos* to the female, and influences her impressions of men as well as ideas and spiritual matters. The wise old man, when encountered or projected by the female subject, is usually not an 'independent' archetype, Jung suggests, but a manifestation of the animus (*CW 9i* 229). In such cases, the great mother may appear singly.

All these figures are connected and related to each other by virtue of a primary, central archetype. Over the course of its encounters with the figures of the collective unconscious, the conscious subject itself usually assumes or develops an archetypal guise, which represents it in relation to the other archetypes and which is in turn moulded and influenced by them. Jung calls this the *supraordinate personality* or the *self.* This archetype functions as the hypothetical centre of the psyche, the archetypal anchor of consciousness, and the principle of balance and coherence one strives to acquire through negotiation with the other archetypes. It typically takes the form of a heroic central figure, a young saviour or warrior, or quite often, Jung says, simply a child. The *puer aeternalis* or *filius sapientiae* aspect of Christ or the Buddha, or the miraculous childhoods of various classical heroes, are prime examples. Where a virgin or maiden figure is an aspect of the anima when projected by the male subject, in the case of a female subject it is her archetype of the self, and traverses a similar arc of development as the male's. Just as the male's supraordinate personality develops toward and through its supreme sacrifice to or death-struggle with the chthonic mother, the maidenhood of the female self dies into its wifehood and motherhood through a hierogamy with the animus. The principle of futurity that is the primary symbolism of a child or youthful character, Jung insists, is actually emblematic of the growth potential of the self, as the centre of the conscious psyche, in interaction with the other aspects of the collective unconscious. The growth of a hero or heroine in myth or fiction, he writes,

> may be regarded as illustrating the kind of psychic events that occur in the entelechy or genesis of the 'self.' The 'miraculous birth' tries to depict the way in which this genesis is experienced. Since it is a psychic genesis, everything must happen non-empirically, e.g., by means of virginal birth, or immaculate conception, or by birth from unnatural organs. The motifs of 'insignificance,' exposure, abandonment, danger, etc. try to show how precarious is the psychic possibility of wholeness, that is, the enormous difficulties to be met with in attaining this 'highest good' ... More especially the threat to one's inmost self from dragons and serpents points to the danger of the newly acquired consciousness being swallowed up again by the instinctive psyche, the unconscious ... The hero's main feat is to overcome the monster of darkness: it is the long-hoped-for and expected triumph of consciousness over the unconscious. (*CW 9i* 166–7)

Such remarks suggest that the unfolding order of Jungian archetypology is essentially the structure of romance, the conventional story-arc of individual heroic development and victory. Recognizable in Jung's assortment of archetypes are the main character-types of romance: the dark antagonist, the paternal king, the maternal queen, the eroticized princess-bride, and the young knight-hero. Jung would doubtless insist that essential types and images of Christian (particularly Catholic and Anglican) theology – the Father God, the Mother Church, the Virgin Bride, and the Son – are related to this structure as well, as are several figures from the Tarot, for instance. Just as Eliade's elemental archetypes cohere into a cosmology, prompting him to give primary importance to creation myths, Jung's model of the self's journey among the other archetypal figures expresses his belief that the essential and most important structure of myth is the romance quest. It is not surprising, then, that Jung finds the great mythic cipher of the mandala to be reflective not of the planes of the cosmos, as Eliade argues, but of the romance structure of the collective unconscious. The circular mandala, with its many layers and its typically fourfold or 'squared' centre, is for Jung not a diagram of the levels of the universe, but the archetype of the self in relation to the other major archetypes. In his essay 'Concerning Mandala Symbolism' (1950), he writes:

> [The] basic motif is the premonition of a centre of personality, a kind of central point within the psyche, to which everything is related, by which everything is arranged, and which is itself a source of energy. The energy of the central point is manifested in the almost irresistible compulsion and urge to *become what one is*, just as every organism is driven to assume the form that is characteristic of its nature, no matter what the circumstances. This center is not felt or thought of as the ego but, if one may so express it, as the *self*. Although the centre is represented by an innermost point, it is surrounded by a periphery containing everything that belongs to the self – the paired opposites that make up the total personality. This totality comprises consciousness first of all, then the personal unconscious, and finally an indefinitely large segment of the collective unconscious whose archetypes are common to all mankind. (*CW 9i* 357)

The mandala appears in therapeutic, religious, and artistic contexts 'in connection with chaotic psychic states,' Jung says, because it serves 'the purpose of reducing the confusion to order' (*CW 9i* 360). It is itself 'the archetype of wholeness,' an *imago Dei* in the human unconscious (*CW 9i* 388).

This contrast with Eliade brings two other issues in Jung's theory into specific relief. First, we can see that just as Eliade's archetypology is more accommodating to elemental and cosmological symbolism and less to mythic figures (particularly human ones), Jung's is more apt to recognize the significance of mythic characters than cosmological symbols. By his own admission, Jung gives priority to archetypes that 'can be directly experienced in personified form,' which include the archetypes as they appear in *theriomorphic* or animal guises (*CW 9i* 37). He also acknowledges the existence of what he calls *archetypes of transformation,* which 'are not personalities, but ... typical situations, places, ways and means' (*CW 9i* 38). While he does not enumerate or incorporate these into his archetypal structure, they are present by implication and indicate the degree to which Jung, in contrast to Eliade, is interested in understanding the mythic resonances of the phenomenologically perceived human world. But while he makes occasional offhand remarks about the ocean as a symbol for unconscious, or garden-imagery as being associated with the anima archetype, Jung has little to say about cosmogonic myths or elemental symbolism (an oversight at least one major Jungian has sought to correct).[6]

Second, and more important, we can see that Jung's archetypology has an inverse but equally problematic relationship to the question of evil. While Eliade's theories try to disavow the presence of evil in myth through a sanitizing Platonism, Jung's theories essentialize evil in myth by making it an inexorable fact of human psychology. It is not simply that Jung designates the shadow archetype, or the demonic aspect of the anima, to be essential features of myth and the collective unconscious: it is the combination of this and his belief that the projection of the archetypes is an autonomous or 'authochthonous' process. Faced with the apparent constancy of evil in life and myth, it is certainly tempting to theorize it as a metaphysical constant or an essential principle of human behaviour, and we must never pretend that myth does not depict titanic struggles and conflicts between forces of various kinds. But to suggest that evil is an inalienable facet of myth, to affirm evil as essential human nature, places real limits on what myth can do in and for culture, and is profoundly pessimistic from the point of view of human destiny. In such a view mythic experience becomes the story of a never-ending and unwinnable struggle between the destructive and creative instincts of the unconscious, an ongoing narrative in life and art of humanity's emergence from and collapse back into its darker nature. As Volodymyr Odajynk recognizes, 'there is a kind of symbiosis between internal psychological forces and those of the external environment,' such that when the psyche 'is at war with itself, class, racial and national wars will follow' (Odajynk 65). Or as Jung himself puts it, 'man's war-like instincts are ineradicable' because he 'harbours within himself a dangerous shadow and adversary who is involved as an invisible helper in the dark machinations of the political monster' (*CW 10* 225, 299). Thus Odajynk accurately deduces that

> Jung does not believe that a state of perfect peace, whether individual or social, is possible or even desirable; for in any more or less perfectly balanced condition 'one is threatened with suffocation and unbearable ennui,'[7] so that a perfect balance seeks an imbalance and a perfect peace breeds war ... for the natural condition of man is to be in a state of war. (Odajynk 112)

There is pragmatic wisdom here, to be sure, but it clearly is too pragmatic. The danger lies in committing humanity to a state where conflict and war are accepted as inevitabilities by enshrining evil and destructiveness as essential and permanent attributes of human psychology. Jung suggests at various points in his writing that the *ouroboros,* the ancient circular symbol of the serpent eating its own tail, is the image of the undifferentiated psyche, a consciousness that has not yet begun the romance of archetypal encounter. One speculates that the *ouroboros* then becomes the mandala, dividing and splitting like an embryonic cell as this process unfolds. If we are right in our sense of the implications of Jung's essentializing of evil, we can see that it seems to be the destiny of the mandala to perpetually dissolve into its original ouroboric state, to devour itself over and over again. For Jung, myth is a cultural entity at war with itself, divided against itself, a constant cycle of internal (and hence external) strife. A myth that eats its own tale, so to speak, is as much a curse as an empowerment to the conscious subject, however, and it is little wonder therefore that the advent of Jung's theories was followed by ardent calls, such as those made by Rudolf Bultmann and Roland Barthes, for the 'demythologizing' of culture. It is little wonder, too, that Jungian commentators often find themselves debating whether the dominant influence on his thought was Gnostic spirituality or Nietzschean philosophy, with some arguing it is a fusion of the two. As J.J. Clarke writes, Jung 'tended, rather as Nietzsche did, to see society as little more than a thin veneer stretched over the surface of primitive instincts' (Clarke 157).

This and the other problematic dimensions of Jung's theory that we have cited weigh heavily on his sense of the overall function of myth. By virtue of these dimensions Jung is required to theorize that manifold function as being as much one of containment and restraint as one of affirmation and liberation. Jung believes that the role of myth, the purpose of the romance of archetypal encounter, is to facilitate the process of *individuation.* He broadly defines individuation as 'the maturation process of personality induced by the analysis of the unconscious' (*CW 9i* 159). Individuation 'throws a bridge between present-day consciousness ... and the natural, unconscious, instinctual wholeness of primeval times' (*CW 9i* 174). Its goal is to develop the archetype of the self and bring it into harmony with the conscious psyche, and in doing so establish the existence of the other archetypes. The process reveals to the conscious mind that its primary perceptions, including its perceptions of itself, are the projected contents of the collective unconscious. Individuation 'dissolve[s] the projections' as such, 'in order to restore their contents to the individual who has involuntarily lost them by projecting them outside himself' (*CW 9i* 84), leading to the realization that human subjectivity constitutes the world. Individuation, Jung suggests, is a contemporary psychoanalytical means of establishing what medieval alchemy called the *unio mentalis* ('unified mind') or the *unus mundus* ('one world'): 'the assumption that the multiplicity of the empirical world rests on an underlying unity,' which in Jung's theory is the god-imago or mandala of the collective unconscious (*CW 14* 537–8).

This process sounds wholly commendable until one remembers that the structure of this *unus mundus* is something that has been metaphysically predetermined for man, something over which he has no direct influence or understanding. As Jung maintains, in a passage that rivals any by Otto or Eliade in its abasement of human life,

> Nobody ever feels himself as the subject of such a process, but always as its object. He does not perceive [it], it takes him captive and overwhelms him; nor does he behold it in revelation, it reveals itself to him, and he cannot even boast that he has understood it properly. Everything that happens is apparently outside the sphere of his will, and these happenings are the contents of the unconscious. (*CW 11* 152)

As the recognition and recovery of projected archetypes, individuation is therefore at best a hazy spectacle for the audience of the conscious mind, and at worst an exercise in *post-factum* self-restraint and damage control. The latter becomes particularly necessary by virtue of the presence and action of the negative or oppositional archetypes, such as the shadow. As Odajynk concludes:

> A certain amount of consciousness and acceptance of the shadow helps avoid ... potentially dangerous development[s]. It checks the projection of the psyche's negative qualities upon others and the involuntary need for and creation of enemies, and it promotes a degree of modesty and humility and an increased sense of personal responsibility. (Odajynk 77)

Jung's gothic conception of myth as a foreboding otherness and an imposing authority inscribes the need for the adoption of such abstinent attitudes and demeanours, just as conservative social policy often does by configuring the authority and hierarchy of the state and nominating its others. One cannot help but cringe, in fact, to see Jung, as a German-speaking Swiss, writing in 1938 that individuation is a state of 'open conflict and open collaboration' with myth and 'an urgent question of psychic hygiene' (*CW 9i* 288, 93). Like conventional conservative social policy, individuation, true to its terminological promise, ascribes an ultimate *individualism.* It is, Jung insists, 'the process by which a person becomes a psychological "in-dividual," that is, a separate, indivisible unity or "whole" (*CW 9i* 275). There is in other words no real provision in Jung's thought for the mythic coherence of anything beyond the individual.[8] The archetypes may be collective in the sense of being common to all humanity, but Jung intends for them to play out their drama on the stage of the individual's conscious and unconscious mind, not least because the reckless projection of them presents the prospect of larger social conflicts and war. It is indeed one of the great ironies of intellectual history that the great theorist of the 'collective unconscious' should have developed a conservative's suspicion of and resistance to appeals to the social collective. 'Any large company of wholly admirable persons,' Jung claims, nevertheless 'has the morality and intelligence of an unwieldy, stupid and violent animal. The bigger the organization, the more unavoidable is its immorality and blind stupidity' (*CW* 7 150).

Jung once wrote that myth affords the opportunity for 'an inner colloquy with one's good angel' (*CW 9i* 40). But another remark of his, which inverts this image, is more indicative of his perspective: 'One does not become enlightened by imagining figures of light, but by making the darkness conscious' (Wehr 55). Such a remark serves as a reminder that Jung is evidently less interested in theorizing myth as something that benefits human consciousness, and more interested in it as the expression of dark instincts and primal drives that are destined to upend and oppress it, products of a region of the mind 'where reason, will and good intentions never penetrate' (*CW 16* 15). As a result of this inclination, he regards myth not as a fortunate consequence of consciousness but consciousness as an unfortunate consequence of myth. In drafting a theory of myth that presents it as an *a priori* and autonomous entity, Jung, like Eliade, is forced to resign conscious human life to the status of a mere object of culture, and forced again to deny that culture the larger unities it often seeks: unities which myth itself often seems to encourage. As with Eliade, in Jung we are presented with a set of archetypes that help illuminate the structures of myth, for they are recognizable as categories of our mythic experience. But we cannot accept the phenomenology of myth he offers to account for these archetypes if we hope to advance the cause of human agency, or speak for more than the individual right, or assuage the lust for *Götterdämmerung* that must become the ephemera, not the essence, of human life. For mythographies that are more congruent with these priorities, we must turn from those which fret in the shadow of the Old World's philosophical traditions to those that cleave to the freedoms of the New.

three

The Inner Reaches of Outer Space: Joseph Campbell and the Two Faces of Myth

What we are looking for is a way of experiencing the world that will open us to the transcendent that informs it, and at the same time forms ourselves within it.

Joseph Campbell, *The Power of Myth* (61)

If C.G. Jung is the most influential mythologist of the twentieth century, the most popular, in every sense of the word, is surely Joseph Campbell. Thoroughly committed to myth's existential value and suspicious of the narrowness of academic standards, Campbell continually sought ever-wider audiences for his writings and ideas. From his co-authorship of *A Skeleton Key to Finnegans Wake* (1944), a study of Joyce's myth-infused masterwork, to his reputation-building *The Hero with a Thousand Faces* (1949), to his magisterial four-volume survey of world mythology *The Masks of God* (1959–67), Campbell's career was one of steadily growing public fame. This notoriety was increased exponentially and sealed in the popular consciousness by two documentary television series on his ideas that were broadcast to large audiences after his death in 1987: the interview-based *The Power of Myth* (1988) and the lecture-based *Transformation of Myth through Time* (1990). Joseph Campbell has since become one of the few academics, and perhaps the only mythologist, of whom the literate layman is likely to have heard. As Walter Gulick observes, 'Campbell is taken by many with the seriousness that is generally accorded the prophet, the priest or the guru' (Gulick 29). Numerous as Jungian institutes and societies might be, even Jung's work has not attained the public popularity and acceptance necessary to provoke the bookstore discussion groups and self-help retreats that Campbell's has. *The Hero with a Thousand Faces* has sold nearly a million copies, which is remarkable for a work of cultural theory.[1] The book even celebrated its fortieth anniversary by making an appearance on the bestseller lists, after the publication of *The Power of Myth* interviews in book form drew it back into the public eye (Manganaro 151). Of the second generation of modern mythologists, Campbell alone has managed to recapture the ability of the foundational theorists to not simply illuminate but actually inspire works of art. Just as the books of Frazer and Weston were midwives for the most acclaimed literary works of their time, novels of Joyce and Lawrence and the poetry of Eliot and Yeats, so Campbell's books have breathed life into the most popular cinematic works of his time, the films of George Lucas and Steven Spielberg.[2]

When compared to that of the other mythologists of the present study, the arc of Campbell's career somewhat resembles Jung's, in that he too began by studying myth in an academic environment, gained broader repute at Eranos, and ended up as something of a public mystagogue. The shared pattern of ascension and Campbell's sidelong engagement with archetypal psychoanalysis have prompted some to label him outright a Jungian, which is inaccurate. Campbell's life and work actually bears more resemblance to that of Northrop Frye. Both Campbell and Frye were raised in fundamentalist religious traditions[3] from which they eventually broke, in hopes of finding a more liberal, myth-inspired spirituality. Both studied in Europe for their master's degrees, and were influenced by a virtually identical group of movements and thinkers: the Romanticism of Blake, the modernism of Joyce and Eliot, the philosophy of Vico and Spengler, and the mythography of Frazer, Freud, and Jung. Both forsook the doctoral degree, believing that excessive specialization would limit the breadth and relevance of their work. Both were motivated to write their first books by the conflagration of the Second World War (cf. *Hero* 389, *FS* iii), and both were staunchly committed to the vocation of teaching. But Campbell and Frye differed in many ways as well, and often in the stereotypical ways in which Americans and Canadians are said to differ. While Campbell has been called a 'prophet' of the myth of 'American individualism,' Frye has been described as a 'national oracle' in Canada (K. King 69, Richter 677). In youth, Campbell played jazz saxophone, while Frye mastered classical piano. In their later years, Campbell resisted the influence of the biblical tradition, while Frye increasingly moved the Bible to the centre of his critical interests. By Jung's categories of personality, Campbell identified himself as an 'extrovert,' while Frye saw himself as an 'introvert.' Thus Campbell was probably the more engaging speaker and lecturer, while Frye was unquestionably the superior writer (although he too could captivate large audiences). Over the course of their careers, both moved, in the words of Marc Manganaro, 'into progressively more powerful positions, from literary critic to mythologist to ... guru' (Manganaro 158). But while this development was deliberate in Campbell's case, it was consequential in Frye's. Frye never abandoned literary criticism as Campbell did, and was a mythologist only by virtue of the theories he derived from literature, and not by sole intent. Frye resisted the notion that he had 'disciples' or that a 'school' had formed around his work (*SM* 100), whereas Campbell found the notion of a broad circle of influence quite congenial (*Journey* 175). Given these similarities and differences, it is perhaps not surprising that Frye's primary impact has been on the study of myth and the arts inside the academy, and has filtered out into popular culture, while Campbell's primary impact has been on the study of myth and the arts in popular culture, and has filtered into the academy. Both men happily addressed just about any forum into which they were invited, but they clearly had their centres of gravity on opposite sides of the campus fence. A survey of 950 academic journals, for instance, found Frye to be the eighth most cited author in the arts and humanities (after such giants as Marx, Aristotle, Shakespeare, Lenin, Freud, Plato, and Barthes [Garfield 56]). Campbell's work, on the other hand, 'has been reviewed and discussed primarily outside the academic field' (Doty, 'Dancing' 5). Gulick's statement that Campbell's work 'has not encouraged wide-spread theoretical criticism ... because it has been regarded as facile, pontificating, derivative or confused' is an exaggeration (Gulick 34). But William Doty's assessment of Campbell's impact on the academic study of myth as 'soft' is probably fair (Doty, 'Dancing' 4).

This comparison is not an idle one, for it gives us some insight into the unusual character of Campbell's main contribution to modern mythography, *The Hero with a Thousand Faces*, his most popular and (in his own estimation) most important book. Many of the circumstances described above have been generated by the combination of that work's existential focus and its critical laxity, which are its strength and weakness respectively, and those circumstances in turn continue to influence its reputation. *The Hero with a Thousand Faces* is a remarkably unrigorous and diffuse volume, and contains passages of almost gnostic intensity; there is something to Stanley Edgar Hyman's review of the book as 'amiably befuddled' and 'mystical' (Hyman 457). Campbell presents his argument through brief but incisive theoretical statements that are punctuated by spiritual reflections and wrapped in large swathes of quoted myth and story. His penchant for citing source material at every opportunity rivals Frazer's, and as with Frazer the citations are usually far in excess of what is necessary to make the case, evincing instead a regard for the myths themselves. The mystical overtones, furthermore, give the text an almost poetic inscrutability, such that the book takes on at times the complexion of a modernist mythic pastiche. One suspects that this is precisely the point, that the making of and encounter with myth are as important as the analysis of it. But it does make it challenging for the scholarly reader to assemble a functional theory of myth from the book, let alone critically examine that theory in a comparative context. It can be done, however, and in fact such an exercise prepares us to discuss Frye's works, which make use of some the same alternative modes of discourse (although Frye blends them more seamlessly and in more equal proportion). Once done, this scholarly reader discovers that *The Hero with a Thousand Faces* advances what is simultaneously a more tenable and a more impossible theory of myth than Jung's. Campbell divides and radicalizes the two aspects of Jung's conception of myth, bringing the archetypes of myth into consciousness as actual phenomenological objects, but also re-literalizes their metaphysical basis. Campbell finds archetypes actually to be accessible and beneficial to consciousness through encounters with the unconscious, but holds their ultimate origin and destination to be something very like the sacred. The former development represents a step toward Frye's phenomenology of myth, but the latter position represents a step back to the problematic metaphysics of Eliade. Campbell's relentless focus on the lived experience of myth allows him to reveal its existential authority, but the effort is undercut by his uncritical acceptance of the tradition of metaphysics. The result is a theory of myth that is suitably phenomenological on the one hand, but hopelessly and finally transcendental on the other.

Like Eliade, who starts with his pairing of the sacred and the profane, and Jung, who starts with his distinction between the unconscious and the conscious, Campbell also begins by postulating a mythic/nonmythic binary. Like Jung's, Campbell's binary breaks down further into a trinary, but where the distinction Jung makes between the personal and collective unconscious is of little real importance in his theory of myth, the dual nature of Campbell's mythic source is central to his. As with the other mythologists, there is for Campbell a historical, material 'everyday' consciousness that is only potentially mythic. But Campbell regards the complement it engages to generate mythic experience as actually being twofold. These two aspects of myth are introduced in a passage on the book's first page which, in addition to establishing this duality, gives a sense of Campbell's cultural purview and functions as a kind of thesis statement for the volume:

> Throughout the inhabited world, in all times and under every circumstance, the myths of man have flourished; and they have been the living inspiration of whatever else may have appeared out of the activities of the human body and mind. It would not be too much to say that myth is the secret opening through which the inexhaustible energies of the cosmos pour into human cultural manifestation. Religions, philosophies, arts, the social forms of primitive and historic man, prime discoveries in science and technology, the very dreams that blister sleep, boil up from the basic, magic ring of myth. (*Hero* 3)

Myth for Campbell boils 'up,' in the form of dreams and other personal and cultural activities, from some deeper zone of human consciousness, but it and all the phenomena it inspires are really and firstly expressions of 'the inexhaustible energies of the cosmos.' From the perspective of human life and culture, in other words, myth has a deep psychological rooting, but its source and referent is ultimately metaphysical. Campbell wants these two dimensions of myth to have hermeneutic equivalency, so that myth might have an internal, immediately human significance as well as an external, objective cosmic one: the two sources of myth, Campbell often said, combine to reveal 'the inner reaches of outer space' (a phrase he took as the title of his essay collection of 1986). But as the discussion of *The Hero with a Thousand Faces* unfolds, Campbell makes it clear that he regards the psychological root of a myth, which dictates its perceived, phenomenal nature, to be an extension of its transcendent source. In order to have the full experience of myth, he claims, human consciousness must engage the mythic unconscious, and then move back still further, beyond the psychological meaning, to its primary metaphysical meaning. The first task is most effectively achieved through the psychoanalytic process, obviously, while the second requires a reversing of the central analogy upon which psychoanalysis operates:

> Heaven, hell, the mythological age, Olympus and all the other habitations of the gods, are interpreted by psychoanalysis as symbols of the unconscious. The key to the modern systems of psychological interpretation therefore is this: the metaphysical realm = the unconscious. Correspondingly, the key to open the door the other way is the same equation in reverse: the

> unconscious = the metaphysical realm. 'For,' as Jesus states it, 'behold, the kingdom of God is within you.' Indeed, the lapse of supraconsciousness into a state of unconsciousness is precisely the meaning of the Biblical image of the Fall ... Redemption consists in the return to supraconsciousness. (*Hero* 259)

The aim is to bring consciousness into an awareness of the human, psychological relevance of myth, and then to use this as a springboard to reach absolute, transcendent reality. At the beginning of the second part of *The Hero with a Thousand Faces,* entitled 'From Psychology to Metaphysics,' Campbell outlines the goal in more detail:

> [T]o grasp the full value of the mythological figures that have come down to us, we must understand that they are not only symptoms of the unconscious ... but also controlled and intended statements of certain spiritual principles, which have remained as constant throughout the course of human history as the form and nervous structure of the human physique itself. Briefly formulated, the universal doctrine teaches that all the visible structures of the world – all things and beings – are the effects of a ubiquitous power out of which they rise, which supports and fills them during the period of their manifestation, and back into which they must ultimately dissolve. This is the power known to science as energy, to the Melanesians as *mana,* to the Sioux Indians as *wakonda,* the Hindus as *shakti,* and the Christians as the power of God. Its manifestation in the psyche is termed, by psychoanalysis, *libido.* And its manifestation in the cosmos is the structure and flux of the universe itself. (*Hero* 257–8)

It is interesting to note that the culturally particular names for this 'universal doctrine' cited by Campbell are largely the same as those evoked by Eliade in his definition of the metaphysical sacred in *Patterns in Comparative Religion* (cf. *Patterns* 20). But Campbell adds to them the human psychological energy that Jung after Freud called the libido. In doing so, Campbell seems to be suggesting that there is a human connection to or manifestation of this transcendent reality, back through which consciousness may move to reach it. Thus Campbell defines myth as 'a vehicle of the profoundest moral and metaphysical instruction' whose 'patterns are consciously controlled' to facilitate this (*Hero* 256–7).

Campbell provides a second definition of myth a few pages later which also reflects the phenomenological and metaphysical postulates of his theory, but which provides more information as to how this 'instruction' and these 'patterns' are communicated: 'Myth is a directing of the mind and heart, by means of profoundly informed figurations, to that ultimate mystery which fills and surrounds all existences' (*Hero* 267). Like Jung, Campbell throws the net as wide as possible when it comes to defining what myth is and can be, and he likewise suggests that any aspect of life can be a manifestation of myth. Besides his uselessly broad qualification that myth is 'the living inspiration of whatever else may have appeared,' Campbell regularly cites religion, the arts, philosophy, social theory, and even science as the inflections or reflections of myth. But when he speaks of myth's usage of 'figures' and 'figurations,' as he does in the above, he is foregrounding the inseparable relationship of pictorial and verbal symbols and myth, a relationship which makes the arts the first-born of mythology. The development of the arts, particularly literature, out of myth is something that is theorized in greater detail in Frye's writings, but Campbell also acknowledges literature as myth's most direct inheritor. In fact, he often blurs the line between the two in order to enhance the understanding of both (a technique that is pushed to its extreme in Frye's work, where it becomes a full-blown hermeneutic principle). For instance, Campbell finds it useful to reapply the literary genres or categories of comedy and tragedy, which developed out of myth, back to it in order to clarify in greater detail what myth is actually 'intended' to do:

> The happy ending of the fairy tale, the myth, and the divine comedy of the soul, is to be read, not as a contradiction, but as a transcendence of the universal tragedy of man ... Where formerly life and death contended, now enduring being is made manifest – as indifferent to the accidents of time as water boiling in a pot is to the destiny of the bubble, or as the cosmos to the appearance and disappearance of a galaxy of stars. Tragedy is the shattering of the forms and our attachment to the forms; comedy, the wild and careless, inexhaustible joy of life invincible. Thus the two are the terms of a single mythological theme and experience which includes them both and which they bound: the down-going and the up-coming (*kathodos* and *anodos*), which together constitute the totality of the revelation that is life, and which the individual must know and love if he is to be purged (*katharsis* = *purgatorio*) of the contagion of sin (disobedience to the divine will) and death (identification with the mortal form) ... It is the business of mythology proper, and of the fairy tale, to reveal the specific dangers and techniques of the dark interior way from tragedy to comedy. (*Hero* 28–9)

The literary dimension of Campbell's mythography also requires him to develop or adopt something for which Eliade had no use, and which concerned Jung only tangentially, but which becomes a cornerstone of Frye's thought: a theory of signification, or a semiotic. As we will discover when we examine the experience of Campbell's mythic subject, a theory of signification is both explicitly stated and implicitly assumed in *The Hero with a Thousand Faces,* and is no less problematic as a result. The relevant point to be understood at this juncture, however, is that Campbell's theory of myth has its archetypes issuing from transcendence, into the mythic unconscious, and then into human life and culture through the medium of language and narrative. The attainment of mythic experience, predictably, involves a return trip along the same axis by the same means.

The fact that Campbell's theory of myth involves such a protean process means that he is, as Robert Segal observes, 'finally not Jungian,' but rather 'a mystic' (Segal, *Joseph Campbell* 58). Both points in turn influence the conception of the term *archetype* that he develops in *The Hero with a Thousand Faces.* Because his theory of myth is so multivalent, and has myth taking on so many different incarnations and ramifications, Campbell finds it necessary to develop a working definition of the archetype that is both flexible and diverse. He thus conceptualizes the archetype only loosely in the actual body of his text (so as to proceed unburdened by a single precise definition), but works to demonstrate the diversity and universality of the notion over two pages of footnotes (*Hero* 18–19). In both settings, however, Campbell can be observed moving from psychological to philosophical to religious and mystical conceptions. In his text proper, he declares an acceptance of the Jungian definition, but relates it to *viveka* (Sanskrit, 'discrimination'), a term from Hindu and Buddhist philosophy that refers to the yogic process of distinguishing the real from the unreal. In his footnotes, the first citation again goes to Jung, but he moves on to cite Nietzsche's notion of dream regression, Adolf Bastian's concept of *Elementargedanken* (German, 'elementary ideas'), Franz Boas's 'unity ... of the mental characteristics of man,' Frazer's 'universal constitution of the human mind,' Freud's 'unconscious ideation' of folklore and myth, Cicero, Pliny, the *Corpus Hermeticum,* Augustine, and the *logoi spermatikoi* (Greek, 'seminal reasons') of Stoic philosophy, and arrives finally at the Sanskrit *antarjñeyarūpa* ('subjectively known forms') and the Australian aboriginal word *altjira* ('dream-ancestor-story'). Both sets of references, particularly the longer notational one, evince the mélange of psychological, mystical, metaphysical, and literary concerns at work in Campbell's theory of myth, as well as his desire that the reader of myth should be free to interpret an archetype as any or all of these things.

Some of these conceptions are welcome configurations of the archetype as a tool of phenomenological awareness and inquiry, as a real object of consciousness, indicative of the desire to theorize an actual phenomenology of myth. Campbell's augmentation of the variants of archetype that come down from the Western tradition of rational philosophy with some analogues from Eastern and aboriginal mysticism (*viveka, antarjñeyarūpa, altjira*) seems designed to provide this, for the latter appear to be more centred in conscious experience. Indeed, there is no question that Campbell is interested in developing a theory of myth that is phenomenologically rooted and has the modulations of human consciousness at its centre, and he often theorizes from this basis. Sometimes his phenomenology is stated in rather modest and pragmatic terms, as when he remarks that myth 'link[s] the unconscious to the fields of practical action, not irrationally, in the manner of neurotic projection, but in such a fashion as to permit a mature and sobering, practical comprehension of the fact-world' (*Hero* 257).[4] But more often his comments reveal that it is a more romantic and even epiphanic phenomenology that he has in mind. In the experience of myth, Campbell writes, 'the objective world remains what it was, but because of a shift of emphasis in the subject, is beheld as though transformed' (*Hero* 28). Mythic experience allows consciousness to resolve what he calls 'the paradox of the dual focus':

> From the perspective of the source, the world is a majestic harmony of the forms pouring into being, exploding and dissolving. But what the swiftly passing creatures experience is a terrible cacophony of battle cries and pain. The myths do not deny this agony (the crucifixion); they reveal within, behind, and around it essential peace (the heavenly rose). (*Hero* 288)

Faced with this bold claim, we must stop to ask how it is possible, or rather, *whether* it is possible, given that the conditions of human consciousness are embodied but that the perspective of Campbell's 'source' of myth is metaphysical. The answer can be found through a close reading of the one paragraph in which Campbell ventures, in specific terms, his phenomenology of myth:

> The apprehension of the source of this undifferentiated yet everywhere particularized substratum of being is rendered frustrate by the very organs through which the apprehension must be accomplished. The forms of sensibility and the categories of human thought, which are themselves manifestations of this power, so confine the mind that it is normally impossible not only to see, but even to conceive, beyond the colorful, fluid, infinitely various and bewildering phenomenal spectacle. The function of ritual and myth is to make possible, and then to facilitate, the jump – by analogy. Forms and conceptions that the mind and its senses can comprehend are presented and arranged in such a way as to suggest the truth and the openness beyond. (*Hero* 258)

This last notion, that myth is a special presentation and arrangement of the categories of human consciousness and the senses upon which they are based (and is designed to expand them), is precisely the phenomenological redemption of myth that can be found in the work of Northrop Frye, and here Campbell is on the right track. But the idea becomes contradictory within the context of his theory by virtue of his necessary formulation of consciousness and the senses as limiting and oppositional to the transcendent. If the 'apprehension of the source' is 'rendered frustrate' by the 'forms of sensibility and the categories of human thought,' how can those things then be 'arranged in such a way as to suggest the truth and the openness beyond'? The answer is that they cannot be. Consciousness can never be conscious of something beyond consciousness. As the phenomenological principle of intentionality has it, consciousness is consciousness *of* something, even if that something is the state or product of consciousness itself. The idea that the objects of consciousness can be arranged to dissolve the objects of consciousness is an impossibility. Though subject to all manner of expansion, consciousness is ultimately ultimate to itself.

Campbell recognizes this insofar as he configures myth as a transformation of consciousness, but unfortunately he has already committed myth to being a vehicle of metaphysics, issuing from and returning to the transcendent. Many of his admittedly provocative and beautifully phrased characterizations of myth and archetype therefore become theoretical contradictions and self-erasures. Campbell's remark that 'mythology direct[s] the mind to the unmanifest which is just beyond the eye' is precisely of the type obviated by the contradiction cited above (*Hero* 267). His reminder that the archetypes 'are to be regarded as no more than shadows of the unfathomable reach beyond, where the eye goeth not, speech goeth not, nor the mind, nor even piety' not only makes them subject to the same critique that Eliade's Platonism invites, it even contradicts the statement just quoted (on the issue of where the mind can and cannot 'go'). Campbell's desire to theorize mythic experience as phenomenological is blocked by his belief that myth's source is transcendent. As a result, he is forced to make the same resignation in the face of myth as metaphysical mystery that Jung makes, and in virtually the same terms: 'The paradox of creation, the coming of the forms of time out of eternity,' Campbell writes, 'is the germinal secret of the father. It can never be quite explained' (*Hero* 147; cf. *CW* 7 69).[5]

It is probably this mystified position on the question of mythogenesis that prompts Campbell to qualify that *The Hero with a Thousand Faces* 'is a comparative, not genetic study' (*Hero* 39n). But a comparative study of myth as extensive as his can hardly proceed without at least a provisional sense of how myth originates, and thus Campbell does offer some telling speculations. Like his definition of myth and archetype, Campbell's implied mythogenesis is also a fusion of Jungian and Eliadean, psychological and metaphysical accounts, with secondary consideration given to the romantic humanism that fuels his phenomenological imperative. Early in *Hero*, for instance, Campbell writes that 'the symbols of mythology are not manufactured; they cannot be ordered, invented, or permanently suppressed. They are spontaneous productions of the psyche' (*Hero* 4). Leaving aside that this seems to contradict his other statements about how myth is 'consciously controlled,' what is most noticeable here is the echo of Jung: and as in Jung, there is the implied backing-up of the mythic initiative to an abstraction *a priori* of human consciousness (and ergo metaphysical). But in another Jung-influenced speculation, Campbell seems to suggest that while the mythic unconscious may be prior and even threatening to consciousness, it seems also to be subject and beneficial to it. Campbell writes:

> The unconscious sends all sorts of vapors, odd beings, terrors and deluding images up into the mind – whether in dream, broad daylight, or insanity; for the human kingdom, beneath the floor of the comparatively neat little dwelling that we call our consciousness, goes down into unsuspected Aladdin caves. There not only jewels but also dangerous jinn abide: the inconvenient or resisted psychological powers that we have not thought or dared to integrate into our lives. And they may remain unsuspected, or, on the other hand, some chance word, the smell of a landscape, the taste of a cup of tea, or the glance of an eye may touch the magic spring, and then dangerous

> messengers begin to appear in the brain. These are dangerous because they threaten the fabric of the security into which we have built ourselves and our family. But they are fiendishly fascinating too, for they carry keys that open the whole realm of the desired and feared adventure of the discovery of the self. (*Hero* 8)

The mythic unconscious is 'beneath' consciousness, but it is still part of 'the human kingdom,' with figures that can actually 'appear in the brain.' These are qualifications that the gothic Jung would not make so readily, and while they do not correct the loss of agency or phenomenological authority that the presumption of the mythic unconscious entails, they do reflect Campbell's desire to configure myth as productive to and of consciousness.

Near the end of *Hero*, however, Campbell offers a second, rather Eliadean account of the origin of myth which attributes the presence of the archetypes in the unconscious to a prime encounter with the objective, natural world. Like Eliade, Campbell suggests that the lineaments of the external universe, particularly plants and animals, impressed the structures of myth on to human consciousness, presumably through the authority of the abstract categories, processes, and principles they embodied. But we also detect, beneath the surface of the account, signs of a human agency which he would like to credit with mythogenesis, but which has been metaphysically subordinated:

> For the primitive hunting peoples of those remotest human millenniums when the sabertooth tiger, the mammoth, and the lesser presences of the animal kingdoms were the primary manifestations of what was alien – the source at once of danger, and of sustenance – the great human problem was to become linked psychologically to the task of sharing the wilderness with these beings. An unconscious identification took place, and this was finally rendered conscious in the half-human, half-animal, figures of the mythological totem-ancestors. The animals became the tutors of humanity. Through acts of literal imitation – such as today appear only on the children's playground (or in the madhouse) – an effective annihilation of the human ego was accomplished and society achieved a cohesive organization. Similarly, the tribes supporting themselves on plant-food become cathected to the plant; the life-rituals of planting and reaping were identified with those of human procreation, birth, and progress of maturity. Both the plant and animal worlds, however, were in the end brought under social control. (*Hero* 390)

The external, conceptual world possesses the first authority of form, apparently, but there is also the suggestion of human powers of identification that help bring myth into being. These powers, however, are neither sufficiently emphasized nor sufficiently scrutinized by Campbell. In any case, as we will discover through our discussion of Frye's *Fearful Symmetry*, Campbell has here configured the genesis of myth backwards. In mythic experience, the natural and animal worlds do not become the tutors of humanity: humanity becomes the tutors and domesticators of the natural and animal worlds. Mythic experience is not the structuring of human consciousness in accordance with the facts of the natural world: it is the restructuring of the natural world in accordance with the facts of human consciousness. The mysterious process that Campbell glosses over at the end of his account, of how the 'the plant and animal worlds' were 'brought under social control,' is not the end of the mythic process, but the beginning of it.

When Campbell introduces us to his mythic subject, the ubiquitous universal 'hero' of the book's title, we again observe him trying to fuse, as well as humanistically expand, the Jungian and Eliadean models. Campbell chooses a more romantic appellation for his mythic subject than the other mythologists, both to emphasize his greater belief in the redemptive power of mythic experience and to reinscribe his concern for the literary. He characterizes the hero's experience as something very like Jungian individuation, but with a metaphysical goal similar to the eternal return of Eliade's *homo religiosus*. He does this, however, while simultaneously implying that these are not necessarily encounters with alien forces, but might involve recovered aspects or real experiences of consciousness (which facilitate its expansion). Campbell states:

> [T]he first work of the hero is to retreat from the world scene of secondary effects to those causal zones of the psyche where the difficulties really reside, and there to clarify the difficulties, eradicate them in his own case (i.e., give battle to the nursery demons of his local culture) and break through to the undistorted, direct experience and assimilation of what C.G. Jung has called 'the archetypal images' ... The hero ... is the man or woman who has been able to battle past his personal and local historical limitations to the generally valid, normally human forms. Such a one's visions, ideas, and inspirations come pristine from the primary springs of human life and thought. Hence they are eloquent, not of the present, disintegrating society and psyche, but of the unquenched source through which society is reborn. The hero has died as a modern man; but as eternal man – perfected,

> unspecific, universal man – he has to be reborn. His second solemn task and deed therefore ... is to return then to us, transfigured, and teach the lesson he has learned of life renewed. (*Hero* 17–20)

The 'hero's first task is to *experience consciously* the antecedent stages of the cosmogonic cycle; to break back through the epochs of emanation,' Campbell explains (*Hero* 320, italics added). 'His second is to return from that abyss to the plane of contemporary life, there to serve as the human transformer of demiurgic potentials.' Campbell thus encouragingly describes the hero as 'the waker of his own soul,' the 'one who, while still alive, knows and represents the claims of supraconsciousness' (*Hero* 259–60). Through mythic experience, he says, the hero finds 'all the forces of the unconscious at his side,' for the archetypes 'signify the support of our conscious personality by that other larger system' (*Hero* 72–3). In myth, the hero comes into 'the presence rather of immense consciousness than of darkness' (*Hero* 257).

Yet, in those passages where Campbell details the hero's progression from psychological to mystical-religious awakening, we run aground not only of his sense of psychoanalysis as being of limited value, but, more importantly, of the consciousness-erasing implications of his commitment of the myth to the metaphysical. There is a 'close relationship ... between myth, psychology and metaphysics,' Campbell states, but 'the aims of the two teachings – the traditional and the modern – are not exactly the same' (*Hero* 164):

> Psychoanalysis is a technique to cure excessively suffering individuals of the unconsciously misdirected desires and hostilities that weave around them their private webs of unreal terrors and ambivalent attractions; the patient released from these finds himself able to participate with comparative satisfaction in the more realistic fears, hostilities, erotic and religious practices, business enterprises, wars, pastimes and household tasks offered to him by his particular culture. But for the one who has deliberately undertaken the difficult and dangerous journey beyond the village compound, these interests, too, are to be regarded as based on error. Therefore the aim of the religious teaching is not to cure the individual back again to the general delusion, but to detach him from delusion altogether; and this not by readjusting the desire (*eros*) and hostility (*thanatos*) – for that would only originate a new context of delusion – but by *extinguishing* the impulses to the very root ... (*Hero* 164–5)

Campbell hopes the hero will 'experience consciously' an epiphanic renewal in myth, but this is surely impossible if his impulses are to be extinguished for the purpose of attaining some 'thought-transcending emptiness,' if the hero's 'experiences of ego, form, perceptions, speech, conceptions and knowledge' are barriers to what Campbell calls a 'thought-transcending truth' (*Hero* 165–6). There is no truth transcending thought, for thought is the creation of truth. As Merleau-Ponty explains, in a theoretical axiom that will fully come to bear in the next chapter, thought 'is not the reflection of a pre-existing truth, but, like art, the act of bringing truth into being' (*Phenomenology* xx).

It is precisely this dichotomy that dooms Campbell's theory of signification. Campbell wants the archetype, as a symbol, to have efficacy and reality, be an experience in itself to the subject and therefore have consciousness-transforming potency. But inevitably, the Campbellian archetype, by virtue of its metaphysical basis, has to be declared empty and provisional, a mere conveyance designed to lure the subject away from its perceptible, phenomenal world and into the presence of the transcendent guarantor of all experience and language (which, naturally, itself exceeds experience and language). As Campbell puts it:

> The gods as icons are not ends in themselves. Their entertaining myths transport the mind and spirit, not *up to*, but *past* them, into the yonder void; from which perspective the more freighted theological dogmas then appear to have been only pedagogical lures: their function, to cart the unadroit intellect away from its concrete clutter of facts ... (*Hero* 180)

Drawing upon the terms of literary theorist I.A. Richards, Campbell thus reduces the symbol as perceived to a mere signpost for consciousness on the one hand, and pushes its real referent out of the reach of consciousness on the other: 'Symbols are only the vehicles of communication; they must not be mistaken for the final term, the tenor, of their reference,' he writes. 'No matter how attractive or impressive they may seem, they remain but convenient means, accommodated to the understanding' (*Hero* 236). The mixture of admiring and diminutive tones in this characterization is telling, for Campbell is of two minds on the nature of the symbol, and has committed it to contradictory purposes. Because one of those purposes is metaphysical, however, the fate of the symbol is sealed. When he suggests that 'mistaking a vehicle for its tenor may lead to the spilling not only of valueless ink, but of valuable blood,' we applaud the sentiment as a condemnation of the same simple-minded descriptive literalism against which Frye's theories incline (*Hero* 236). The problem is that the only alternative to such literalism in Campbell's theory is instead to regard the symbol as hollowly referential of a transcendental signified. Thus we find Campbell proffering a final definition of myth which actually demotes it, and contains the inevitable contradictions to and devaluations of phenomenal consciousness:

> Myth is but the penultimate; the ultimate is openness – that void, or being, beyond the categories - into which the mind must plunge alone and be dissolved. Therefore, God and the gods are only convenient means – themselves of the nature of the world of names and forms, though eloquent of, and ultimately conducive to, the ineffable. They are mere symbols to move and awaken the mind, and to call it past themselves. (*Hero* 258)

Another account of this particular effect provided by Campbell in a later essay points up more clearly the difficulty in our accepting it, for it makes reference to what we know to be a highly problematic theological concept: Campbell writes that, at this point in the mythic process, the hero's 'mind, disengaged from the protection of the symbol ... meet[s] directly the *mysterium tremendum* of the unknown' (*Flight* 169). How is it the knowable may refer to the unknowable? If the knowable symbol falls away, does not consciousness go with it, since the symbol is the object of that consciousness? If merely a 'name,' how can the archetype be 'eloquent of' and 'conducive to the ineffable' (Latin, *ineffabilis*, 'not utterable')? These questions become merely rhetorical in the face of the realization that myth cannot simply be a getting-beyond of names to reach the unnameable. If the word 'redemption,' the focus of so much mythic and religious thought, means anything, it means to *re-deem*, to reclaim, recover, or restore.

Campbell openly admits that his theory of myth holds language to be inadequate. In *Myth, Rhetoric, and the Voice of Authority*, Marc Manganaro offers an insightful deconstructive reading of Campbell's methodology that demonstrates why it is so, and culminates in a citation from *The Power of Myth* where the mythologist makes just such a concession:

> Campbell's drive to strip away the linguistic peel to get to the metaphysical fruit, witnessed in both *A Skeleton Key* and *The Hero with a Thousand Faces*, typifies the logocentric search for origins that poststructural efforts condemn. Indeed, Michel Foucault's description of how the search for

absolutes 'necessitates the removal of every mask to ultimately disclose an original identity' not only aptly assesses Campbell's efforts but echoes his metaphor for the procedure. Campbell's fluoroscope functions like the X-ray machine in *A Skeleton Key:* both are required to close the gap between word and spirit, between signifier and signified, and hence to reach what Derrida calls the 'lost presence.' The last words of the recent Public Broadcasting interviews by Bill Moyers make only too clear the metaphysics of presence at work:

MOYERS: The meaning is essentially wordless.
CAMPBELL: Yes. Words are always qualifications and limitations.
MOYERS: And yet, Joe, all we puny human beings are left with is this miserable language, beautiful though it is, that falls short of trying to describe –
CAMPBELL: That's right, and that's why it is a peak experience to break past all that, every now and then, and to realize, 'Oh ... ah.' (Manganaro 159–60)

What Manganaro's critique and citation reveal is that Campbell does not recognize that there is no peak experience beyond language: it is only through a renovation of language that anything like peak experience might become possible. But such a renovation would require a phenomenological and not a transcendental theory of signification. This is, unfortunately, not in the offing in Campbell's theory, for as Manganaro goes on to observe:

> At the heart of Campbell's conception of the commonality of poetry and myth ... is his version of transcendental semiotics: the poetic mind, in tune with myth, intuitively recognizes 'mere trope' and casts it aside ... Poetry, like myth, is not in essence figural but transcendent; thus the poet does not negotiate meaning through the medium of language ... but, rather, follows a beeline to an ultimate meaning that is eminently nonlogical and subjective (associated, after all, with the 'heart' over the 'eyes,' and one can surmise, the head). (Manganaro 168–9)

Manganaro is overstating the case in citing the 'nonlogical' and 'subjective' faculties as obviously problematic, for they have their function, we will discover, in phenomenological signification. Manganaro gives no further consideration to the possibility that there might be such a thing, since poststructuralist critique assumes all theories of stable linguistic meaning to be transcendental:[6] but insofar as Campbell does commit himself to a transcendentalism, Manganaro is right to call attention to his shirking of the task of negotiating meaning through the figural. Where there is no negotiation of meaning through the figural, there can be no consciousness. Thus Campbell's hero reluctantly lies down beside Eliade's *homo religiosus* and Jung's 'modern man' as another model of human subjectivity bilked of its modicum of consciousness and agency by metaphysical mythography.

When we turn our attention to Campbell's mythic structure, the much-applied, much-maligned *monomyth,* we find that it, like so many other aspects of his theory, is equally reflective of his focus on phenomenological process as of his transcendental semiotics. Campbell borrows the term itself from *Finnegans Wake,* to underscore his point that the arc of the hero's journey into mythic consciousness has a single, essential form that is informed by, or assembled out of, the archetypes of myth and literature: he frequently refers to the monomyth as the 'nuclear unit' of myth (*Hero* 30). As Doty observes, the monomyth has become 'an analytic tool for literally hundreds of secondary studies' (*Mythography* 176), to the extent that he claims to have once heard of a journal having to declare a 'temporary moratorium' on articles making critical use of it ('Dancing' 4). Folklorist Alan Dundes warns, however, that the monomyth is a 'synthetic, artificial composite which [Campbell] fails to apply *in toto* to any one single hero,' and which is therefore not 'verifiable ... by means of inductively extrapolated incidents from any one hero's biography' (Dundes 232).[7] Given Campbell's bifurcated theoretical approach, it may be that the monomyth is both a preconceived, abstract pattern into which he compresses myth and literature, and a structure that the writers and readers of myth themselves strive to assemble (but which, for whatever reasons, seldom appears in its entirety).[8] The fact that there have been many highly acclaimed and popular post-Campbell novels and films which illustrate the monomyth with greater fidelity than any of the myths he cites may be evidence of the latter. In any case, it is interesting to observe that while many parts of the monomyth detail supposed engagements with higher levels of metaphysical being, many are also presented as phenomenological expansions of consciousness. The stages of the monomyth are 'thresholds of transformation,' Campbell tells us, or as Robert Ellwood simply refers to them, 'intriguingly-named experiences' (*Hero* 10, Ellwood 143). At first glance, the structure of the monomyth seems to be a detailed elaboration of Jungian individuation, but with some curious rearrangements, and with more emphasis thrown on the positive development of the subject. The arc is tripartite, a progression through the three phases of *departure, initiation,* and *return*: 'A hero ventures forth from the world of common day into a region of supernatural wonder: fabulous forces are there encountered and a decisive victory is won: the hero comes back from this mysterious adventure with the power to bestow boons upon his fellow man' (*Hero* 30). The archetypal phases of this cycle are familiar and recognizable to the student of myth and literature, even without the citation of particular examples.

The first occurrence in the departure phase is the 'Call to Adventure,' which presents the hero with the prospect for growth or transformation in the form of a crisis or opportunity: it is the discovery that 'the familiar life horizon has been outgrown' and that 'the old concepts, ideals, and emotional patterns no longer fit' (*Hero* 51). A failure to respond to this archetype, which Campbell refers to as 'The Refusal of the Call,' can lead to the sudden apprehension of intolerable strictures or even a paralysis of consciousness (manifested, for example, as a sleeping or spellbound character or 'frozen world'), which further augments the need for development and the imperative of the call. When originally or finally heeded, however, the call leads to the revelation of 'Supernatural Aid,' in which consciousness discovers guidance and assistance (often in a personified form similar if not identical to Jung's 'wise old man') and the means to continue the journey (*Hero* 71–3). This continuance in turn presents the hero with the task of 'Crossing the First Threshold,' in which an apotropaic faculty is triggered, creating an archetypal barrier, or something very like the Jungian shadow (which Campbell calls the 'threshold guardian' [*Hero* 82]), to inhibit progress; but as the mythologist writes, 'it is only by advancing beyond those bounds ... that the individual passes ... into a new zone of experience' (*Hero* 82). The reaching of this new zone is symbolized by the hero's descent into 'The Belly of the Whale,' a common image of the transition. Such descents mark the hero's symbolic expansion beyond restrictions of consciousness like the ego; these archetypes 'illustrate the fact that the devotee, at the moment of entry ... undergoes a metamorphosis. His secular character remains without; he sheds it' (*Hero* 92).

The initiation phase begins with what Campbell calls 'The Road of Trials,' a series or sequence of archetypal challenges which indicate that the hero is now wandering 'the crooked lanes of his own spiritual labyrinth' (*Hero* 101). Campbell's characterization of this experience (which is also applicable to the monomyth as a whole) is particularly relevant, given our sense of his conflicting philosophical loyalties:

> In the vocabulary of the mystics, this is the second stage of the Way, that of the 'purification of the self,' when the senses are 'cleansed and humbled,' and the energies and interests 'concentrated upon transcendental things'; or in a vocabulary of more modern turn: this is the process of dissolving, transcending, or transmuting the infantile images of our personal past. (*Hero* 101)

Predictably, the progression through these challenges prepares the hero (the male hero, obviously) for Campbell's archetypes of hierogamy, 'The Meeting with the Goddess' and 'Woman as Temptress,' which, respectively, correspond to the appearance of the eroticized 'maiden' and the 'terrible mother' aspects of a Jungian *anima*.[9] The first of these archetypes presents the hero with the challenge of being worthy of a union with the feminine ideal, while the second forces him to endure the inevitable (s)mothering by the *mate*rial world that accompanies such a union. If the hero can endure this 'moment of revulsion' where the fact that 'everything we think or do is necessarily tainted with the odor of the flesh' and becomes 'intolerable to the pure, pure soul' (*Hero* 122), he is ready to experience a real and final dispensation of the ego: the 'Atonement with the Father.' Here, the reflex-driven 'ogre-aspect of the father' conducts an 'ego-shattering initiation,' which allows him to be seen rather as a benevolent father-god to which the hero might be atoned. In this moment, the hero, Campbell writes, 'open[s] his soul beyond terror to such a degree that he will be ripe to understand how the sickening and insane tragedies of this vast and ruthless cosmos are completely validated in the majesty of being' (*Hero* 147). Having 'experienced' a metaphysical realm whose nature obviates the facts of the phenomenal world, the hero is now understood to have become one with his god, and an 'Apotheosis' is said to have occurred. The hero is now in possession of the enlarged perspective of recovered paradise, which Campbell calls 'The Ultimate Boon,' and it then becomes the hero's task to return to his society with this newfound knowledge.

The first part of the return phase of monomyth may, however, actually be a 'Refusal of the Return.' The hero's new wisdom may be so blissful as to make it difficult for him to resume apprehension of his original setting, and so he balks at the notion of return. When he finally resolves to return, he may have to do so via 'The Magic Flight,' especially if his 'trophy has been attained against the wishes of its guardian.' In such circumstances, 'the last stage of the mythological round becomes a lively, often comical pursuit ... complicated by marvels of magical obstruction and evasion' (*Hero* 197). In other situations, the hero may require 'Rescue from Without,' which is to say, 'the world may have to come and get him ... for the bliss of the deep abode is not lightly abandoned in favor of the wakened state' (*Hero* 207). In either case, 'The Crossing of the Return Threshold' then occurs, which presents to the hero the challenge of how to 'accept as real, after an experience of the soul-satisfying vision of fulfillment, the passing joys and sorrows, banalities and noisy obscenities of life,' of how to 'make plausible, or even interesting, to men and women consumed with passion, the experience of transcendental bliss' (*Hero* 218). If he is able to retain and disseminate his perspectival 'boon brought from the transcendent deep' (*Hero* 218), he becomes 'The Master of Two Worlds.' Now in possession of 'the freedom to pass back and forth across the world division, from the perspective of the apparitions of time to that of the causal deep,' the hero 'no longer resists the self-annihilation that is prerequisite to rebirth in the realization of truth' (*Hero* 229, 237). At this point, he 'no longer tries to live but willingly relaxes to whatever may come to pass in him' (*Hero* 237). Paradoxically, Campbell calls this final stage 'Freedom to Live,' which, he says, is marked by the hero's 'realization of the true relationship of the passing phenomena of time to the imperishable life that lives and dies in all' (*Hero* 238).

Like the arc of Jungian individuation, Campbell's monomyth is basically the structure of romance, but as Ellwood remarks, 'Campbell [is], if conceivable, even more romantic in spirit than Jung or Eliade' (Ellwood 130). Richard A. Underwood's observation that 'Campbell both builds upon and goes beyond the work of Jung' is more to the point (Underwood 16). Jung typically presents individuation as the unconscious confronting consciousness with a series of archetypal guises. Campbell's monomyth seems to be this, but the impression is also given that it may be a case of consciousness expanding into and harnessing the unconsciousness, if the aspects of the unconscious that are discovered are really unconsolidated dimensions of consciousness. There are frequent signs of what we have called Campbell's humanism at work. Where Eliade's archetypes tend to be elemental, and Jung's tend to be personifications, Campbell's tend to be experiential and initiatory or transformational: one has difficulty imagining Eliade's or Jung's theories of myth making an archetype out of a crisis or the experience of disillusionment, isolation, or wisdom. Many of these archetypal experiences are magnificent empowerments, too, as witnessed by such stages as the 'Apotheosis' and 'The Ultimate Boon.' As Segal writes, 'where a Jungian hero is chastened by his confrontation with the unconscious, Campbell's is emboldened.' The Jungian self, Segal notes, returns 'humbled rather than elevated, wary rather than brash, the saved rather than the savior' (Segal, *Joseph Campbell* 22, 64). Where Jung's individuation reveals its Freudian inheritance in the overtones of ironic Oedipal *agon* that colour many of its stages, Campbell's monomyth, with episodes like 'Atonement with the Father,' reveals itself to be more of a Telemachan comedy, a reunification of the archetypal family. Campbell thus grandly characterizes the monomyth as 'effecting a reconciliation of the individual consciousness with the universal will' (*Hero* 238). The claim is both encouraging and troubling, and we must again ask, this time in the context of the monomyth structure, whether it is possible. Our previous experience with Eliade and Jung has taught us where to look for an answer.

In the same way that Eliade and Jung see their totalities of myth reflected in the image of the mandala, Campbell, too, finds this prime effect of the monomyth enacted in that venerable icon. As was the case with the other mythologists, Campbell's interpretation of this symbolic complex is indicative of the strengths, weakness, and real destination of his theory. He does not explicitly relate his monomyth to the mandala in *The Hero with a Thousand Faces*, as Eliade and Jung do in their main writings, but all three of the conceptual diagrams in *Hero* strongly suggest the connection (*Hero* 30, 245, 266). In his later essay 'The Symbol without Meaning' (1957), however, Campbell raises the issue of the mandala, suggesting that it is not structured after absolute cosmology, as in Eliade, or after the form of the collective unconscious, as in Jung, but has to do with the structure of the human world:

> We have to ask ourselves whether it can be properly claimed that these geometric forms, which have become the commonplaces of our modern psychological discussion of archetypal symbols, actually do represent basal structures of the human psyche, or may not, rather, be functioned only of a certain type or phase of social development. (*Flight* 141)

Almost as if he were prescient of the poststructuralist critique of metaphysics that was on the horizon as he was writing, Campbell exhorts us to leave behind the mandala as a symbol of objective order, as something that reflects the otherness of the heavens or the unconscious, and plumb the resources of human creative power for some other structure or experience:

> Today, when the mandala itself, the whole structure of meaning to which society and its guardians would attach us, is dissolving, what is required of us all, spiritually as well as corporeally, is much more of the fearless self-sufficiency of our shamanistic inheritance than the timorous piety of the priest-guided Neolithic. (*Flight* 189)

But we are left to wonder what structure or experience might result from our becoming 'fearlessly self-sufficient,' 'spiritually as well as corporeally,' for Campbell, disappointingly, does not speculate. When he addresses again the meaning of the mandala in *The Power of Myth* interviews, however, we learn that he has settled on a conventional and problematic interpretation that confirms what we have already discovered about his theory of myth:

> 'Mandala' is Sanskrit for 'circle,' but a circle that is coordinated or symbolically designed so that it has the meaning of a cosmic order. When composing mandalas, you are trying to coordinate your personal circle with the universal circle. In a very elaborate Buddhist mandala, for example, you have the deity in the center as the power source, the illumination source. The peripheral images would be manifestations or aspects of the deity's radiance. In working out the mandala for yourself, you draw a circle and then think of the different impulse systems and value systems in your life. Then you compose them and try to find out where your center is. Making a mandala is a discipline for pulling all those aspects of your life together, for finding a center and ordering yourself to it. [Then] you try to coordinate your circle to the universal circle. (*Power* 271)

Campbell's remarks are more conversational than theoretical here, but they are nevertheless salient for our purposes. On the human level, the mandala is *created*; it is not something that reflects what *is* in the heavens or the unconscious, but something human consciousness makes of and for itself. But this has always to be 'coordinated' with the pre-existent, higher mandala, the mandala as the 'universal circle,' a 'cosmic order' that sounds very like the Eliadean configuration. What form might a coordination of these two circles take? The question is moot, for in conventional geometry (or signification, as the case may be) there is no equation that allows for the intersection of two-dimensional surfaces in three-dimensional space. Any arrangement is therefore hierarchical, and again the promising prospect of phenomenological process is trumped by the metaphysical assumption. If Eliade's cosmological mandala becomes the Möbius, the closed circuit, and Jung's mandala of the unconscious becomes the *ouroboros*, the worm that consumes itself, Campbell's two (sur)faces of myth become the *parallelepipedon*, the parallel planes that the mathematician Euclid tells us can never, by definition, meet (*Elements* XI, def. 8).

As Karen L. King recognizes, Campbell wants to 'replac[e] the notion of ontological hierarchy with democratic principles,' but in fact 'the whole metaphysical schema he presupposes is based on a socio-political pattern of hierarchy not acceptable to modern Americans' (K. King 75). This leads necessarily to what Segal understands is 'a devaluation of the everyday world' (Segal, *Joseph Campbell* 63), a subordination of the human sphere not unlike that suffered by Eliade's profane. Thus we have the hero enduring his 'moment of revulsion' at the nature of the material world in order to make way for 'The Atonement with the Father,' an establishing of metaphysical authority over it. We have Campbell's remark that the hero's 'basic problem' is to reach a state where 'the body with its attendant personality will no longer obstruct the view' (*Hero* 189). We have Campbell's acceptance of the conventional reading of the Hindu and Buddhist concept of *nirvana* as an extinguishing of desire (as opposed to, say, the full satisfaction of it), a dispensing with the libido which we know to be the manifestation of creative energy on the human plane (*Hero* 163n). We have Campbell's emphasis on *amor fati*, which is not actually a love of fate but the resignation to it, for the initiated hero 'no longer tries to live' but accepts 'whatever may come to pass' (*Hero* 27, 237). We have Campbell's unabashed 'preference of the mystical to the ethical' (Gulick 32). We have the hero's triumphant return become, as Segal recognizes, a 'sham,' for the human world is now 'worthless,' and 'he is returning only to apprise others of that fact' (Segal, *Joseph Campbell* 63).

Campbell's sense of myth as having an ultimately transformative purpose is romantic and optimistic, even utopian, and his motivations for wanting to realize that purpose cannot be criticized as such. They should in fact be applauded, for as he nobly declares in the preface to *The Hero with a Thousand Faces*:

> My hope is that a comparative elucidation [of myth] may contribute to the perhaps not-quite-desperate cause of those forces that are working in the present world for unification, not in the name of some ecclesiastical or political empire, but in the sense of human mutual understanding. (*Hero* viii)

Campbell understands that 'if God is a tribal, racial, national, or sectarian archetype, we are the warriors of his cause,' but that 'if he is the lord of the universe itself, we then go forth as ... brothers' (*Hero* 162). But because for him that 'lord of the universe' is first a metaphysical principle and only later something which the brothers, as questing heroes, might create of themselves, the 'transmutation of the whole social order' that he wants to occur cannot be everything he hopes it to be (*Hero* 389). Indeed, in Campbell's arrangement of myth, it becomes a 'transcendent force ... which lives in all, in all is wonderful, and is worthy of our profound *obeisance*' (*Hero* 44, italics added). Even if this were possible, we would remain, however blissfully, however developed in our own right, subjects to a higher object, or objects to a higher subject.

Campbell's theory holds that mythic experience leads to the 'destruction of the world that we have built and in which we live, and of ourselves within it; but then a wonderful reconstruction, of the bolder, cleaner, more spacious, and fully human life' (*Hero* 8). As we will discover, Frye's *Fearful Symmetry* reaches out, often through similar rhetoric, toward a similar apocalyptic realization. Both mythologists have in mind the notion of the universal body of man, the Joycean Everyman to which they both periodically allude. From his account, we feel Campbell very nearly understands the goal, the dialectic and interpenetration of particular and universal, of individual and collective, of part and whole. But something also seems amiss:

> In his life-form the individual is necessarily only a fraction and distortion of the total image of man. He is limited either as male or female; at any given period of his life he is again limited as child, youth, mature adult, or ancient; furthermore, in his life role he is necessarily specialized as craftsman, tradesman, servant or thief, priest, leader, wife, nun or harlot; he cannot be all. Hence, the totality – the fullness of man – is not in the separate member, but in the body of the society as a whole; the individual can be only an organ. (*Hero* 383)

The goal cannot be fulfilled in relation to the field of the absolute that Campbell presumes, which subtly inflects everything as a question of positive and negative, meaningful and meaningless, better and worse, more and less worthy. 'The great figure of the moment,' Campbell writes, 'exists only to be broken' (*Hero* 337). The dream of transcendence actually serves to reinforce its unattainability. He therefore somewhat tiredly intones:

> The tribal ceremonies of birth, initiation, burial, installation, and so forth, serve to translate the individual's life-crises and life-deeds into classic, impersonal forms. They disclose him to himself, not as this personality or that, but as the warrior, the bride, the widow, the priest, the chieftain; at the same time rehearsing for the rest of the community the old lesson of the archetypal stages. All participate in the ceremonial according to *rank* and function. (*Hero* 383, italics added)

Thus we come to the curiously deflated coda of *The Hero with a Thousand Faces*, which implies, rather as Jung's conclusions did, that an insoluble tension persists between the community and the individual, whose first obligation is to a 'higher' destiny that codifies his individualism and guarantees an uncomfortable degree of personal isolation:

> The modern hero, the modern individual who dares to heed the call and seek the mansion of that presence with whom it is our destiny to be atoned, cannot, indeed must not, wait for his community to cast off its slough of pride, fear, rationalized avarice, and sanctified misunderstanding ... It is not society that is to guide and save the creative hero, but precisely the reverse. And so every one of us shares the supreme ordeal – carries the cross of the redeemer – not in the bright moments of his tribe's great victories, but in the silences of his personal despair. (*Hero* 391)

We will not go so far as to sanction such *ad hominems* as Segal's labelling of Campbell as 'unabashedly elitist' (Segal, *Joseph Campbell* 149), or the many conservative proclivities and indiscretions discussed by Ellwood. Our focus has been on Campbell's mythography rather than his biography, and we have gone some way, in the recognition of his humanism, toward dispensing with such questions. But in its misconfigurations of myth's departure point and its destination, Campbell's theory itself, in the final analysis, lends some legitimacy to Manganaro's admittedly harsh assessment that its 'drive toward the absence of nation, gender, and religion effectively functions as a logocentric tactic of assimilation' (Manganaro 175).

But the sense of existential empowerment that abides in the work of Joseph Campbell is not false, not a function of rhetorical inflation. It comes as a result of his recognition of the real apocalyptic potential of mythic consciousness. Campbell's theories become bogged down, however, on the broken ground of what Frye after Blake calls the 'cloven fiction,' the supposition that man and God, body and spirit, world and word, might not initially or finally share the same substance. If acute and deliberate cultivations of this type of thinking, such as poststructuralism, serve any purpose, it is to discern the unknowing cultivations of it, so that both might be identified and then redeemed within a more genuinely unifying vision. Such is the relationship between the methodology we have employed here and *The Hero with a Thousand Faces.* If some aspects of Campbell's theory must be resigned to the apocrypha of mythography, alongside elements of Eliade's and Jung's, solace is to be found in the fact that many others may be carried forward as reconcilable with the more far-reaching and yet more tenable project of Frye. Like Eliade's cosmology and the personae of Jung, Campbell's monomyth, we will discover, is well contained and well used in Frye's immense archetypology. Moreover, Campbell's phenomenology of myth has prepared us to engage the more radical aspects of Frye's theories of mythic consciousness and signification, which share many of the same goals. Above all, we will find Campbell's ambitions extended and fulfilled in the titanic vision of Frye. It is to that vision, in its various incarnations, that the foregoing work is commended, and the remainder of our work is devoted.

four

Cleansing the Doors of Perception: Northrop Frye's *Fearful Symmetry*

If the doors of perception were cleansed everything would appear to man as it is: Infinite.

William Blake, *The Marriage of Heaven and Hell*

I. Perception and Imagination

The origin of *Fearful Symmetry* can be traced back to a cold night in February of 1934, when the then twenty-two-year-old Northrop Frye was working on a paper on William Blake for a graduate school seminar. As he sat in an all-night cafeteria on Bloor Street in Toronto called Bowles Lunch, working on a reading of Blake's *Milton*, something unusual happened, which he would later recount at least three times in three different settings. 'I ... started working on [the paper] the night before I was to read it,' Frye told interviewer David Cayley. 'It was around three in the morning when suddenly the universe just broke open, and I've never been, as they say, the same man since.' Pressed to describe the experience further, Frye could only say that it was 'just the feeling of an enormous number of things making sense that had been scattered and unrelated before,' the result of 'a mythological framework taking hold' (*NFC* 47). Another account of that night which he gave in a letter to his friend and mentor Pelham Edgar is interesting for its reverse angle on the epiphany, and some minor discrepancies in detail:

> At about two in the morning some very curious things began happening in my mind. I began to see glimpses of something bigger and more exciting than I had ever before realized existed in the world of the mind, and when I

> went out for breakfast at five-thirty on a bitterly cold morning, I was committed to a book on Blake. (Ayre 92)

In his essay 'The Search for Acceptable Words' (1973), Frye provides a third account of the evening in question, this time in terms that tap its critical significance for him:

> I was assigned a paper on Blake's *Milton*, which I sat down to write, as was my regular bad habit in those days, the night before. The foreground of the paper was commentary, which was assuredly difficult enough for that poem, but in the background there was some principle that kept eluding me. On inspection, the principle seemed to be that Milton and Blake were connected by their use of the Bible ... If Milton and Blake were alike on this point, that likeness merely concealed what was individual about each of them, so that in pursuing the likeness I was chasing shadow and avoiding the substance. Around about three in the morning a different kind of intuition hit me, though it took me twenty years to articulate it. The two poets were connected by the *same* thing, and sameness leads to individual variety, just as likeness leads to monotony. I began dimly to see that the principle pulling me away from the historical period was the principle of mythological framework. The Bible had provided a frame of mythology for European poets: an immense number of critical problems began to solve themselves as soon as one realized this. (*SM* 17)

These disclosures not only illuminate the compositional context of *Fearful Symmetry*; they also serve as an effective introduction to its central idea. The equation of *cosmos* with *consciousness*, the principle that the universe appearing to break open is, rather, a 'curious thing' occurring 'in the world of the mind,' is the book's first principle. The volume goes on to propose that the discovery that reality is a function of consciousness is a perceptual shift that allows for the revelation and comprehension of the mythological framework that gives form to art and culture. Within this framework, the particularities of a given historical period, from great poets and important realizations, to the smallest details (like whether it is two or three o'clock in the morning and whether one is inside or outside an all-night diner), come into their ultimate significance through being perceived and humanized by the essential patterns of consciousness: the archetypes of myth. Particularly at issue in the book is the question of *identification*, the possibility of things being recognized and connected across space and time, the process of subjects and objects achieving a unity. In *Fearful Symmetry*, Northrop Frye presents Blake's poetics as a renovation of human consciousness that makes such identifications possible, with the grander intention of showing myth to be a framework of identifications that is continually incarnate in literature and, more broadly, in culture at large.

If further contexualization of the book is desired, it is worth noting that *Fearful Symmetry* not only theorizes myth as a matrix of cultural identifications: by all accounts, it enacts many of its own. Frye's own comments on his book, as well as those of his first circle of readers and most respondents afterward, testify to its standing at the nexus of a host of identifications. The book has been said to consolidate the voice of Northrop Frye with that of William Blake, its own structure with that of Blake's poetry, Frye's persona with his own text, Blake's poetry with all of literature, theory with criticism, theory *and* criticism with literature, and, of course, literature with myth. In his private correspondence, Frye writes 'I know Blake as no man has ever known him,' and says of his manuscript 'If it's no good, I'm no good' (*NFHK* 435, 414). 'My criticisms are not, properly speaking, criticisms at all, but synthetic recreations,' he explains, and quotes one of his professors as remarking that his 'theoretical re-construction of Blake was a damn sight more interesting than the original' (*NFHK* 435). In his diaries, he often assumes a complete coincidence of his thought with Blake's, occasionally catching himself doing so, as when he speaks of ideas that come 'out of Blake – I mean, FS' (*D* 125). In one diary entry, he refers to *Fearful Symmetry* as a 'subjective academic lyric,' a 'hymn to the Father' which he felt had allowed him to symbolically merge with the poet he regarded as his 'spiritual preceptor' (*D* 215, *SM* 15): 'It occurs to me that what I did with FS was perform the act described in much the same way by Freud and Jung,' he writes. 'This is the act of swallowing the father, integrating oneself with the wise old man' (*D* 94). As this chapter unfolds, we will discover that Frye's use of bodily or corporeal metaphors to articulate spiritual relationships is neither insignificant nor inconsistent; Frye also speaks of having 'anatomized [Blake] with pincers,' of having 'stretched my mind over passages [of Blake] as though it were on a rack,' and jokes that the resulting study might appear to have 'cultural high blood pressure' (*NFHK* 414, Ayre 194). When asked whether he had any substantial intellectual differences with Blake, Frye would only say that 'Blake was perhaps certain of a lot of things I am much less certain of'; other than this, he said, his only dispute with Blake was over the poet's lack of appreciation of the painter Rubens (*NFC* 60). In the preface to the Beacon Press reprint of *Fearful Symmetry* (1962), Frye speaks of his book as advancing a set of 'critical theories that I have ... been trying to teach ... in Blake's name and my own' (ii).

Significantly, these identifications were the not illusory apprehensions of Frye's own mind, but have been acknowledged by readers and commentators of *Fearful Symmetry*, early and late. After reviewing an early manuscript of the book, Frye's colleague Kathleen Coburn, an eminent Coleridge scholar, observed little in the way of an 'obvious separation' between Blake and Frye (Ayre 187). Carlos Baker, a Shelley scholar who reviewed Frye's first submitted manuscript for Princeton University Press, said it was 'impossible to distinguish between Frye's commentary and the paraphrasing of Blake' (Ayre 193). Baker opined further that Frye 'appears to know more about Blake than any living critic,' that he 'knows the Bible as few scholars do' such that the book is as much 'a treatise on the unity of western poetry' as a study of Blake (and, as the latter, 'requires as much of the reader as Blake's Prophetic books themselves'). Like Frye himself, Baker recognized the book's simultaneously critical and creative nature, referring to it as 'a diffuse epic in prose,'[1] and even prophesied that, through its 'most acute perceptions and insight' and its 'super-intellectual' nature, Frye might have been 'creating his own tragedy by knowing and seeing so much' (Ayre 192–3). In one of the first published reviews of *Fearful Symmetry*, Marshall McLuhan, the University of Toronto's other emerging man of letters, remarked that Frye had somehow managed to 'speak ... as we might suppose Blake would have spoken' (McLuhan 711).

Later readers and critics echo these impressions.[2] Frye's biographer John Ayre maintains that in *Fearful Symmetry* the poet and his critic 'merge and produce a coordinated statement' (Ayre 195). Ian Balfour writes that 'the line between Frye's own thought and the exposition of Blake is so fine as to be indistinguishable,' that 'Frye, rather like Blake in his epic *Milton*, merges with the subject of his writing and speaks with a double persona' (Balfour 3). Robert Denham remarks that the book contains as much 'practical criticism' as 'theoretical speculation' and observes that it is 'difficult ... to determine whether the theory exists for the commentary or vice versa' (Denham, *Critical Method* 157). Joseph Adamson acknowledges the 'difficulty of knowing where Frye's commentary ends and Blake's poetic thought begins' but suggests that disputing this apparent fusion of the two is 'the inevitable resistance of less imaginative practitioners of a discipline to a revolutionary reorientation of its central tenets' (Adamson 42). A.C. Hamilton resolves the matter by simply recognizing that Frye's 'ambition as a critic may be expressed in what he says of Blake by substituting his name for Blake's, and "criticism" for "poetry"' (Hamilton 204). It is hard not to see *Fearful Symmetry*'s ability to establish and maintain these identifications, to speak in several voices about several bodies of writing in several modes of discourse, as a striking demonstration of the tenability and authority of its own theory. This genius for identification is no doubt one of the many meanings to the book's Blakean title. We are right to ask how such identifications are made possible and how far they extend, for this inquiry is the prime subject of the book and takes us to the heart of Frye's theory of myth.

In one of his letters of 1935 quoted earlier, the young Frye reminds himself 'You're not working with realities, but with *phenomena*' (*NFHK* 435, italics added); the fact that he grasped the difference between the two, and recognized early his own focus on the latter, was an important factor in his development as a thinker, and is critical to the comprehension of his theories. In his late notebooks, an aging Frye looks back on *Fearful Symmetry* as being a product of his 'existential period' (*LN* 594). Between these two remarks comes a passage from 'The Search for Acceptable Words' which closely follows the paragraph from the essay quoted above:

> [T]he Bible preoccupied me, not because it represented a religious 'position' congenial to my own, but for the opposite reason. It illustrated the imaginative assumptions on which Western poets had proceeded; consequently the study of it pointed the way towards a phenomenological criticism which would be as far as possible free from presuppositions. (*SM* 18)[3]

Frye is referring here to the tendency of phenomenology to 'bracket' its subject from the assumption of terms and standards from other disciplines. His notes to himself in his early letters and late notebooks, however, suggest that he also understood and had in mind the other priorities of phenomenological inquiry as he penned his first book. *Fearful Symmetry*, as we will discover, is relentlessly phenomenological: it is phenomenological in subject, as its subject is consciousness as prior to ontological reality; it is phenomenological in methodology, as it studies that subject without presumption of its nature or limits; and it is phenomenological in utility, as its theory aspires to existential application. As Michael Dolzani observes, Frye is proceeding in 'the later phenomenological tradition,' by which he means the post-metaphysical phenomenology of which Heidegger and Merleau-Ponty are the best-known practitioners (*TBN* xxxv).

Where Eliade, Jung, and Campbell began by postulating mythic/nonmythic binaries where the mythic pole or source is exterior to consciousness and acts upon it, Frye recognizes that the mythic and nonmythic are actually two aspects of human consciousness. One is constantly in the presence of the objects and operations of consciousness in the work of Northrop Frye, and herein lies much of the existential and humanistic authority of his theories. Where our other mythologists were committed to theorizing myth as something which originates externally and proceeds to structure consciousness, Frye is able to invert this model and theorize myth as something that originates in consciousness and structures the external world. The nonmythic aspect, in this case, is that which prevents or hinders this process, committing one, for example, to the highly problematic theories of myth that we have been discussing. For Blake and hence for Frye, the theories of seventeenth-century empirical philosopher John Locke are *de facto* the foremost apologies for the nonmythic functions of human consciousness: Blakean poetics, on the other hand, provides convincing proof and an argument in favour of its mythic aspect. *Fearful Symmetry* thus opens with a chapter entitled 'The Case against Locke' in which Frye outlines and clarifies Blake's answer to empirical philosophy. A compact, revolutionary reappraisal of the nature of consciousness, the chapter sees Frye marshal out of Blake a pointed refutation of Locke's conservative epistemology and an alternative that forms the basis of a radical phenomenology of myth.

The fundamentals of Locke's thought are familiar to anyone who has studied the tradition of empirical philosophy. In his *Essay Concerning Human Understanding*, Locke takes as his first principle the Cartesian assumption that human consciousness is a pure mental subjectivity that stands apart from the objective world, engaged (he appends) in reserved contemplation of the impact and intrusions that the objective world makes upon it. Locke sees the human mind as an empty receptacle, which he variously compares to a blank sheet of paper (the infamous *tabula rasa*) or an unfurnished room or cabinet which is gradually filled by the data of sensory stimuli. Consciousness, as the occupant of the room or the reader of the page, examines this datum in the process of gathering knowledge. Sensations, impressions of the external world received through the senses of the body, are accepted by the mind as pure objective facts, which consciousness then analyses by the process

Locke calls 'reflection.' Reflection is a process of empirical analysis that the rational mind conducts upon these objective facts, which leaves them external as things and bodily sensations, but extracts from them abstract ideas and general concepts (Locke 15–25). These ideas and concepts, Locke maintains, become the basis of our understanding of reality. The theory has the ring of intellectualized common sense, and seems to accord with what most of us already feel we know about the operation of our own minds. Upon closer examination, however, it is highly problematic. Locke's assumptions that the sensations that inform ideas 'enter by the senses simple and unmixed,' and that he need not 'meddle with the physical consideration of the mind,' are found by Blake and Frye to be presumptive errors that literally carry the sting of death (Locke 90, 5). 'Locke, along with Bacon and Newton,' Frye observes, 'is constantly in Blake's poetry as a symbol of every kind of evil, superstition and tyranny' (*FS* 14).

Frye recognizes that Blake's main objection to Locke is that, in his assumption that human consciousness passively accepts sensation, the pre-existent form of the objective world and the subjective alienation of the human subject are confirmed. The presumption of Lockean epistemology that sensation is passively received by consciousness means that sensation automatically stands as proof of an *a priori* objective world over and against which the human mind languishes in a subjective, anterior state. Reality, from this perspective, is something dictated to and deduced by human consciousness, rather than something created by it or for it. While there are doubtless situations where it is necessary to accept this theory, this does not alter the fact that it is inherently hostile to the creative artist or anyone else engaged in cultural production. What appears from one perspective to be the natural accommodation of thought to the seemingly self-evident fact of an objective reality is, from another perspective, human consciousness willingly putting itself at a marked disadvantage before the world, placing itself perpetually distant or belated in relation to it. In fact, Frye follows through Blake a line of reasoning that reveals the broad acceptance of the Lockean theory of consciousness to constitute a cultural death-impulse, particularly from the point of view of the arts:

> Reflection on sensation is concerned only with the mere memory of the sensation, and Blake always refers to Locke's reflection as 'memory.' Memory of an image must always be less than the perception of the image. Just as it is impossible to do a portrait from memory as well as from life, so it is

> impossible for an abstract idea to be anything more than a subtracted idea, a vague and hazy afterimage ... Locke's 'reflection' is designed to withdraw the subject from the object, to replace real things with the shadowy memories of them which are called 'spectres' in Blake's symbolism. (*FS* 15, 18)

Because Lockean reflection divides reality and recesses the mind from it, Blake refers to it, with poetic zest, as 'Two Horn'd Reasoning, Cloven Fiction' (*FS* 18, Blake 268).[4] His reference to abstract ideas as 'spectres' (*FS* 73) underscores their status as what would now be called signs of 'lost presence': this accounts for why Jacques Derrida, the philosopher who coined this term and theorizes it most thoroughly, adopted Blake's trope in his book *Specters of Marx* (1994) in order to meditate again on the dilemmas of a culture that compulsively abstracts. The mania and melancholia of isolation that Derrida has consistently observed in the abstracted subject have a precedent in the fate Frye observes Blake ascribing to the habitual practitioner of Lockean reflection; having lost the presence of the world, he has also lost the presence of others. Blake therefore speaks of him as being confined to 'Selfhood,' which Frye aptly describes as 'a state of animal self-absorption' (*FS* 58). In its extreme form, this 'Selfhood' is a Cartesian hell where the only reality of which one can be certain is the reality of one's own doubts about reality. In its more common and moderate form, it is the alienated perspective that sees everyone and everything beyond one's own mind as a mere object: 'Our Selfhoods,' Frye explains, are 'our verminous crawling egos that spend all their time either wronging others or brooding on wrongs done to them' (*FS* 67). Deprived of real presence long enough and thoroughly enough, the Selfhood reaches a point where, 'when [it] is asked what it wants to do, it can only answer, with the Sibyl in Petronius, that it wants to die,' for death is its last chance at experiencing something real (*FS* 195).

Intent on dislodging the commonplace assumption of Lockean reflection, Frye ushers out of Blake a model of thought based on *active* perception that is as productive as Locke's is terminal, and which leads to ever broader frames of reference for human consciousness. Frye notices that Blake's thinking has some similarity to that of idealist philosopher George Berkeley, who questioned the independence of the objective world granted to it by Locke and was thus read approvingly by Blake. But Berkeley's dictum of *esse est percipi* ('to be is to be perceived') does not tell the whole story for Frye, and would not have satisfied Blake, for it leaves too much emphasis on the object (note the verb remains in its *passive* voice). Frye therefore recasts it as he expects Blake would have it, as *esse est percipere* ('to be is to perceive'), so as to shift agency and the ground of being entirely to the subject (*FS* 14–18). To substantiate this, Frye brings out of Blake a thinker whose approach is as congruent with the phenomenological approach that the mythologists of Frye's era hoped to mobilize as it is with the idealist philosophy of the poet's own age. This Blake not only shares the desire of English and continental Romanticism to achieve a mediation between the 'faculties' of the 'intellectual' and the 'sensible.' This Blake aims to rout out Locke's 'Cloven Fiction' by pulling it up by its cloven root, the Cartesian assumption of a schism, a difference in substance, between mind and body, and thereby push the limits of Romanticism, and, indeed, of all human experience, beyond its conventional strata.

'Man has no body distinct from his Soul,' Blake writes; 'for that call'd Body is a portion of Soul discern'd by the five Senses' (*FS* 19, Blake 34). Frye points out that in using the word 'Soul' here, Blake is not using it for its 'theological overtones [of] an invisible vapor locked up in the body and released after death' (*FS* 18): he means rather something more akin to 'mind' in its conventional usage as the counterpart of the body. Blake's point, however, is that the parts do not at all run counter, but are in fact one, such that the poet sometimes uses the word 'mind' to refer to the whole of man in the act of perceiving. The senses of the body are not to be regarded as independent and objective of the mind, but are united with and in the mind, and actively employed by the mind. Frye explains that:

> We use five senses in perception, but if we used fifteen we should still have only a single mind. The eye does not see: the eye is a lens for the mind to look through. Perception, then, is not something we do with our senses; it is a mental act. Yet it is equally true that the legs do not walk, but that the mind walks the legs. *There can be therefore no distinction between mental and bodily acts* ... The only objection to calling digestion or sexual intercourse mental activities is the hazy association between the mind and the brain, which latter is only one organ of the mind, if mind means the acting man ... The abstract reasoner attempts to give independent reality to the qualities of the things he sees, and in the same way he tries to abstract the quality of his perception. It is to him that we owe the association of mind and brain. The intellect to him is a special department concerned with reasoning, and other departments should not meddle with it. Emotion is another department, formerly ascribed to the heart, and still retaining a fossilized association with it. As for the sexual impulse, that is 'bodily'; that is, it belongs to a

> third department called 'body' by a euphemism ... All this pigeonholing of activity is nonsense to Blake. (*FS* 19–20, italics added)

For Blake, the senses and organs of the body are not objective or external to the perceiving mind, but are fully connected with it and extensive of it. This position, Frye recognizes, holds the potential to reverse the erroneous Lockean equation and its gloomy prospect. The Lockean assumption of the objectivity of the body and the senses means that the external world that is perceived by the body and the senses is also necessarily objective: if there is instead a continuity of the body and senses with consciousness, as Blake suggests, then the external world is not objective but actually contingent upon the senses of the perceiving subject for its existence. The subject and his senses become the means by which the world comes into being. Many of Blake's epigrams, Frye reminds us, are intended to emphasize this 'relativity of existence to perception' (*FS* 19): 'The Sun's Light when he unfolds it / Depends on the organ that beholds it,' writes Blake (*FS* 19, Blake 260). This effectively means, Frye writes, that 'man perceiving is a former or an imaginer,' and thus 'imagination' becomes 'the regular term used by Blake to denote man as an acting and perceiving being' (*FS* 19). The word 'imagination,' for Blake and Frye, has a place in the discussion of not only the smallest and most basic acts of perception, but also, as we will outline later, of the grandest totalities of human thought. The essential point is that if 'to be perceived ... means to be imagined ... therefore nothing is real beyond the imaginative patterns men make of reality ... [R]eality is as much in the eye of the beholder as beauty is said to be' (*FS* 19).

The ramifications of this alignment of perception with imagination are remarkable, as we will shortly see. The most immediate, however, is that it means the subject exercises creative agency in the act of perceiving, that the act of perception is also an act of creation. The Lockean 'fool,' Blake insists, 'sees not the same tree that a wise man sees,' for 'the clearer the organ the more distinct the object' (*FS* 21, Blake 35, 541): in other words, the more direct and fluid the connection between body and mind is made to be, and the more the notion of the whole man as 'imagination' is embraced, the more complete and intelligible the perceived object becomes. This is what Blake means when he speaks of how 'the doors of perception' might be 'cleansed' (Blake 39). Frye details the operation of this principle in a memorable passage that sees him smoothly adopting Blakean tropes and rhetoric to elucidate Blakean verse and ideas:

> Hence if existence is in perception the tree is *more* real to the wise man than it is to the fool. Similarly it is more real to the man who throws his entire imagination behind his perception than to the man who cautiously tries to prune away different characteristics from that imagination and isolate one. The more unified the perception, the more real the existence. Blake says:
>
> 'What,' it will be Question'd, 'When the Sun rises do you not see a round disk of fire somewhat like a Guinea?' O no, no, I see an Innumerable company of the Heavenly host crying 'Holy, Holy, Holy is the Lord God Almighty.'
>
> The Hallelujah-Chorus perception of the sun makes it a far more real sun than the guinea-sun, because more imagination has gone into perceiving it. Why, then, should intelligent men reject its reality? Because they hope that in the guinea-sun they will find their least common denominator and arrive at a common agreement which will point the way to a reality of the sun independent of their perception of it. The guinea-sun is a sensation assimilated to a general, impersonal, abstract idea. Blake can see it if he wants to, but when he sees the angels, he is not seeing more 'in' the sun but more of it. He does not see it 'emotionally': there is a greater emotional intensity in his perception, but it is not an emotional perception: such a thing is impossible, and to the extent to that it is possible it would produce only a confused and maudlin blur – which is exactly what the guinea-sun of 'common sense' is. He sees all that he can see of all that he wants to see; the perceivers of the guinea-sun see all that they want to see of all that they can see ...
>
> Blake's objection to Locke is that he extends the involuntary action into the higher regions of the imagination and tries to make perceptive activity subconscious. Locke does not think of sight as the mind directing itself through the eye to the object. He thinks of it as an involuntary and haphazard image imprinted on the mind through the eye by the object. In this process the mind remains passive and receives impressions automatically. We see the guinea-sun automatically: seeing the Hallelujah-Chorus sun demands a voluntary and conscious imaginative effort; or rather, it demands an exuberantly active mind which will not be a quiescent blank slate. The imaginative mind, therefore, is one which has realized its own freedom and understood that perception is self-development. (*FS* 21–3)

Read carefully and with an eye for implication, this passage is more than just the commonplace articulation of the Romantic theory of the imagination, though it is not incompatible with some specifications of it (in particular, what M.H. Abrams calls theories of the 'natural genius' may be reconcilable with or implicit in it [Abrams, *Mirror* 167–218]). But even Coleridge's *Biographia Literaria*, with the portentous but cryptic remarks of its thirteenth chapter, does not proceed from such a wholesale redefinition of the imagination and/as the perceiving subject as Frye's interpretation of Blake entails (and so is considerably less useful). Coleridge's promising characterization of what he calls the 'primary imagination' as 'the living power and prime agent of all human perception' seems entirely consistent with Blake's and Frye's thinking (Coleridge, *Oxford Authors* 313). But when the younger poet further describes it as 'a repetition in the finite mind of the eternal act of creation' of God, one is unsure whether this is congruent with his first remark, or whether it affirms an *a priori* reality (or implies a distance between man and God: both notions for which Blake and Frye, as we will shortly discover, had no patience).[5] Coleridge's muddled delineation of two other derivative and apparently aesthetic forms of imagination, which he calls 'secondary imagination' and 'fancy,' further complicates things, for it obscures if not demotes the status of art.

In Frye's presentation of Blake, the imagination is scrupulously theorized as nothing less than the total reversal of the Lockean model of reflective thought, such that the whole consciousness and physical being of the subject is thrust outward in a singularly creative act. We can better understand what this entails if we invert Frye's characterization of the reflective mode: if the 'guinea-sun is a sensation assimilated to a general, impersonal, abstract idea,' then the Hallelujah-Chorus sun is *a sensation projected as a specific, personal, concrete image.* This complete opposite of the abstract idea or 'Spectre' is what Blake appropriately calls an 'Emanation' (*FS* 73). There is a difference of degree if not of kind between the potency of this principle and the standard Romantic doctrine of the imagination, in that neither Blake nor Frye equivocates on questions of idealist philosophy or aesthetics, and theirs is more than a genetic or expressive theory concerned with how images in works of art are created. This core postulate of *Fearful Symmetry* is a radically phenomenological principle that compares to if not extends what that discipline, after Heidegger, calls the condition of *Dasein* or 'Being-in-the-world.' It involves the literal re-purposing of sensation by the imagination into a fuller image of the object in question, which then, by virtue of the totality of the imagination, comes into perceptible existence to be experienced anew. The sceptic or rationalist no doubt responds to this prospect by saying it is simply a case of the subject seeing what he wants to see, but this is to forget that the passive and partial act formerly known as 'seeing' (which Frye continues to speak of only for the purposes of parallelism) has since been redefined and enfolded into the active and total act of *making*, which involves the entire being, or imagination, of the subject. The re-purposing of sensation through the imagination is thus an actual creation or recreation of reality. This is not to say that it therefore has nothing to do with art: it has everything to do with art, because it means that every act of perception is also a work of art, with the most effective acts of perception by the most effective imaginations becoming what we conventionally understand to be aesthetic objects.

This swallowing of Romantic philosophy and aesthetics into phenomenology occurs as a matter of course in Frye's further theorization of the principle of the imaginative recreation of reality. As he clarifies this fundamental imperative of the Blakean consciousness, the notion of art as its prime achievement emerges:

> Sense experience in itself is a chaos, and must be employed either actively by the imagination or passively by the memory. The former is a deliberate and the latter a haphazard method of creating a mental form out of sense experience. The wise man will choose what he wants to do with his perceptions just as he will choose the books he wants to read, and his perceptions will thus be charged with an intelligible and coherent meaning ... It thus becomes obvious that the product of the imaginative life is most clearly seen in the work of art, which is a unified mental vision of experience. (*FS* 24)

'Art is based on sense experience,' Frye recognizes, but 'it is an imaginative ordering of sense experience' (*FS* 24). Just as the practitioner of Lockean reflection inevitably develops into a 'Selfhood,' the practitioner of Blakean creation develops into the vaunted figure of the artist, or more generally, the 'visionary,' 'vision' being the activation of that perceptual totality of which the passive sense of sight was formerly a separate part. In *Fearful Symmetry*, those ubiquitous concerns of Romantic theory, the power of vision and the role of the visionary, are theorized as radical but real existential possibilities on the level of the lived, for Frye shows how they may be developed in each person, as aspects of what will eventually constitute a total mythic subject. Frye writes:

> [W]e derive from sense experience the power to visualize ... we do not visualize independently of sense ... But what we see appearing before us on

> the canvas is not a reproduction of memory or sense experience but a new and independent creation. The 'visionary' is the man who has passed through sight into vision, never the man who has avoided seeing, who has not trained himself to see clearly, or who generalizes among his stock of visual memories ... To visualize, therefore, is to realize. The artist is *par excellence* the man who struggles to develop his perception into creation, his sight into vision; and art is a technique of realizing, through an ordering of sense experience by the mind, a higher reality than linear unselected experience or a second-hand evocation of it can give. (*FS* 25–6)

We should notice that there is implied in this account a total of three possible developments, for just as the Jungian and Campbellian mythic binaries break down into trinaries, so too does Frye's. Frye thus speaks of three possible worlds; the created world of vision, the observed world of sight, and the abstracted world of memory:

> The world of memory is an unreal world of reflection and abstract ideas; the world of sight is a potentially real world of subjects and objects; the world of vision is a world of creators and creatures. In the world of memory we see nothing; in the world of sight we see what we have to see; in the world of vision we see what we want to see. (*FS* 26)

However, 'these are not three different worlds' in an ontological sense, Frye reminds us, such as we have in the work of the other mythologists: 'they are the egocentric, the ordinary and the visionary ways of looking at the same world' (*FS* 26). In other words, they are modes of consciousness.

The world of vision is the world we want to 'see' because the visionary that creates and dwells in it is the Blakean subject whose subjectivity has been broadened to include his body and its senses: Blake's and Frye's reappraisal of the subject to include his physical being not only neutralizes the objectivity of the external world and renders it malleable through the senses, but also provides the structuring factor of its recreation. This factor is *desire*, which is the physical, material needs and expressions of the body as recognized and developed by consciousness. The reason why the world of sight and the world of memory are worlds of alienation and eventually death is that the mental consciousness of Locke can only produce the principle of reason. The Cartesian *cogito* is a disembodied entity that can neither make sense of desire nor abide its source, and thus seeks to ignore or extinguish it. For the unified Blakean consciousness, however, desire provides the pre-rational motivation and the post-rational form of the imagined world of vision. 'All thought' for the Blakean subject is 'the fulfillment of desire,' and therefore, 'the world of vision or art ... is a world of fulfilled desire' (*FS* 26–7). The role of desire in art and thought suggests that these things have nothing to do with abstract ideas or metaphysical states, but are rather higher or more consolidated levels of phenomenological being. This is what Frye means when he writes that 'perceptions form part of a logical unfolding organic unit,' that 'there is no causality that is not part of the organic process' (*FS* 23, 36): or as Blake aphoristically puts it, 'Energy' (a Blakean synonym for desire) 'is the only life, and is from the Body; and Reason is the bound or outward circumference of Energy' (*FS* 27, Blake 34). The way up to higher realms of being, it turns out, is the way down to a phenomenological body-consciousness. 'Imagination creates reality,' Frye concludes, 'and as desire is part of the imagination, the world we desire is more real than the world we passively accept' (*FS* 27).

Frye's theorization of the Blakean imagination is such a radical reassessment of the nature and creative potential of human consciousness that it may be fairly asked whether it is tenable and whether there is any philosophical elaboration or corroboration of it. A survey of the theories of Maurice Merleau-Ponty, the foremost phenomenologist after Heidegger, suggests an affirmative answer to both questions. In his masterwork *Phenomenology of Perception* (which was written even as Frye was finishing *Fearful Symmetry*),[6] and elsewhere in other writings, Merleau-Ponty seeks to ground Husserlian transcendental phenomenology, even more thoroughly than Heidegger had, through a theory of 'embodied' or 'corporeal' consciousness. The results of his research provocatively underwrite, if not quite match, the extraordinary implications of Frye's model of imaginative consciousness.

A necessary first step of theorizing the nature of consciousness in the world, Merleau-Ponty argues, is to theorize its relationship with the body, which is the interface between consciousness and the world. This is a task to which he felt previous philosophy, including even Heidegger's phenomenology of *Dasein*, had failed to attend. 'The soul is not merely in the body like a pilot in his ship; it is wholly intermingled with the body,' Merleau-Ponty recognizes: 'The body, in turn, is wholly animated, and all its functions contribute to the perception of objects – an activity long considered by philosophy to be pure knowledge' (*Primacy* 5). The philosopher confirms Blake's and Frye's point that our perceptions of the world are not 'simple and unmixed' as Locke would have it; perception is rather a matter of cooperation between consciousness and the senses. Consciousness both informs and is informed by physical being. The corporeal setting of consciousness possesses it with what Merleau-Ponty variously calls the 'body image,' the 'body schema,' or the 'phenomenal body,' the coordination of which produces an expanded and unified subjectivity not unlike what Blake refers to as 'mind' or 'imagination.' 'Objective thought is unaware of the subject of perception,' Merleau-Ponty complains, in the spirit of Blake and Frye: 'This is because it presents itself with the world ready made, as the setting for every possible event, and treats perception as one of those events.' But in fact the embodied or perceiving subject is himself 'the place where these things occur,' for the interaction of the objective world and consciousness through the senses is 'a re-creation or re-constitution of the world at every moment' (*Phenomenology* 207).

Merleau-Ponty sees the body itself as an irrefutable argument against the presumption of a subject-object fissure in epistemology and experience. To understand why, one need only ponder the difficulty of determining precisely when and where objects like a swallowed piece of food or an in-breathed molecule of air stop being objects and become part of the subject. It is both arbitrary and extreme to say a bit of food does not become part of the subject until it is transformed from chemical matter into electricity in the brain. Why not when it is chemically digested into the bloodstream? If the bloodstream, why not when it enters the stomach? If the stomach, why not the mouth? If the mouth, why not the hand? If the hand, why not the eye? The relation of subjects to objects, in other words, is rendered completely fluid by the presence of the body. To cite one of Merleau-Ponty's favourite illustrations, if one shakes one's own hand, is the right hand the object of the left, or is the left hand the object of the right? If autonomic physical functions such as swallowing, digestion, and breathing blur the supposed barrier between subject and object, does not the conscious outward-bound employment of the senses by the mind completely shatter it, rendering such categories obsolete?

Merleau-Ponty insists that in fact the grandest either/or categories of empirical philosophy become useless once perception is understood as the cooperative activity of body and consciousness. 'We cannot apply the classical distinction of form and matter to perception,' he writes; 'the quasi-organic relation of perceiving subject and the world involves, in principle, a contradiction of immanence and transcendence' (*Primacy* 2). In the place of these oppositions there is only the question of being, and what can be made to be. The 'body is the potentiality for a certain world,' Merleau-Ponty explains, a potentiality which is then fixed or developed in one way or other by consciousness (*Phenomenology* 106). 'The essence of consciousness,' therefore, 'is to provide itself with one or several worlds, to bring into being its own thoughts *before* itself as if they were things' (*Phenomenology* 130). The dialectic of perception that is opened between consciousness and the world through the mediating presence of the body renders sensations intentional, which is to say, as real objects or engagements of consciousness in the direction of its fulfilment. Merleau-Ponty explains this in a rich meditation that invites comparison to Frye's discussion of Blake's Hallelujah-Chorus sun:

> Sensation is intentional because I find that in the sensible a certain rhythm of existence is put forward ... following up this hint, and stealing into the form of existence which is thus suggested to me, I am brought into relation with an external being, whether it be in order to open myself to it or shut myself off from it. If the qualities radiate around them a certain mode of existence, if they have the power to cast a spell ... this is because the sentient subject does not posit them as objects, but enters into sympathetic relation with them, makes them his own and finds in them his momentary law.
>
> Let us be more explicit. The sentient and sensible do not stand in relation to each other as two mutually external terms, and sensation is not an invasion of the sentient by the sensible. It is my gaze which subtends the object's colour, and the movement of my hand which subtends the object's form ... and in this transaction between the subject of sensation and the sensible it cannot be held that one acts while the other suffers the action ... Apart from the probing of my eye or my hand, and before my body synchronizes with it, the sensible is nothing but a vague beckoning ... Thus a sensible datum which is on the point of being felt sets a kind of muddled problem for my body to solve. I must find the attitude which *will* provide it with the means of becoming determinate ... I must find the reply to the question which is obscurely expressed. ... The sensible gives back to me what I lent to it ... As I contemplate the blue of the sky I am not *set over against* it as an acosmic subject; I do not possess it in thought, or spread out towards it some idea of blue such as might reveal the secret of it, I abandon myself to it and plunge into this mystery, it 'thinks itself within me.' I am the sky as it is drawn together and unified, and as it begins to exist for itself ... [T]he geographer's or the astronomer's sky does not exist for itself. But of the sky, as it is perceived or sensed, subtended by my gaze which ranges over it and resides in it, and providing as it does the theatre for a certain living pulsation adopted by my body, it can be said that it exists for itself. (*Phenomenology* 213–15)

Merleau-Ponty's self-interrogating account lacks the metaphorical power of Blake and the theoretical power of Frye, but the same principle by which the poet transforms the sun into a chorus of angels is what allows the philosopher to transform the sky into 'the theatre of a certain living pulsation.' This is the principle of perception-as-creation that Blake and Frye call the imagination, which Merleau-Ponty more modestly refers to as 'creative receptivity.'

The principle is more potently illustrated by another of Merleau-Ponty's favourite examples: if a subject is presented with a cube, he or she can only see three of its six sides. The other three sides remain hidden from view on the opposite side of the cube. The subject is nevertheless conscious that it is indeed a whole cube that is present before him. The awareness is instantaneous, and so cannot be attributed to analytical reasoning, and the notion that the laws of geometry might somehow be innate to the mind, like Jung's archetypes, is absurd. In fact the cube is constituted as whole by consciousness because consciousness possesses a 'body image,' a sense of its own extensive concrete form and modes of action, and has already taken the cube into that field of subjectivity. Consciousness envisions itself either handling the cube or viewing it from another perspective, thereby verifying its hidden sides:

> I should not say that the unseen sides ... are simply possible perceptions, nor that they are the necessary conclusions of a kind of analysis or geometrical reasoning. It is not through an intellectual synthesis which would freely posit the total object that I am led from what is given to what is not actually given; that I am given together with the visible sides of the object, the nonvisible sides as well. It is, rather, a kind of practical synthesis: I can touch [it], and not only the side turned toward me but also the other side; I have only to extend my hand to hold it. (*Primacy* 14)

The embodied consciousness possesses the ability and experience of reach, and thus it can imaginatively 'subtend' (*sub* + *tendere*, to extend beneath) the cube to take (or rather *make*) account of its hidden sides. Merleau-Ponty presents this action as a more complete theorization of what Heidegger after Longinus calls *ekstasis*, the comprehensive out-reach of the subject into the external world (*Phenomenology* 70); it is a concept we will meet again in the conclusion to this study, in a discussion of the theory of metaphor in Frye's *Words with Power*. The point here is that consciousness inherently possesses and uses an ecstatic or projective process to develop a perception of a part into a perception of a whole, reconstructing the cube, in this case, and perceiving it as complete. 'I cannot see a cube, a solid with six surfaces and twelve edges; all I ever see is a perspective figure of which the lateral surfaces are distorted and the back surface completely hidden,' Merleau-Ponty explains; 'If I am able to speak of cubes, it is because my mind sets these appearances to rights and restores the hidden surface' (*Sense and Non-Sense 50*).

The quotidian nature of Merleau-Ponty's examples should not keep us from recognizing the remarkable operation of consciousness they demonstrate: they reveal the ability of consciousness to expand its own perceptions and envision what it cannot see, to fulfil its own expectations, to complete and, indeed, *create* reality. '[T]he thing which falls to our perception is ... only an invitation to perceive beyond it,' writes Merleau-Ponty *(Phenomenology* 233). This operation is in fact the kernel or root of the Blakean imagination, for it depicts the subject's first passage from sight into vision. Northrop Frye would probably suggest that the human capacity to experience 'the substance of things hoped for, the evidence of things not seen' (his favourite scriptural definition of faith, as found in Hebrews 11:1) begins here (*FS* 28). If the embodied subject of Merleau-Ponty automatically creates for itself the three sides of a cube which are hidden from it, it stands to reason that the embodied and *desiring* subject of Blake and Frye would create a good deal more, and make a grander structure of the cube in the disciplined act of reordering the experience of it. Merleau-Ponty refutes Descartes's claim that consciousness is a transcendent matter of 'I think' and 'I am,' insisting it is rather an embodied matter of 'I can' (*Phenomenology* 137). Frye would probably remind Merleau-Ponty that the human subject is not merely able but also motivated, and that consciousness is therefore an imaginative matter of 'I need' and 'I want.' The latter is nothing less than a theory of the origin and liberating power of art and culture. 'Once we begin to think in terms of wish and desire,' writes Frye, 'we find ourselves beating prison bars' (*FS* 40).

The implications of embodied consciousness with regard to culture are not lost on Merleau-Ponty, however, even as his theorization of it is more hesitant and less ambitious than Blake's and Frye's, and tinted at times with the philosopher's *skepsis.* In one telling passage, he exhibits an awareness of how the ramifications of the phenomenology of creative perception exceed the conventional language of philosophy and require a system of larger concepts and metaphors for their significance to be grasped:

> The subject of sensation is neither a thinker who takes note of quality, nor an inert setting which is affected or changed by it, it is a power which is born

> into, and simultaneously with, a certain existential environment, or is synchronized with it ... Just as a sacrament not only symbolizes, in sensible species, an operation of Grace, but is also the real presence of God, which it causes to occupy a fragment of space and communicates to those who eat of the consecrated bread, provided that they are inwardly prepared, in the same way the sensible has not only a motor and vital significance, but is nothing other than a certain way of being in the world suggested to us from some point in space, and seized and acted upon by our body, provided that it is capable of doing so, so that sensation is literally a form of communion. (*Phenomenology* 211–12)

Merleau-Ponty's reference to creative perception as a 'communion' is an example of the observation with which Frye concludes 'The Case against Locke': 'the material world provides a universal language of images ... and each man's imagination speaks that language with his own accent,' Frye explains. 'Religions are grammars of this language' (*FS* 28). This is to say, religion is the cultural system that serves to unify and develop our phenomenological acts of perception (which, remember, are also works of art), to render them comprehensible and significant, and allow their creative potential to be tapped. 'Religion is the social form of art, and as such both its origin in art and the fact that its principles of interpretation are those of art should be kept in mind' (*FS* 28). The phenomenological basis of the imagination, in turn, gives the otherwise abstract concepts of religion their existential reality. The failure to recognize this results in the perversion of religion that Blake refers to when he uses the word pluralized or capitalized, as in the 'dark Religions' of *The Four Zoas*, or when he speaks, as Frye does, of 'state religion' (Blake 407, *FS* 61, 271). The second chapter of *Fearful Symmetry*, 'The Rising God,' and several of the chapters that follow it elucidate how and why the greater ramifications of perception-as-creation can be understood only as analogies and, indeed, actualizations of religious concepts; or, in other words, how and why imaginative consciousness is mythic consciousness.

II. God and Grammar

The most important of these analogies is the one that functions as the cornerstone of Blake's and Frye's thought (and is the issue raised by Coleridge but on which he equivocates): if perception is creation, and reality comes into being when and as imagined by man, then man must be the Creator, which is to say, God. More specifically, the imagination in man must be the creative power that religion conventionally attributes to God, since it is the principle that creates reality itself. 'Man in his creative acts and perceptions is God, and God is man,' Frye writes; 'God is the eternal self, and the worship of God is self development' (*FS* 30). 'Man is not wholly God,' however, 'otherwise there would be no point in bringing in the idea of God at all,' Frye explains; 'The identity of God and man is qualified by the presence in man of the tendency to deny God by self-restriction' (*FS* 31). But the visionary, as we know, is the man who has overcome this tendency and committed himself to the development of his imagination. Having done so, he is not simply worshipping or experiencing God, or repeating his work, as Coleridge and other Romantic thinkers seem to suggest:[7] he is himself enacting the divine *fiat* and thereby becoming an aspect of or taking up a place within God. This is not simply a spiritual merging or meeting of man and God, as in the *unio mystica* of various Neoplatonic, alchemical, and Gnostic systems (of which the encounter with the Jungian unconscious is a late variant), for these by necessity postulate an *a priori* God that is initially if not perpetually external to human consciousness. For Frye and Blake, as for Ovid, *est deus in nobis*, but this God in us is the only God. 'The only God that exists exists in man,' Frye writes (*FS* 217): anything else requires some form of pre-existent reality, which would take us back to the fragmented consciousness of Locke and the lost presence of Derrida. 'God is not only the genius [in man] but the genus of man,' Frye intones, in what is very much an elaboration of Blake's memorable christening of man as the 'Human Form Divine' (*FS* 31, Blake 32). The truth of both phrases is well illustrated in Frye's point that as 'we cannot perceive' (that is to say, *imagine*) 'anything higher than a man, nothing higher than Man can exist. The artist proves this by the fact that he can paint God only as a man ... There is no form of life superior to our own' (*FS* 32). Man, in other words, is the necessary phenomenological form of God, the perceiving and perceptible body of God. 'To perceive the particular and imagine the real is to perceive and imagine as part of a Divine body,' Frye writes (*FS* 32). The whole of this body, of course,

> is ultimately God, the totality of the imagination. But even men who cannot reach the idea of God believe in the reality of larger human bodies, such as nations, cities or races, and even speak of them as fathers or mothers. It takes genuine faith to see a nation or race as a larger human being, or form

> of human existence, and a good deal of such faith is undoubtedly idolatry. Still, there is the partial idea of God in it, and in a Utopia or millennium it would become direct knowledge or vision. (*FS* 43)

Frye's point here is that human beings are in the habit of identifying themselves with other human beings and groups of human beings, which demonstrates at least a latent or partial ability to take others into their subjectivity (into their 'body image,' to use Merleau-Ponty's term) and form a larger human body. Anyone who has ever found himself or herself wincing or thrilling at the pain or pleasure experienced by a friend or family member, or even a complete stranger, has already revealed a capacity to do this: these are sympathetic mental and physical responses that demonstrate that one has phenomenologically identified oneself with another and is experiencing that other's being, however faintly, as their own. The visionary is a man who insists on taking *all* human beings into his imagination in this way, and wants all human beings to do the same, for in doing so they would become the imaginative totality that is the phenomenological reality of God. It goes without saying that such a God would be as different as possible from the *ganz andere*, the 'wholly other' God of conservative theology and mythography, for this God would be the sum of ourselves and a manifestation of being beyond the assumed dialectic of immanence and transcendence. It would also be a God that permits no exclusion, not because *extra ecclesium nulla salus* (which is an ideological principle intended to separate one group of people from another), but because once this God is realized, there is no longer any 'outside' that may be spoken of. From the imaginative perspective of the visionary, 'the infinite variety of men is no argument against the unity of God' (*FS* 31).

The idea of God as the 'totality of the imagination,' a sum of visionaries galvanized into a single body, corresponds to the conception of the resurrected Jesus of Christianity, which is that same greater body as viewed and experienced from the human world. This conception functions better as an image of Frye's total mythic subject because it illustrates more tangibly that imaginative development is not spiritual abstraction but phenomenological concretion and consolidation on a higher, broader level. In Blake's and Frye's view, as we know, there is no question of abstraction, only the choice between the death or birth of the imagination: 'Man's body may remain a natural hell of unsatisfied desire, or it may become an imaginative purgatory, a crucible from which the purified mind emerges' (*FS* 291). This emergence is the concept religion understands as resurrection, and it is robbed of its potency and relevance if it is seen as a mere abstraction rather than a concretion of the imagination. 'The body is the form of the soul,' Frye writes, and thus the risen body of Jesus 'is not an abstraction or aggregate, but a larger human body or human being' (*FS* 200, 125):

> The imagination cannot exist except as a bodily form, but the body is only what others on the same plane of existence see of the soul or mind ... Christianity has always insisted on the resurrection of the body, though the two facts that the risen body is spiritual and that it is a body are hard to keep both in mind at once. All belief in ghosts or shades or in any form of spirit conceived as less than bodily is superstitious ... (*FS* 38–9)

Understood imaginatively and phenomenologically, the notion of resurrection does not involve a soul 'imprisoned within the body evaporating at death,' but rather 'living man armed with all the powers of his present body infinitely expanded' (*FS* 194). This total resurrected subject is neither an abstract political entity nor a metaphysical or Platonic form. It is a conception of 'all human "Beings" united in a larger human being,' a 'completely integrated body of imaginative men' that fulfils 'the Biblical and Christian idea of a Church or City of God' (which would, Frye says coyly, 'be difficult to find in Plato' [*FS* 248, 128]). He explains the working of this conception further in a passage that also points out that such a development alters our perceptions not only of ourselves, but of the world:

> The relation of soul to body is that of an oak to an acorn, not of a genie to a bottle. And there are no natural laws which the risen body must obey and no compulsory categories by which it must perceive. It is impossible to picture this except in terms of what we now see, and providing angels with wings is about as far as we can get ... [B]ecause we perceive on the level of this body we see an independent nature in a looming and sinister perspective. We are still living in an age of giant stars just as the ants are still living in an age of giant ferns; the natural man is a mole, and all our mountains are his molehills. In the resurrection of the body the physical universe would take the form in which it would be perceived by the risen body, and the risen body would perceive it in the form of Paradise. (*FS* 194–5)

This last point brings us to a third crucial analogy of religion and art: 'The realization that the world we desire and create with our imaginations is both better and more real than the world we see leads us to regard the latter world as "fallen"' (*FS* 40). '[T]he end of art,' conversely, 'is the recovery of Paradise' (*FS* 41). There is a functional similarity, in other words, between what religion sees as 'faith' in the existence of a spiritual world and what Coleridge (in another moment of hedged brilliance) understood as 'the willing suspension of disbelief' solicited by the aesthetic proposition (Coleridge even suggested that such a response constitutes what could be called '*poetic* faith' [Coleridge, *Oxford Authors* 314]). Whatever access is to be had to the paradises, heavens, and higher spiritual worlds of religion comes through the imaginative experience of the reality of art:

> Faith, Jesus said, can remove mountains. But mountains in the world of experience are entirely motionless; what kind of faith can remove them? Well, a landscape painter can easily leave one out if it upsets his imaginative balance. And that kind of vision, which sees with perfect accuracy just what it wants to see, pierces the gates of heaven into the unfallen world. (*FS* 81)

Thus:

> Vision is the end of religion, and the destruction of the physical universe is the clearing of our own eyesight. Art, because it affords a systematic training in this kind of vision, is the medium through which religion is revealed. The Bible is the vehicle of revealed religion because it is a unified vision of human life and therefore, as Blake says 'the Great Code of Art.' And if all art is visionary, it must be apocalyptic and revelatory too: the artist does not wait to die before he lives in the spiritual world ... (*FS* 45)

The higher spiritual world of religion is the imagined world of art because the perspective sought after in the former, that of the eternal and the infinite, is attainable only in the latter. This is because 'eternity is not endless time, nor infinity endless space,' Frye explains; 'the religious idea of "salvation" depends on transcending this view' (*FS* 47, 46). The eternal and the infinite are, rather,

> entirely different mental categories through which we perceive the unfallen world ... Real space ... is the eternal here; where we are is always the center of the universe, and the circumference of our affairs is the circumference of the universe, just as real time is the 'eternal Now' of our personal experience. (*FS* 46, 48)

Eternity is a perpetual present, just as infinity is perpetual presence, and this is their ultimate value as perspectives: together they constitute a state of being in which the objects of desire are always available, and not destined to be drawn away into the linear continuum of time and space by the mental processes that are native to time and space (and, indeed, which *create* time and space), memory and abstraction. The corporeal basis of the imagination is what creates and provides the perspective of eternity: 'Just as it is necessarily "here," the body necessarily exists "now"; it can never become "past,"' writes Merleau-Ponty (*Phenomenology* 140). 'My body takes possession of time,' he explains; 'it brings into existence a past and a future for a present' (*Phenomenology* 240). 'We hold time in its entirety, and we are present to ourselves because we are present to the world' (*Phenomenology* 424). In life the body's senses, needs, and desires are *omnipresent*, and they ensure that the imagination is perpetually bringing the objects of desire into being before itself, into presence. It is the presence of body that allows what Frye calls 'the imaginative control of time' (*FS* 292). The corporeal senses and desire, the roots of the imagination, have a constant, vital immediacy: they are always there (or rather, *here*), and will always develop an intentional object rather than tolerate absence. The lineaments of the embodied imagination are therefore the lineaments of eternity, for 'eternity,' Frye explains, 'is simply that plane of existence on which joy, or the fulfillment of desire, becomes possible' (*FS* 72); 'Heaven *is* this world as it appears to the awakened imagination' (*FS* 83); 'The higher state of heaven is achieved by those who have developed the God within them,' God, we remember, being the human imagination as the principle of creation (*FS* 81).

The expansion of the circumference of the human imagination that occurs as groups of human beings phenomenologically unite not only galvanizes them into larger and larger bodies: the burgeoning imagination also perceives the elements of the external world as objects of desire and so 'swallows' them into itself (this is where the corporeal metaphor of 'taste' as artistic refinement comes from), and digests them into the total body of Man. If this process sounds supernatural, it is because it is, and if that word sounds like a synonym of 'impossible' it is only because it has been appropriated by the discourse of the occult and the paranormal. 'Civilization is in more than one sense supernatural,' Frye points out; 'it is something which man's superiority over nature has evolved' (*FS* 36): 'The totality of imaginative power, of which the matrix is art, is what we ordinarily call culture or civilization' (*FS* 89). Imaginative expansion is in fact the process by which culture has always developed in response to the consciousness-fragmenting prospect of objective nature. In clarifying the sources and workings of this process, Blake and Frye are showing how far it could conceivably extend (and, indeed, from the perspective of religion, how far it is *supposed* to extend). 'If the whole of mankind were ... integrated in a single spiritual body the universe as we see it would burst' (*FS* 44). This is the radical of the vision of human life presented in the Bible, and fulfilled particularly in the New Testament: 'For all Jesus' teaching centers on the imminent destruction of this world and the eternal permanence of heaven and hell, these latter being not places but states of mind' (*FS* 80). Nothing, therefore, is actually (that is, ontologically) destroyed, but everything is actually (that is, phenomenologically) recreated, and unified within a total structure. This includes, again, formerly disparate and competing groups of human beings: theorists of the so-called politics of inclusion should take note of Frye's point that 'The most inclusive vision possible ... is to see the universe as One Man' (*FS* 125). In a climate of outright hostility, the principle is even more salient: 'a genuine culture does not murder its neighbors but attempts to unite with them into a larger human body' (*FS* 263). In his essay 'Blake after Two Centuries' (1957), Frye characterizes the structure and nature of this universe of the Blakean imagination in a summary that is as useful and compact as any laid out in *Fearful Symmetry* itself. The imagination, ultimately, creates a world where

> all forms are identified as human. Cities and gardens, sun moon and stars, rivers and stones, trees and human bodies – all are equally alive, equally parts of the same infinite body which is at once the body of God and of risen man ... It is a world of forms like Plato's except that in Blake these forms are images of pure being seen by a spiritual body, not ideas of pure essence seen by a soul, a conception which would rule out the artist as the revealer of reality. (*FI* 143–4)

III. Archetype and Apocalypse

It will have been noticed that, while we have been elaborating at length the complex nature of Frye's mythic subject and his theory of mythogenesis, we have not yet developed conceptions of the term 'myth' and its component 'archetype' as they are used in *Fearful Symmetry*. We have had to forego doing so thus far because Frye himself is reluctant to provide definitions: 'no literary critic of any experience,' Frye maintains, 'will make much effort to define his terms' (*FS* 316).[8] But in two of the core chapters of *Fearful Symmetry*, 'A Literalist of the Imagination' and 'The Word within the Word,' he addresses the nature and substance of myth more directly, such that it becomes apparent that his earlier theorizations have developed working or implicit definitions that we are now in a position to intuit and discuss.

Proceeding from the above, therefore, we may say that myth for Northrop Frye is the process of the phenomenological realization of the universal subject (*subject-as-universe, universe-as-subject*). It is the development of human consciousness into the total imagination or body that is Jesus as the incarnation of God. It is the expansion and concretization of human consciousness into the eternal world that is the abode and perspective of God. It is what Frye finds recreated in the poetry of Blake: 'a rigorously unified vision of the essential forms of the creative mind' (*FS* 143). Insofar as this body and perspective tends to abide as latent potential in our individual lives and culture, at the level of our very perceptions, it is something we are always moving away from: insofar as it is the conceivable end or logical conclusion of this latent potential, it is something we are always developing toward. This suggests that myth has, or rather *is*, an arc, the human descent from and ascent to the experience and perspective of the divine. This in turn suggests that myth has, or rather is, a narrative form or structure, the experience and actions of its central figure. Frye thus embraces (though he does not specifically cite it in *Fearful Symmetry*, as he often does later) Aristotle's definition of myth in the *Poetics* as *mythos* (story, plot, narrative), which he develops into a notion of myth as 'a certain kind of story, generally about a god or other divine being,' a 'conventionalized or stylized narrative' in which 'some characters are superhuman beings' ('Literature and Myth' 27, *AC* 366). In the prolegomena of *Fearful Symmetry*, Frye theorizes myth as the literalization in human experience of a narrative form, the concretion of the phenomenological reality of a story-structure, the recovery of the identity of human consciousness with/as the divine character. We do not mean 'literalization' in the sense in which it is used in religious hermeneutics, however, as the opposite of 'spiritualization,' for it is the precisely the spiritual dimension that is being literalized: this is yet another conceptual binary that no longer holds. Blake and Frye see this narrative form in the Bible, whose main character is God, and see its literalized or concretized form as art and culture (and, therefore, the perceived world), whose main character and inhabitant is Man. Frye details this rather profound formulation of myth in a dense paragraph that sees his first significant (albeit variant) use of the term 'archetype' and a subtle allusion to the issue of language that has been lurking beneath the surface of his study (both of which will be engaged more fully as a matter of course):

> When we perceive, or rather reflect on, the general, we perceive as an ego: when we perceive as a mental form, or rather create, we perceive as part of a universal Creator or Perceiver, who is ultimately Jesus. Jesus is the Logos or Word of God, the totality of creative power, the universal visionary in whose mind we perceive the particular. But the phrase 'Word of God' is obviously appropriate also to all works of art which reveal the same perspective, these latter being recreations of the divine vision which is Jesus. The archetypal Word of God, so to speak, sees this world of time and space as a single creature in eternity and infinity, fallen and redeemed. This is the vision of God (subjective genitive: the vision the God in us has). In this world the Word of God is the aggregate of works of inspired art ... Properly interpreted, all works of art are phases of that archetypal vision ... [T]he greater the work of art, the more completely it reveals the gigantic myth which is the vision of this world as God sees it, the outlines of that vision being creation, fall, redemption and apocalypse.
>
> The Bible is the world's greatest work of art and therefore has primary claim to the title of God's Word. (*FS* 108)

This is not a fundamentalist or evangelical privileging of Christian-biblical myth as the sole source of art and culture: it is rather a theory that proceeds from the recognition that, among the often fragmentary and episodic sources of myth, the Bible constitutes as complete a corpus (bibliographically and therefore literally) and as full a cycle of myth as has ever been compiled. In its vision of the full diversity of human experience as nevertheless contained in a single narrative arc, the Bible is rivalled only by the Homeric and Hindu epics (the former of which still require two separate narratives to transcribe the arc that the Bible does in one, and the latter of which tends to resist the discovery of a single continuous narrative). As a result of this panoramic perspective of diversity-in-unity, the Christian Bible has been the central mythic influence on art and culture. 'The most complete form of art is a cyclical vision, which, like the Bible, sees the world between the two poles of fall and redemption,' Frye writes (*FS* 109–10). Even so, the Bible does not 'exhaust the Word of God' (*FS* 110), and therefore it does not eclipse other sources of myth, nor is it to be regarded as particular property or inheritance of one group or segment of culture:

> [W]hile 'The Old & New Testaments are the Great Code of Art,' to regard them as forming a peculiar and exclusive Word of God is a sectarian error ... All myths and rituals hint darkly and allegorically at the same visions that we find in the Bible, which is why they have such strong resemblance to the Christian myths and rituals, a resemblance explained by the Church Fathers as diabolic parodies or Bibles of Hell, as Blake calls his own prophecies. There are many great visions outside the range of the Bible, such as the Icelandic Eddas and the *Bhagavadgita,* almost equally faithful to the central form of the Word of God, and the Bible no less than Classical legends comes from older and more authentic sources. (*FS* 110)

All myths, in other words, may be seen to point in the same direction. The qualification 'almost' is a rare example in Frye's writings of an unexplained and unnecessary equivocation. His point, which will be borne out when we turn to his elucidation of the structure of the Blake's *mythos,* is precisely that:

> The difference between Christianity and other religions is not the difference between truth and falsehood, for the gods of the Christian pantheon are, to the imaginative eye, the same white-whiskered tyrant, the same tortured dying god, the same remote and ineffable Queen of Heaven, that we find in all religions. (*FS* 120)

The progression to higher vision (i.e., reality) that is myth is common to many (and perhaps all) cultures, and intelligible between cultures, so long as the total form of that vision is understood and approached as such.

For Blake and Frye, however, the Bible is unique not only for its providing the total vision or form of myth more effectively than other sources, but because it comes complete, particularly in its New Testament, with guidance on how myth is to be read and understood in order to fulfil that vision. This has to do with the process alluded to above, of grasping and literalizing the spiritual meaning of myth through the phenomenological imagination, the discussion of which will illuminate for us Frye's conception of the archetype. Frye begins to outline this process when he explains that:

> The Gospel teaches us not to despise the letter of the law, but to read it as 'letters,' spiritually, with the full energy of an active and intelligent mind. The law tells us to offer our first fruits to God. The [Selfhood][9] interprets

> that as a command to waste our best efforts in an attempt to bribe a ravenously greedy demon of the sky. The least touch of the imagination releases us from the act, and gives us the anthropologist's insight into its meaning. The full imagination transforms the offering of first fruits into one of the archetypes of the human mind: the identification of the created thing with the God who made it. The Bible teaches us to read like this: it is the primer of a cultured and civilized man. It teaches us to see the sun not as a polished guinea but as a company of angels, and it teaches us to see in the records of all past time not a chaos of tyrannies, but the eternal and eventually emerging form of human life, a form which is the larger body of Man and of God. (*FS* 342)

The visionary, as we know, is one who has learned to 'touch' things with his full imagination: the visionary poet in particular is in the best position to further the Bible's methodology of reading through his own written works, and so enable participation in its vision and the development of the greater mythic subject. The function of the poet, therefore, Frye writes,

> is to concentrate on the myths of that religion, and to recreate the original imaginative life of those myths by transforming them into unique works of art. The essential truth of religion can be presented only in its essential form, which is that of imaginative vision ... [T]he poet is a seer of the apocalyptic vision and the expounder of the Word of God; he sees in every object of nature an 'augury of innocence,' and unites it to a name from the Bible which is evidently the human spirit within it. (*FS* 118, 176)

This uniting of an object with 'a name from the Bible' is the beginning of the process of establishing an archetype as unit or building block of myth, for to do so is to perceive-create that object in the manner of the total imagination which is Man-as-God: this is why Frye speaks of 'archetypes of the human mind.' He is not suggesting that each object must receive a *specific* name from some mythological lexicon; more that an object is made comprehensible through a formal, imagistic or verbal association with some element of myth. There are in fact advantages, he says, to a poet's avoiding traditional mythological names and creating original ones, which was Blake's well-known habit with regard to his own poetic characters. '[W]hen a character is presented as an individual or god and his relationship to an archetype is left to take care of itself, an advantage of vividness is often gained' (*FS* 143): this is because it prompts the reader to discover and recreate the archetype for himself, rather than simply informing him of it. It is the very process of naming and verbally identifying objects that is crucial, because this is a 'putting' of things into words, a dispensation of objects within the malleable system of language, where they can be recreated in association with an element of myth, that is, as an archetype. Frye details the beginning of this process in a passage of *Fearful Symmetry* that sees him positing his semiotic, which is remarkable for its answering of the argument of poststructuralism some twenty years before that approach to language was to develop:

> Those who accept the ... Lockian principle that words are the spectral ghosts of real things existing outside the mind will be hampered by several misconceptions which will forever prevent them from understanding what poetry is and why it exists. It is characteristic of people with vague minds and wandering attentions to speak of literature as 'just a lot of words,' meaning that words are inadequate and misleading substitutes for real things which the weakness and opacity of our minds compel us to adopt. But the assumption is false. If a tree fell in an uninhabited forest, would there be any sound? If sound means only waves set up in the air, yes; if it means waves set up in the air and striking a mind through its ear, no. But the latter meaning of sound is the only one that has any sense as well as sound. On the same principle, an object that has received a name is more real by virtue of it than an object without one. A thing's name is its numen, its imaginative reality in the eternal world of the human mind. That is another reason why Jesus is called the Word of God. Reality is intelligibility, and a poet who has put things into words has lifted 'things' from the barren chaos of nature into the created order of thought. (*FS* 114)

Frye's use of the word 'lifted' recalls Merleau-Ponty's peculiar verb 'subtend.' We should also note Frye's pushing of *numen* away from its conventional metaphysical usage and toward reference to 'imaginative reality': this makes sense to the extent that the word is in fact a corporeal metaphor that descends from the Latin *nutare*, meaning 'to nod' (as a means of summoning or beckoning). It is easy to see how the metaphor developed into a metaphysical concept as the power of creation was assumed to be divine and not human. Frye's intention, obviously, is to restore something of its original meaning, since in his view divine and human creation are the same thing. The point is that the use of the language is crucial aspect of the phenomenology of creative perception, and furthers or refines the expansion of what we have been calling the body image. Merleau-Ponty's own discussion of the act of naming in *Phenomenology of Perception* explains how this is so, and bears out Frye's assumption that the use of language, particularly in mythic and literary contexts, is a corporeal extension and not the exercise in metaphysics or abstraction it is often assumed to be by the theorists and practitioners of poststructuralism:

> The denomination of objects does not follow upon recognition; it is itself recognition. When I fix my eyes on an object in the half-light and say: 'It is a brush,' there is not in my mind the concept of the brush, under which I subsume the object, and which moreover is linked by frequent association with the word 'brush,' but the word bears the meaning, and, by imposing it on the object, I am conscious of reaching that object. As has often been said, for the child the thing is not known until it is named, the name is the essence of the thing and resides in it on the same footing as its colour and its form. For pre-scientific thinking, naming an object is causing it to exist or changing it: God creates beings by naming them and magic operates upon them by speaking of them. These 'mistakes' would be unexplainable if speech rested on the concept, for the latter ought always to know itself as distinct from the former, and to know the former as an external accompaniment ... [But] speech, in the speaker, does not translate ready-made thought, it accomplishes it. (*Phenomenology* 177–8)

Here, as above, Merleau-Ponty's discussion may be understood as underwriting Frye's point, which carries it through to its logical conclusion. If the denomination of an object as a conventional tool allows it to be recognized and brought to hand as such, Frye would suggest that a grander effect could be achieved through application of a mythological name or reference: this raises the object to a level of broad if not universal intelligibility and reveals its place and relevance in the eternal economy of human desire. If the embodied subject of Merleau-Ponty names and therefore reaches a brush, then the embodied and desiring subject of Frye can, by the same token, name and reach the 'bow of burning gold' or mount the 'chariots of fire' of Blake's 'Jerusalem' preface to *Milton* (Blake 95). The same phenomenology of creative perception underwrites both experiences. The only difference between them is the potency of the desire and the discipline of the imagination employed in the perception. This difference, however, makes *all* the difference. In both cases the object is made real by its entrance into the system of language as a word, which functions therefore as a metaphor for it. But the metaphor 'brush' is derived from a quality of its raw or original objectivity (in this case, its practical function) and so does not rise above this significance. It is a metaphor only in the most modest sense, a simile of what may be done with it in its most basic usage (cf. *FS* 123–4). The application of a mythological or religious metaphor, however, in the mode of mythopoeic poetry transubstantiates the material base of an object itself through the projection of desire upon it, recreating it in its universal significance ('Behold, I make all things new' [Rev. 21:5]). Lest this phrase be misunderstood as a political or hegemonic gesture, we should notice that Frye speaks of 'universal significance' for its precise meaning of 'signifying the universe,' for mythological metaphors are the building blocks of a new and humanized cosmos where, as we have shown, egocentric concerns have no reality and selfish or individualistic motives are no longer operative (*FS* 121). As is well implied in the very form of the infamous Blakean metaphors cited above, the imaginative effort to bring them to hand as such is what Blake calls a 'Mental Fight' (Blake 95). They are weapons in the spiritual and imaginative defence of all (as one) against what we have shown to be the threatening concept of an objective universe, and not weapons that men may use against each other. 'Art protects us from nature' and 'enables us to undertake its imaginative conquest,'[10] Frye explains; art 'does what all civilization does: it transforms nature into a home' (*FS* 265).

It may be objected that this apocalyptic potential resides only in the archetypally inclined speaker or writer and does not extend to the reader, that it is just a personal delusion or (to cite a common phrase in Blakean criticism against which Frye braces) a kind of 'private symbolism.' A survey of Merleau-Ponty's corporeal phenomenology of reading and linguistic experience reveals that this is not the case, and suggests rather that the reader participates in the experiential reality of metaphor as fully as a writer. The philosopher observes:

> It is my body which gives significance not only to the natural object, but also to cultural objects like words. If a word is shown to a subject for too short a time for him to [reflect upon][11] it, the word 'warm' for example, induces a kind of experience of warmth which surrounds him with something in the nature of a meaningful halo. The word 'hard' produces a sort of stiffening in the back of the neck, and only in a secondary way does it project itself into the visual or auditory field and assume the appearance of a sign or a word. Before becoming the symbol of a concept it is first of all an event which grips my body, and this grip circumscribes the area of significance to which

> it has reference. One subject states that on presentation of the word 'damp' ... he experiences in addition to a feeling of dampness and coldness, a whole rearrangement of the body image, as if the inside of the body came to the periphery, as if the reality of the body, until then concentrated in his arms and legs, were in search of a new balance of its parts. The word is then indistinguishable from the attitude which it induces ... Words have a physiognomy because we adopt towards them, as towards each person, a certain form of behaviour which makes its complete appearance the moment each word is given ... What is particularly brought out by the word's behaviour is its indissoluable identity with something said, heard and seen ... In short, my body is not only an object among all other objects, a nexus of sensible qualities among others, but an object which is sensitive to all the rest, which reverberates to all sounds, vibrates to all colours, and provides words with their primordial significance through the way in which it receives them. It is not a matter of reducing the significance of the word 'warm' to sensations of warmth by empiricist standards. For the warmth which I feel when I read the word 'warm' is not actual warmth. It is simply my body which prepares itself for heat and which, so to speak, roughs out its outline ... We are not, then, reducing the significance of the word, or even the percept, to a collection of 'bodily sensations' but we are saying that the body, in so far as it has 'behaviour patterns,' is that strange object which uses its own parts as a general system of symbols for the world, and through which we can consequently 'be at home' in that world, 'understand' it and find significance in it. (*Phenomenology* 235–7)

This passage, as we might expect, can stand as a rich elucidation of Frye's own phenomenology of language[12] if we are prepared to fortify its philosophical modesty with a transfusion of red-blooded Blakean vigour. When Merleau-Ponty speaks of embodied consciousness experiencing a word in 'indissoluble identity with something said, heard and seen,' Frye would, in speaking of the Blakean imagination, hasten to add 'or *desired*.' We must also offset the philosopher's qualification that the physical impression of warmth created by the word 'warm' is not 'real' warmth, but the mere 'outline' of the sensation; such hair-splitting ignores the necessary tautology that for a sensation of warmth to be recognizable as such, it must at least be that. But this is not to say that the experience of warmth prompted by the word is 'empirical' in any sense, as Merleau-Ponty recognizes, for such objectively derived conceptual standards are neither relevant nor applicable. The word 'warm' conjures the real sensation of warmth to a degree (pardon the pun) and in a fashion determined only by the potency of the imagination. The crucial point, from the perspective of archetypal theory and existential mythography, is that the incarnate imagination 'provides words with their primordial significance in the way in which it receives them.' The human body, in its provision of a 'general system of symbols,' constitutes what Merleau-Ponty calls a 'nascent *logos*' (*Primacy* 25).

The objection that a demonstration of how one reader may read or experience language corporeally does not mean that other readers may do so is answered in the status of universal discourse to which myth itself aspires, and often achieves. Even Stanley Fish's largely poststructuralist notion of 'interpretive communities' assumes that strategies of reading become standardized. Merleau-Ponty himself inquires 'whether plenary objectivity can be conceived,' or, more precisely, 'whether my experience and that of another person can be linked in a single system of intersubjective experience': 'There may well be,' he hesitantly allows, 'either in each sensory experience or in each consciousness, "phantoms" which no rational approach can account for' (*Phenomenology* 220). His falling back upon Blake's spectral metaphor here is telling, for it indicates the point at which his philosophical notion of 'creative receptivity' falters while the mythic imagination marches onward. But in fact the philosopher's later speculation that the human body could conceivably develop from a nascent *logos* into a *sensorium commune* (which is precisely what is actualized in Frye's notion of the total imagination or universal body) obviates his own scepticism and makes the argument for myth's universal intelligibility on the basis of extensive cultural diffusion a complementary one. '[The] body is the fabric into which all objects are woven,' Merleau-Ponty explains, 'and it is, at least in relation to the perceived world, the general instrument of [our] "comprehension"' (*Phenomenology* 235).

It is, therefore, the standard theoretical objection to the universal intelligibility of the body itself that must finally be met, and this is the one mounted most notably by Michel Foucault. Once a student of Merleau-Ponty, Foucault has theorized the fragmentation of the subject amid the power relations of history as consistently and thoroughly as Derrida has theorized it in language. Surprisingly, Foucault does not deny outright the possibility of universal experience through what he calls the 'productive body and [the] subjected body' (Foucault 173); it is the work of more radical theorists in cultural materialism that has sponsored this moratorium. What Foucault denies, however, is that we can ever have access to or a development of universal experience in thought:

> Forms of experience may perfectly well harbour universal structures; they may well not be independent from the concrete determinants of social existence ... Neither those determinants nor those structures can allow for experiences (that is, for understandings of a certain type, for rules of a certain form, for certain modes of consciousness or oneself and others) except through thought. There is no experience that is not a way of thinking, and which cannot be analyzed from the point of view of the history of thought ... Thought has a historicity which is proper to it. That it should have this historicity does not mean it is deprived of all universal form, but instead that the putting into play of these universal forms is always historical. And that this historicity should be proper to it does not mean that it is independent of all the other historical determinations (of economic, social, or political order), but that it has complex relations with them which always leave their specificity. (Foucault 335)

In recognizing that 'experience may perfectly well harbour universal structures' and that 'there is no experience that is not a way of thinking,' Foucault seems to be opening the door into a world of new possibilities of signification. But as we can see, his emergent position is actually that, even if the body engenders forms of universal experience, that experience is conditioned by the historicity of thought, which is itself conditioned by specific economic, social, and political determinants. The 'putting into play' of the universal forms of experience, in his view, does indeed appear to deprive them of their universality, despite his claim to the contrary. In order to make this argument, however, Foucault, we must notice, has surreptitiously reinstated the deadly Cartesian schism and assumed that body and thought are separable: if the body is universal but thought is always historicized, as Foucault suggests, then they do not share the same substance and cannot function in unity. If this is in fact the case, then human beings are fated to fragmentation, and Foucault and the theorists who follow his lead are merely negotiating the particulars of our damnation. On the other hand, if any aspect of the body is universal, and we observe the obvious *homoousia* of body and consciousness, then some aspect of consciousness must also be universal. This universal aspect of consciousness, extending from corporeal form and experience, is the imagination, myth's mode of production and reception. Foucault's assumption that the universal experience of the body is always conditioned by the historicity of thought is often taken to endorse the position of poststructuralist rhetoricians that any universal posited in language is immediately and necessarily recontextualized in the unilinear continuum of time and grammar; by the time it reaches the reader, its meaning has been redefined by its place in the presumably inviolable sequence of history, or as Derrida's mantra of 'toujours déjà' is intended to drive home, it is 'always already' historicized as at best a mere 'trace' of itself and more likely something different altogether (Derrida, *Grammatology* xvii, 65). But in fact the universal presence of the body ensures that some component of consciousness is likewise universal, and that therefore some elements of language have eternal significance or meaning, are 'already always' in reference. As Northrop Frye observes, 'The apocalypse could occur at any time in history if men wanted it badly enough to stop playing their silly game of hide-and-seek with nature' (*FS* 195).

It should be clear by now that the archetype as theorized in *Fearful Symmetry* is unlike any previous conceptualization of the term in religion, philosophy, or psychology, and that therefore the commonplace characterization of it as a mere variant of other theorizations is erroneous and inadequate. A.C. Hamilton's suggestion that Frye's 'definition [of the archetype] does not differ that much from Jung's' and Jonathan Hart's cavalier insistence that it is, rather, 'more Platonic' are unfortunate cases in point, as are the dozens of summaries, glossaries, and anthologies that repeat these wrongheaded generalizations (Hamilton 109, Hart, 'Context' 29). Not only do such accounts ignore Frye's general description of his conception of the archetype as 'indigenous to criticism, not as transferred from Neoplatonic philosophy or Jungian psychology,' they show no awareness of the phenomenology of *Fearful Symmetry* (*StS* 82). Less erroneous but still slightly misleading is Caterina Nella Cotrupi's remark that Frye's theory extends from Blake's 're-elaboration ... of the Plotinian figure of the mind as a ... source of power that "gives radiance out of its own store to the objects of sense"' (Cotrupi 24, quoting Abrams, *Mirror* 59). Plotinus would certainly endorse and is probably the *locus classicus* of Blake's and Frye's position that the human subject himself is the agent of phenomena; this is why the philosopher is sometimes said to have anticipated many of the concerns of phenomenology. But Plotinus's philosophy is generally idealist and transcendental, and his attitude toward embodiment, while complex, is largely negative.[13] The relationship between the mind and phenomenon is prominent among his concerns, but the principle that ultimately governs the emergent form of phenomenon in his philosophy is the ubiquitous 'One' of which he frequently but cryptically speaks, particularly in the sixth *Ennead* (*Ennead* VI 9.6–8). The Plotinian 'Soul,' a living totality of which each human being is a part (which admittedly bears some resemblance to Frye's total imagination), apparently exists to contemplate the One in dutifully bringing its forms into being. The One is, therefore, a metaphysical other, which is why Plotinus's standing as a founder of Neoplatonism is not trumped by his reputation as a proto-phenomenologist. This is also why Frye specifically says that it is only the 'the *lower half* of the mystical system of Plotinus' (*FS* 154, italics added) that is 'similar' to his Blakean theorizations, by which he means the principle of creative perception and unified humanity and not the idea of the One, an abstraction so complete that no name or image attends it (cf. *DV* 64).[14] If the philosophy of Plotinus sponsors any conception of the archetype, it is Joseph Campbell's, not Northrop Frye's.

Fortunately, Cotrupi's *Northrop Frye and the Poetics of Process* proceeds from this slightly ill-fitting characterization of Frye's archetype as Plotinian to a better-suited discussion of it as influenced by the mythopoetics of the Italian philosopher Giambattista Vico (who has a far better claim to the title of proto-phenomenologist than Plotinus). Thus Cotrupi enters into the small company of scholars who have provided useful notes toward the definition of the Frygian archetype. Frye, Cotrupi suggests, adopts from Vico the position that 'human intellection was grounded in the body both literally and metaphorically, for it was through the senses that the first anthropomorphic "ideal" and corporeal mental portraits of the world were contrived ... primarily through metaphor' (Cotrupi 72). Her claim that Frye, like Vico, understood 'poetic class concepts or archetypes' as 'way[s] of seeing' that constitute the 'very condition of reality for the poetic mind' is precisely at issue and very much the case. But while Cotrupi's Viconian cast has the virtue of substantiating an influence that Frye himself acknowledged in his later works, her assumption that Vico was absorbed early by Frye and informs his entire corpus is spurious,[15] and tends to obscure the originality and importance of his first theorization of the mythic imagination in *Fearful Symmetry*. It would be more judicious to say that Frye found late in Vico a confirmation of his theory of mythic language and imaginative creation as rooted in his first book, just as he might have in *Phenomenology of Perception*. In any case, Vico does not (at least not as presented by Cotrupi) underwrite or corroborate the workings of Frye's corporeal imagination as fully or precisely as the contemporaneous researches of Merleau-Ponty, nor does Vico (through Cotrupi) come to bear on *Fearful Symmetry*'s apocalypse of the universal subject. It is a reduction, therefore, to say that Frye's archetypology 'push[es] a Vichian agenda [sic],' though Cotrupi is nevertheless very much on the trail of Frye's post-metaphysical or phenomenological archetype (Cotrupi 51).

To Cotrupi's remarks we may add Thomas Willard's important distinction between Frye's 'archetypes of the imagination' and Jung's archetypes of the collective unconscious. 'Jung's archetypes are fundamentally different from Frye's,' Willard recognizes, because the two thinkers differ on the important question of 'the innate versus the socially constructed.' Willard correctly observes that this does not mean, however, that they are therefore 'incompatible' (Willard 18). Still more useful is the discussion of Frye's conception of the archetype, and his attitude toward other conceptions of it, in Robert Denham's *Northrop Frye and Critical Method.* Denham, Frye's steadiest commentator, devotes his study chiefly to *Anatomy of Criticism,* but it nevertheless contains insightful remarks on *Fearful Symmetry* and Frye's relation to modern mythography. Frye's archetype is not only unique, Denham suggests, but it absorbs other conceptions. Proceeding from Frye's frequent claim[16] that theories of myth and archetype are more at home in literary and cultural criticism than anthropology or psychology, Denham observes that Frye's archetypology swallows several of the others we have looked at: Frye's theory 'works in a centripetal direction,' and ingests Jung and Eliade as 'students of symbolism whose works provide us with a grammar of the human imagination' which helps form the foundation of his broader and more apocalyptic vision (Denham, *Critical Method* 45).[17] As for the specific theory of the archetype in *Fearful Symmetry,* the pinnacle of this vision, Denham aptly describes it as the instrument by which 'things attain human rather than merely natural form,' until the whole world 'is completely possessed by the human mind,' the process by which 'the perceiving subject [becomes] the circumference and not the centre of reality' (Denham, *Critical Method* 55, 54). If Denham missteps it is in his characterization of this process as a reparation of the 'radical disjunction between the phenomenal and the noumenal worlds,' when (as we have demonstrated at length) it is better understood as a renovation and unification of an extensive phenomenal universe. The mythic cosmos, as Blake writes in *Milton,* is 'one infinite plane' (Blake 109).

Frye's archetype, as we have demonstrated, is a verbalization of a desired mythic form or state by the visionary, which is intended to come into being and identity with him through the phenomenological imagination, and which invites, through allusion to the universally intelligible structures of myth, similar identification from readers. At the very least, therefore, it is a verbal postulate of obvious interest to semiotics and literary criticism: as Frye explains in his essay 'Blake's Treatment of the Archetype' (1950), an archetype is, most basically, 'an element in a work of literature, whether a character, an image, a narrative formula, or an idea, which can be assimilated to a larger unifying category' ('Blake's Treatment' 14). It is more broadly and deeply (which is to say, existentially) relevant, by virtue of the radical phenomenology or the 'apocalyptic theory of perception' that underwrites its reality in projection and reception ('Blake's Treatment' 15). From this perspective, the archetype is nothing less than the instrument of apocalypse, a 'clarification of the mind which enables one to grasp the human form of the world' ('Blake's Treatment' 12). Frye's archetype is the catalyst of 'the complete transformation of both nature and human nature into the same form' ('Blake's Treatment' 8). When Frye speaks of 'how important in Blake's theory of art is his conception of the recreation of the archetype,' it is because it is a 'process which unites [the] sequence of visions' that is myth and art into a total vision (*FS* 415). 'Blake's view of art,' Frye explains, 'could almost be defined as the attempt to realize the religious vision in human society' ('Blake's Treatment' 8).

The ways in which Frye's archetype differs from other conceptions are both readily apparent and highly significant. Frye's archetypes are 'essentialist' (an oft-cited criticism of them) only in the sense that human beings possess the natural ability and the ready means to create and comprehend them, and because they account for the presence of some obviously stable base units employed in the creation of art and culture as intelligible structures. But Frye's archetype is fuelled neither by the presumption of an abstract philosophical or conceptual necessity, like the Eliadean archetype, nor by the presumption of an abstract psychological compulsion, like the Jungian archetype (nor, obviously, by the presumption of some combination of the two, like the Campbellian archetype). It is a perceptive and intentional extension of corporeal form, which is therefore rooted or situated in a continuum of phenomenal transformation rather than in the metaphysical or noumenal. As a product of the embodied consciousness, the archetype, as Frye explains in his late notebooks, is born of the physical reality of the body, rises up through and 'beyond Jung's collective unconsciousness into a collective consciousness arrived at through an imaginative consensus[18] and tak[es] on the form of a cultural tradition' (*LN* 633, cf. *RT* 39).[19]

The paradoxical authority of Frye's archetype comes from the fact that it is not, like other conceptions, *a priori* to consciousness and culture; it is co-constitutive of consciousness (which is to say, creating and created by consciousness) and coincident with culture (which is to say, the form of culture). For this reason, and its grounding in the embodied consciousness, the Frygian archetype has the virtue of real presence: it is the backbone of a theory of myth as something 'which addresses the reader in the present tense, as something confronting him with an imperative rather than revealing a mystery out of the past' ('Literature and Myth' 53). This archetype is an intensification of consciousness in the present (and *of* the present), not a dissipation of some originary plentitude never to be fully recovered. Not only are Frye's archetypes socially constructed, which is to say, constructed by and in society, they are themselves the very instruments of social (re)construction at the highest level. It is not, as it is with other theories, through the recognition of a shared source that Frye gives warrant to the archetype: it is its active role in a real but non-objectifying process of social unification. Its rooting in the universal form of the human body is a more verifiable foundation than the assumptions upon which other notions of the archetype rest, but it is its demonstrable function and fulfilment in society that ultimately give Frye's archetype the proverbial (and literal) leg up. The social grounding of Frye's mythography gives it an immediacy and a forward momentum which other theories of myth lack. His archetypology cannot be interpreted, as others can, as a conservative ideology cloaked in the rhetoric of primitivism and reverential God-talk, or an essentialist system of social control that anxiously tethers man to familiar and predictable root behaviours. Its value lies not in its claim to some pre-social authority, but in its being a medium of social exchange, and a system or body of thought that is as radically liberal (in the original sense of that word as *liberating*) and as socially progressive as any theory could conceivably be. From the perspective of criticism, for example, Frye suggests that:

> [T]hose who are incapable of distinguishing between a recognition of archetypes and a Procrustean methodology which forces everything into a prefabricated scheme would be well advised to leave the whole question alone. It is with symbolism as with etymology: the true course is neither to accept all resemblances as proving common descent from a single ancestor, nor reject them all as coincidence, but to establish the laws by which the real

> relationships may be recognized. If such laws exist, it will be quite possible to develop an imaginative accuracy in reading the arts which is not, like the accuracy of pedantry, founded purely on inhibitions. (*FS* 422–3)

And from a broader social and existential perspective, he prophetically thunders:

> The release of the creative genius is the only social problem that matters, for such a release is not the granting of extra privileges to a small class, but the unbinding of a Titan in man who will soon begin to tear down the sun and moon and enter Paradise. The creative impulse in man is God in man; the work of art, or the good book, is an image of God, and to kill it is to put out the perceiving eye of God. God has nothing to do with routine morality or invariable truth: he is a joyous God for whom too much is enough and exuberance beauty, a God who gave every Israelite in the desert three times as much manna as he could possibly eat. *No one can really speak for liberty without passing through revolution to apocalypse.* (*FS* 160, italics added).

Or as he starkly phrases it in his essay on Blake's archetype, Man cannot be truly free until he is everywhere and everything ('Blake's Treatment' 8).

Frye's theorization of the archetype stands outside and beyond the traditional association of myth with mysticism that informs the work of Eliade, Jung, and Campbell. Without dismissing the association, Frye suggests that mysticism, as a 'spiritual communion with God which is by its very nature incommunicable ... and which soars beyond faith to direct apprehension,' is 'difficult to reconcile with ... poetry' and the notion of artistic creation (*FS* 7). Frye's Blakean or visionary archetype, unlike the mystical archetypes of our other mythologists, 'is a perceptive' (which, again, means *creative*) 'rather than a contemplative attitude of mind' (*FS* 8). Mysticism involves an austerity and an asceticism that grate at the sensibilities of creative thinkers like Blake and Frye. While the mystic typically seeks to atone himself to some pre-existent God or truth, the visionary is himself an aspect of God, and creates that truth; where the mystic seeks only to behold, the 'visionary creates, and dwells in, a higher spiritual world where the objects of perception in this one become transfigured and charged with a new intensity of symbolism' (*FS* 8). It is the embodied consciousness or imagination, as we have seen, that empowers this creativity, and bases it in the field of the real; where mystics and ascetics 'go wrong,' Frye writes, 'is in forgetting that all mental activity is also a bodily struggle, because based on sense experience' (*FS* 194). 'Turning from instead of passing through perception is a reduction of life,' Frye insists (*FS* 55). However, if mysticism were redefined, as it is in an endnote to *Fearful Symmetry*, as 'an effort of vision,' the 'realization in total experience of the identity of God and Man in which both the human creature and the superhuman creator disappear,' then he is willing to call Blake's poetry and mythography mystical (*FS* 431–2). But where mysticism involves at best an innocuous withdrawal from the human world, and at worst a suspicious imposition of an assumed transcendent form onto that world, Frye, like Blake, has little time for it. The visionary archetype, unlike the mystical, constitutes uncompromising creative work in and for the lived world, with the aim of transforming it into the world we desire.

Our imagination creates the archetypes of myth as Milton's God creates Adam: in our own image, to be one with us, sufficient to stand but free to fall. As simultaneous inhabitants of the human world, however, we also stand on the other side the archetype, and so it is by our effort in this field that it stands or falls, based on our commitment to the creation of the world it postulates. The best definition of the archetype is thus perhaps the very simple one upon which Frye rests after he has finished presenting the theory of *Fearful Symmetry*, and is about to turn to the mythic structure of Blake's poetry: archetypes are 'images of a higher state of being which is human and divine at once' (*FS* 163). In the context of semiotics and literary criticism, Frye explains, this suggests that the archetype invites or rises to that 'profoundest understanding of poetry' that Dante Alighieri called *anagogy*, which, he says, is the poetic word as taken to have been 'spiritually expounded' (Dante 64). The literal meaning of 'expound,' derived from Dante's Latin verb *exponere*, is relevant here: *ex*, out, out of + *ponere*, to put or place, 'to place or put out.' In this mode of understanding, Dante says, a word, 'even in the literal sense, by the very thing it signifies, signifies again some portion of the supernal things of eternal glory' (*FS* 121, Dante 64). 'The ultimate significance of a work of art,' Frye writes, is therefore 'simply a dimension added to its literal meaning' (*FS* 121): this added dimension being, of course, reality itself, the only dimension into which the literal may expand and still retain its form and reference. The highest level of interpretation and criticism, in other words, is that which fulfils the destiny of myth mentioned earlier, the extension or re-literalization of itself in the realm of human experience. Anagogy is the proper name of the apocalyptic hermeneutic that takes the reader from 'superficial to the complete apprehension of the same thing, the single image of reality which the work of art is' (*FS* 121); it is the mode of reading which fulfils the phenomenological intentionality of the archetype (a point of considerable importance to our understanding of Frye's theory of myth in and after *Fearful Symmetry*, for his formulation of anagogy changed somewhat in *Anatomy of Criticism*).

IV. The Visionary Fourth

The literal meaning of anagogy (Greek, *ana*, up + *agein*,[20] to go or lead = 'leading up' or 'up-going') underscores the productive nature or 'upward thrust' of the archetype, which greatly influences the total structure that Blake and Frye see embodied in myth and mythopoeic literature. The phenomenology of myth that we have outlined led Blake to a unique and original interpretation of the mythological sources (chiefly the Bible) that constituted his reading and inspiration, and that interpretation is reflected in the structure of his own poetry. Blake called this interpretation 'diabolical' or 'infernal,' because it constitutes, as the two words suggest, a revolutionary reading of myth from the perspective of human experience in a lower or fallen world (Blake 44, *FS* 109). In clarifying Blake's mythic phenomenology as such, Frye was able to provide the still-foremost understanding of Blake's poetry as a unified structure that is at once an interpretation and a revelation of the existential form and relevance of biblical (and possibly all other) myth. This structure and form is therefore both a sequence of phases in a total *mythos*, and a progressive heightening and broadening of the plane of imaginative consciousness. With regard to the structure of that *mythos*, Frye explains that:

> The imaginative vision of human life sees it as a drama in four acts: a fall, the struggle of men in a fallen world which is what we usually think of as history, the world's redemption by a divine man in which eternal life and death achieve simultaneous triumph, and an apocalypse. (*FS* 357)

These four acts, which are the major events and episodes of the biblical narrative, are clarified in and align with the four levels or progressive states of imaginative existence that are the settings inhabited by the characters of Blake's mythopoetic verse. The poet calls these Ulro, Generation, Beulah, and Eden.

Before turning to a discussion of these states, we should first observe that there is no independent creation episode in Blake's mythography, or in Frye's elucidation of it. The Romantic notion of *felix culpa* reaches an apotheosis in Blake's sense that consciousness is born into an awareness of its fragmentation, and proceeds from there (this position further emphasizes what we have cited as the upward or 'forward-leaning' quality of Blake's and Frye's mythography). There is in Blake, however, a heuristic (as opposed to an ontological) assumption of a primordial unity of cosmos and consciousness, which serves to emphasize the potential for human unification in the resurrected body of Jesus (as opposed to being an actual mythic departure point). The Blakean *mythos* thus presumes the existence of a primordial Titan-figure named Albion (an ancient name for Britain), a universal God-man within whose body all of humanity and creation is contained. The creation of the objective universe is the result of the fall and fragmentation of Albion; 'the key to much of [Blake's] symbolism,' Frye explains, 'is that the fall of man and the creation of the physical world were the same event' (*FS* 41). There are several accounts of the Fall in Blake's work, but the essential reason for all of them is 'Albion's relapse from active creative energy to passivity. This passivity takes the form of wonder or awe at the world he has created' (*FS* 126). The Fall, in other words, results from the adoption of the Cartesian-Lockean posture of passive perception that assumes the existence of an objective universe, which amounts to an evisceration and scattering of the universal body. Blake's belief that the Fall is a result of this change in consciousness explains his insistence that the biblical tree of knowledge grows 'in the human brain,' there to be either cultivated or pruned (Blake 27). The fall of Albion symbolizes the Fall of Man as the assumption or acceptance of imaginative limitation or constraint, which is in essence the extraction or separation of man from God. It functions simultaneously as a fall myth and a creation myth because it represents an alienation from the universal body (image), which then appears as the objective universe that both stretches out before us and crashes in upon us.

This myth of a primeval giant whose fall creates the universe may seem strange to inhabitants of the Christian tradition, since it is not found in the Bible (though one is tempted to associate its Fall aspect with the Sabbath rest [Genesis 2:1–3]). As Frye explains, however, it is a widespread and venerable form, and though he does not cite its archetypal name, which Plutarch has as *macroanthropos,* he does list some of the best-known examples of it (*FS* 125–6, 287). The figure is preserved in the Jewish Cabbalistic myth of Adam Kadmon, 'the universal man who contained within his limbs all heaven and earth.' In the prose Edda, it appears as the giant Ymir, whose bones become the mountains and whose blood becomes the sea. In classical myth, the figure is Atlas, whose image perfectly captures the situation of the fallen god-man, with the world outside and above him, pressing down upon him. It is also presumably related to the *sparagmos* rituals of the ancient Greek cult of Dionysus. In Egyptian mythology, it can be found in the figure of the vegetative god Osiris, whose body is torn to pieces and scattered along the Nile river. When Frye observes that 'the same imagery is found in the Vedic hymns,' he is almost certainly thinking of the 'Purusha-Sukta' verses of the *Rig-Veda* (10.90.1–16), the hymn to the 'Cosmic Man' who at birth sacrificially multiplies himself into all beings and objects in the universe. Where this myth dovetails most recognizably into the biblical narrative is in the occasion of the flood of Noah, which likewise symbolizes the dissolution of humanity and the world. In particular, Blake aligns the fall of Albion with the flood that drowns the mythical city of Atlantis (which he calls 'the archetype of mighty Emperies / Now barr'd out by the Atlantic Sea'), an association which foreshadows, as Albion himself does, the risen body of Christ, the other metaphorical form of the reunified subject (Blake 55). The sunken city, like the sparagmatic body, implies dissolution and disappearance, but not destruction or death, the point being that the universal subject is only buried and awaiting resurrection.

In Blake's poetry, the Fall of Albion takes human life down through the various levels of imaginative existence until it reaches the lowest,[21] Ulro, the poet's conception of hell. In the Bible, this is the descent delineated in the consistent downward arc of the book of Genesis: the expulsion from paradise, the dispersal of Cainite civilization, the Noahic deluge, the fall of the Tower of Babel, and the arrival and bondage of Israel in Egypt. Other fall and exilic myths, such as the classical *Titanomachia*, or the casting down of the Titans into Tartarus by the Olympians, articulate the same experience. Ulro, for Blake, is the world of total abstraction that gapes threateningly with the discovery of the very ability to abstract. Frye describes Ulro as the state of 'the isolated individual reflecting on his memories of perception and evolving generalizations and abstract ideas' (*FS* 48). It is the world we enter when consciousness yields to the temptation to engage in Lockean reflection, a state where only Blakean 'Spectres,' only the traces of Derrida's 'lost presence,' are apprehended. In the context of modern mythography, this is the world delineated by Mircea Eliade's archetypes, the recollections or generalizations of lost hierophantic experience, articulating a static, hollow universe. It is no coincidence that Eliade saw the apprehension of stone as particularly provocative of *homo religiosus*' tendency to abstract (cf. chapter 1, 30, *Patterns* 216), for as Frye observes, the primary symbols for Blake's hell-state of Ulro are 'the symbols of sterility, chiefly rocks and sand' (*FS* 48–9). Ulro is also the imaginative state in which the supreme sky-god, the pinnacle of Eliade's mythography, comes to bear. The fall of Albion, according to Blake, leads to the appearance of several other characters, which symbolize the contortions and fragmentation of consciousness: Ulro is the realm of Blake's cold and distant figure Urizen, a 'tyrannical old bully' who represents the 'abstraction called Heaven' and 'the imaginative feeling of a hostile mystery in the sky-world' (*FS* 119). Urizen is the archetypal father-god, the result of the state of restrained or repressed consciousness that also creates the wrathful and seemingly arbitrary Jehovah of the Old Testament, the all-powerful Zeus of Hesiod, the Roman Jupiter, and the stern Odin or Wotan of Norse mythology. A 'thundergod of moral law and tyrannical power,' Urizen is a 'projection of the death-impulse' (*FS* 129). His name is apparently derived by Blake through a fusion of the words 'your reason' and 'horizon' (in its connotation of 'limit'), but one also detects in it an echo of what, borrowing from Plato, Eliade calls the 'ouranic' or celestial. The appearance of this white-whiskered tyrant marks the advent of consciousness as rationalism and empirical *skepsis*, akin to Freudian notions of the superego or the 'reality principle'; he embodies in particular the fear and dread, the sense of *mysterium tremendum*, with which human beings perceive the objective and objectifying structures of authority that appear to assimilate them.

In Ulro, the sub-rational dimensions of consciousness, especially the body and forms of desire, are buried, denied, or thwarted by the frozen and purgatorial will of Urizen. Human consciousness inevitably finds this state of deprivation and contraction to be intolerable, and so before long a set of corporeal desires and concerns emerges which resists such a condition. This array of revolutionary impulses, projecting itself along the predictable sensual and socio-political axes, is embodied in the dynamic figure Blake calls Orc, whose name is derived from the Latin *orcus*, meaning 'lower world.'[22] Frye defines Orc as 'the power of human desire to achieve a better world which produces revolution and foreshadows the apocalypse' (*FS* 206). In theoretical terms, Orc is the ameliorating desire and potential of corporeal consciousness expressing itself through its ecstatic tendency, or as Frye more succinctly explains it, 'human imagination trying to burst out of the body' (*FS* 136). Described by Blake as a 'hater of indignities,' the 'terrific form,' and 'Lover of wild rebellion' (Blake 53–4), the fiery Orc personifies the drives that Freud tried to theorize as the id and 'pleasure principle,' and Jung as the archetypes of the collective unconscious, but which are actually the desires of embodied consciousness. With the birth of Orc as a challenge of the dominance of Urizen, human life ascends to the imaginative state Blake refers to as Generation, a name intended to connote the growth potential and cyclical structure of nature.

Where Ulro is the 'single' or solitary world of abstraction, Generation is the double or 'twofold' world of subject and object, as the appearance of Orc is the birth of subjectivity in the teeth of, and in conflict with, the objective universe. Generation is the world of human wandering and struggle in the field of time and nature. Frye describes it as 'the ordinary world we live in,' the world of 'organism and environment' (*FS* 49). What was the tyranny of the abstract in Ulro, presided over by Urizen, becomes in Generation the tyranny of nature and history, the distancing and depriving effects of space and time. Urizen continues to stand behind this structure as the guarantor or enforcer of the physical laws governing these effects, but the structure presents itself in Blake's poetry in the female figures Enitharmon and Vala, the queen of heaven and the body of nature (*FS* 127). The archetypal forms of Generation are, not surprisingly, those of Jung, for Enitharmon and Vala resemble the Jungian chthonic mother in her maternal and maiden aspects just as Orc resembles the Jungian self,[23] and the revolving cycles of time are akin to those of the individuation process. This is why Frye associates the nature of conflicted consciousness in Generation with the *ouroboros*, the self-consuming serpent which is, as we observed, the real form of the Jungian cycle of individuation: 'The serpent with its tail in its mouth is a perfect emblem of the Selfhood: an earth-bound, cold-blooded and often venomous form of life imprisoned in its own cycle of death and rebirth ... It is this serpent, man's ... desire to assert rather than create, that stands between man and Paradise' (*FS* 135, 137). This last remark accounts for the representation of nature as a water-serpent, dragon, or other gigantic beast, or a monstrous, domineering, or consuming female, that is commonplace in myth and literature (it also accounts for Blake's occasional representation of Orc himself as a serpent [*FS* 210–11]): such images are symbolic of the natural world by which consciousness perceives itself to be simultaneously tempted and tormented, but which is actually an unclaimed (or untamed) object or aspect of itself.

This conflicted relationship between Blake's characters unfolds in a recurrent structure found in his poetry which Frye refers to as 'the Orc cycle,' the cycle of repression and rebellion in human consciousness. Blake's *America: A Prophecy*, for instance, opens with Orc chained in the 'dens of Urthona,' the rocky prison of Ulro which contains the buried and germinating imagination; Orc bursts free and forces himself upon Vala, who is briefly animated by him, but Orc is eventually countered and subsumed again under the authority of Urizen (Blake 51–8). In other poems, more significantly, Orc is sacrificed to Urizen, as in the *The Four Zoas* where Orc is hung or 'stretched' upon the 'tree of Mystery,' which likewise begins the cycle anew (Blake 365). The Orc cycle of Blake and Frye, like the Jungian individuation process and Campbell's monomyth, is the romance or quest structure that is the conventional core of myth (although where Jung sees it as a closed cycle, Campbell and Frye are concerned to theorize it as open, or at least openable). It is a manifold depiction of the Frazerian fertility myth that reflects and is reflected in such rise-and-fall rotations as the seasonal cycle and the Oedipal conflict of liberal youth and conservative parentage. Frye's more flexible model observes in it what is a significant and remarkably consistent cosmological image-pattern; the rebel Orc ascends from a rock or stone that is symbolic of Ulro, confronts, crosses, or otherwise engages the water-monster, woman, or wilderness that is symbolic of Generation, and then collapses, through exhaustion or sacrifice, back to either the stone or a tree (another base symbol of Generation). 'Life in this world apparently springs from the lifeless,' Frye writes, 'that is, life seems, in some way we cannot fathom, to form itself out of dead matter. As the rock is the image of dead matter, all new life struggles out of a rock, and relapses back into it at death' (*FS* 225).

This pattern is particularly prevalent in the Bible's Old Testament. Jacob falls asleep upon a stone and dreams up and out of it a ladder ascending to heaven; then he wanders and wrestles in the wilderness, and eventually follows his sons into captivity in Egypt. Moses leads the Israelites out of that Egyptian 'furnace of iron' (Deuteronomy 4:20), across the parted Red Sea (which is imaged in Isaiah as a passage over a wounded dragon [Isaiah 51:9]) and into the desert; but the energy of his rebellion, Frye says, is 'perverted into the Sinaitic moral code' of the Urizenic Jehovah, and he dies upon Mount Pisgah (*FS* 137). Samson breaks free from his bonds atop 'the rock Etam' (Judges 15:8), becomes entangled in the intrigues of Delilah, and dies beneath collapsing ruins. The prosperity of Job comes to an abrupt halt through sufferings that result from his being under the dominion of 'Behemoth' and 'Leviathan,' a land-dwelling and a seagoing beast that together symbolize objective nature. This same fate is later rendered more explicitly in the experience of Jonah's being swallowed by Leviathan. In the New Testament, the great example of the Orc cycle is, of course, the life of Christ: Jesus breaks free from the swaddling clothes of his childhood, wanders the wilderness in his ministry, challenges a narrow orthodoxy, and is crucified on a mound of skulls (specifically upon a wooden cross that resembles a tree).

The cycle is equally common in the classical tradition. Prometheus ascends to his infamous fire-theft, and in punishment is chained by Zeus to the rock of Mount Caucasus, where vultures, symbolic of devouring nature, tear at his regenerating body. For daring to outwit death (with a plan involving an impious wife), Sisyphus is condemned to continually roll a stone to the summit of a mountain, but never over it. Both Homeric heroes, Achilles and Odysseus, are laid low by water, womanly wiles, and Urizenic tyrants, during and after the war at Troy. Adonis, Frazer's favoured figure, bursts forth from a wooden chest or myrrh tree, and is meted between the goddesses Aphrodite and Persephone by Zeus (symbolizing the vegetative cycle); he is eventually killed by a boar sent by Artemis, goddess of the hunt and wild animals, or in some cases, by a jealous and Urizenic Ares, god of war. In Norse mythology, the death of Thor at Ragnarok in battle with the Midgard serpent, and Odin's sacrifice of himself to himself upon the world-tree Yggdrasil, are both resolutions of Orc cycles (the latter example emphasizing, even more than the hanging of Blake's Orc and the crucifixion of Christ, that the hanged god and the hoary tyrant are aspects of the same identity or consciousness). There is evidence that the Orc cycle is functional if not fundamental in mythologies outside the West: many hymns in the *Rig-Veda* celebrate the myth of heroic Indra, who slays the dragon Vritra and frees the waters that are held captive inside him (cf. 1.52.1–15, Weston 25–33). When Frye writes that 'there is frequently a "freeing of the waters"' when the Orcish hero slays a dragon, he is certainly thinking of these hymns (*FS* 284). Significantly, in the later versions of the myth in the *Mahabarata*, Indra suffers for his great deed when a vengeful goddess rises from the dragon's corpse and clings to him until he repents to the supreme Brahma. He is eventually beheaded as penance, in what is sometimes considered to be an Eastern analogue of the crucifixion.

The Orc cycle is the mythic structure of 'the entire process of life and death which goes on in our world, taking in the whole physical world of Generation' (*FS* 234). It is, however, a 'pessimistic view of life,' Frye explains, because it expresses the perspective that 'human and vegetable life is imprisoned in a rock' (from 'the imaginative point of view the physical world *is* a rock,' Frye points out). There is a 'protective aspect' to the rock-symbol, as evinced by such reassuring tropes as the Christian 'Rock of Ages,' which confirms that 'the physical world is solid and permanent, and orderly enough for the imagination to get a grip on it' for the purposes of building upon it. The problem originates rather in the negative or sceptical interpretation of this principle as a limitation rather than a basis for liberation, a perspective that sees the rock as an inescapable burden and 'all life [as] vegetable in the sense of being anchored to it' (*FS* 225). As Paul writes, in the terms of Generation rather than Ulro, 'cursed is everyone that hangeth on a tree' (Galatians 3:13). The Orc cycle, ultimately, expresses a recurrent failure of the imagination to establish an expanded form, a continual collapse of the ecstatic body image back to a purely empirical ground, which is symbolized by the sacrifice or aging of Orc into Urizen.

If the imagination can maintain its broadened, ecstatic form and keep hold of its object, however, human life ascends to the state that Blake calls Beulah, a term derived from the book of Isaiah which means 'married land' (Isaiah 62:4). Where Ulro is the single world of abstraction, and Generation the double world of subject-object conflict, Beulah is the triple or 'threefold' world of 'the lover, the beloved and their mutual creation' (*FS* 50); or, in theoretical terms, the imagination, its former object, and the new reality or body that springs from their union. In Beulah, 'the perceiving consciousness of our world becomes a lover or child and the nature of our world beautiful and beloved, a mistress or mother' (*FS* 229–30). In Jungian or Freudian terms, the ascent to Beulah is the resolution of what was in Generation the family-drama aspect of the Orc cycle, the archetypal *agon* of the Oedipal triangle: in Beulah, the authority and power of Urizen is domesticated or absorbed,[24] the terrible mother is made nurturing, and the tempting maiden becomes a bride. Blake thus describes this state in *Milton* as 'appear[ing] within each district / As the beloved infant in his mother's bosom round incircled,' but also inhabited by 'the Daughters of Beulah / Enraptured with affection sweet and mild benevolence' (Blake 129). The hold of the imagination on the objects of desire of the external world transforms the threatening countenance of objective nature into a welcoming paradisal garden, which is the central symbol of Beulah. The garden as a vision of cultivated comfort, material plentitude, and (through its personifications) sexual satisfaction indicates the place of Beulah in the cosmos of mythic experience as the state of possible imaginative fulfilment, and emphasizes the principle that the desires of the imagination are corporeal in origin and form. 'Every Generated Body,' writes Blake, 'in its inward form / Is a garden of delight' (Blake 123).

The erotic dimension of Beulah, in particular, dispels the fallacious assumption in religion and literature that the pastoral or garden paradise of myth symbolizes a state of asexual abstraction or chaste spirituality. As we mentioned earlier, the expansion of the imagination is analogous to the Christian doctrine of bodily resurrection, and the resurrection of the body, Frye recognizes, must mean 'the resurrection of *all* the body': 'as the physical body has a sexual origin, the sexual life [in Beulah] ... is transformed, not eliminated' (*FS* 195–6). '[T]his life is a transfiguration of the sexual life of the natural world, and has nothing to do with the refined fantasies of spiritual eunuchs' (*FS* 240). This transfiguration applies to the other human desires in addition to the sexual, in all cases turning on the discovery that subjects can merge with objects in the expanding field of the imagination or body image, rather than desiccate them in abstraction (the former discovery constituting redemption as the latter constituted the Fall). If this principle is properly understood, the concern raised by Daniel O'Hara in his critique of *Fearful Symmetry*, that theorizing an ascent to a Beulah-state amounts to a 'visionary polemic against nature' involving its 'symbolic exclusion and death,' becomes recognizable for what it is (O'Hara 153–5): the voice of temptation whispered from the wilderness of Generation by the figure Blake calls the 'Covering Cherub,' whose job it is to keep humanity from entering paradise (Blake 104). The attainment of Beulah is not the destruction of nature but redemption to and through her ideal form, and only appears as hostile to those who would rather struggle in her teeth than rest in her maternal or marital embrace. O'Hara's claim that Frye's imaginative '"dialectic of love" is founded ... upon the exclusion and death of nature' and masks the aggression of '"the domineering male in erection"'[25] repeats the critique of the ecstatic phenomenology of Heidegger and Merleau-Ponty made by feminist theorists like Luce Irigaray and Judith Butler. But this position, and O'Hara's crudely overstated objection that the ascent to Beulah requires that 'the real woman must "die" if the Eternal Feminine is to live' (O'Hara 159), not only wrongly implies that imaginative recreation somehow requires 'actual' destruction; they also forget that a true ecstatic union of subject and object means that ego-driven impulses like aggression and the will to dominate no longer exist. As Alvin A. Lee observes, Frye's theorizations entail neither the 'groveling of the human creature before a deity thought to be transcendent, nor ... any sense of the individual ego asserting itself' (*NFR* xix). This is to say nothing of the fact that the feminist critique of *ekstasis* as male dominance conveniently overlooks that it occurs just as readily as a conventionally feminine act of envelopment as a conventionally masculine act of projection (something the frequent use of metaphors of swallowing and integration in this chapter is intended to demonstrate); the two actions are in fact equivalent, even interchangeable, in their accomplishment of the same end. Blake's Beulah is to some degree a vision of the paradisal garden as sought by a heterosexual male, but everything in the Blakean-Frygian theory of the imagination suggests that the same state, or an analogous one, awaits the female or homosexual visionary at the moment of ecstatic discovery, which is likewise their journeying beyond the narrow contexts of gender and orientation. Far from endorsing 'tacit normative assumptions' about the heterosexual and preferentially masculine priorities of bodily exchange, as Judith Butler has charged (Butler 85–90), genuine ecstatic or imaginative experience is the outgrowing of such normative assumptions and priorities. 'Wherefore are sexes in Beulah?' inquires Blake in *Jerusalem* (Blake 193). In Beulah, he writes, sexual embraces are 'cominglings: from the Head even to the Feet / And not a pompous High Priest entering by a Secret Place' (*FS* 196, Blake 223). 'Man cannot unite with Man but by their Emanations / Which stand both Male & Female at the Gates of each Humanity' (Blake 246).

Beulah, as Frye explains, is 'a middle stage between the spiritual and the temporal world,' a 'stage intermediate between spiritual and physical existence' which marks 'the begetting of new life in a state of love [that] represents a higher phase of existence than we ordinarily enter' (*FS* 227, 232). While the archetypes of Ulro are those of Eliade's *homo religiosus*, and the archetypes of Generation are those of Jung's Sisyphean modern man, it cannot quite be said that the archetypes of Beulah are those of Joseph Campbell. But Beulah is clearly the paradisal state and the Telemachan resolution to which Campbell's hero *aspires*, a thought that occurs particularly as Frye describes it as

> the world of those transient intuitions of eternity which are not hammered into definite form, the fancies that break through language and escape. It is the world of contemplative thought, of the adoration of some vague mystery enveloping us. It is the world of the consolations of religion, of implicit faith and confident hope. It is the world of wonder and romance, of fairy tales

> and dreams. It is the protected world of the child and the world of the lover's 'gratified desire.' It is ... the world of the benevolent father, Providence or Madonna which the gentler visionaries inhabit. (*FS* 230)

The vagaries of this account, which reads like a tolerant gloss on *The Hero with a Thousand Faces*, are employed by Frye as much to evoke the wonder of Beulah as to suggest its precariousness; or, when sought through the compromised theory of Campbell, its untenability. This is because, even when it is actually (which is to say, phenomenologically) attained, Beulah is only a transitional phase of imaginative growth or expansion. It is, as Frye says,

> a place of perilous equipoise ... the region of the imagination which falls short of the disciplined unity of art ... Beulah provides only a temporary escape from the world, not a permanent creation out of it. Wonder that does not stimulate art becomes vacuity: gratifications of appetite that do not build up a creative life become destructive. Everything that enters Beulah must quickly emerge either by the south or the north door; up to Paradise, or back again to this world ... If dwelt in too long, Beulah will soon turn into Ulro. (*FS* 233–4)

This latter fate, of course, is the experience of Campbell's hero: his phenomenological development is undercut by his metaphysical predisposition, and he is left pining for a higher state that his own passive assumptions have made unreal. It is the theoretical manifestation of the imaginative failure that Frye is describing when he explains that:

> In the state of love the divine imagination is passive, contemplating and adoring, and in such passivity there is a deadly danger if it is persisted in too long. If it reposes so long in sleep as to forget on waking up again that its mistress is its own creature, an independent external world begins to separate from that imagination and it is done for. This, Blake says, is what happened to Albion: he adored the nature he had created too long, [and] began to regard it as independent of him. (*FS* 232)

To fail to enter or pass through Beulah, in other words, is to repeat the fall into metaphysical abstraction. Beulah can only be entered and passed through if it is approached as the first stage of the construction of the archetype as Frye theorizes it: a meeting or marriage between subject and object in the field of imagination in preparation for the latter's being renovated through desire and thereby rendered intelligible to other subjects as myth and art. This development raises it above the context of merged subjects and objects to the status of universal or eternal vision.

Predictably, then, many examples of the Beulah state are penultimate phases reached in preparation or expectation of a final form or total vision (which are somewhat less common in myth and literature). The Eden of Genesis provides the original model of human life in Beulah as consisting of *culture*, in the essential sense of that word as it persists in such terms as 'agriculture': that is, something deliberately cultivated out of nature (note the origin of these words in the Latin *colere*, 'to till or fertilize'). Consistent with the humanist argument of *felix culpa*, however, the biblical Eden stands more as an image of what has been lost than of what stands to be regained through imaginative cultivation, or how it takes place. A clearer vision of this is provided by the Song of Songs, 'the wedding song of a king and a bride who is more definitely Isaiah's married land, the parts of her body being frequently compared to parts of a country' (*FS* 230): here the metaphorical interchange of anatomical and geographical features illustrates the absorption of the objective world into the body image, and the wooing of a country maiden by an urban ruler foreshadows the union of their modes of life at the next and final level of human imaginative development (*FS* 276). Other biblical depictions of the ascent to Beulah are examples of how the sacrifice or crucifixion of Orc is, in special cases, ultimately purgatorial, a tearing-free from the constrained realms of Ulro and Generation and a rebirth into a higher state marked by intimacy or identity with the divine. Once Jonah is purged of 'lying vanities' (Jonah 2:8), for example, he is expelled from the bowels of the Leviathan, and his concern for Nineveh has something of the urban destiny of Solomon. Job's declaration 'though after my skin worms destroy this body, yet in my flesh shall I see God' (Job 19:26) is arguably the most self-conscious account in all of myth of the purgatorial growth of body into body image, of the rebirth of flesh into the imagination or spirit. Thus Job is initiated into a total vision of the cosmos, the point of which is that redemption is a function of imaginative perspective and not moral virtue. During this initiation, God points out to Job the Leviathan and the Behemoth, symbolic of Generation, and in doing so confirms that he has (like Jonah) got clear of them and ascended to a state above or outside of them (*FS* 361–2, cf. *GC* 196): in the carefully enumerated livestock and beautiful daughters that are restored to him at the end of the narrative the general elements of the agricultural and feminized paradise of Beulah may be discerned. The most significant example in the Bible of the ascent to Beulah is, however, the resurrection. The crucifixion of Christ, like that of Wotan, illustrates the imagination as having burst out of the material body through the image of an 'empty skin ... left hanging on a dead stripped tree,' the symbol of Generation (*FS* 212). The harrowing of hell, like Solomon's advocacy of Jerusalem and Jonah's of Nineveh, foreshadows the communal value of attaining Beulah. Christ's emergence from hell, which as Frye has pointed out is sometimes pictorially represented as his coming out of the mouth of a monster, connotes escape from the grasping jaws of Generation (*FS* 210, cf. *GC* 191). His rolling back of the stone that bars his tomb indicates the attainment of full freedom from the metaphysical conditions of Ulro, for it is his moving of the thought-to-be-unmovable rock of time and space.

The best known biblical ascents to Beulah – the ecstasies of Solomon, the purging of Jonah, the whirlwind restoration of Job, and the resurrection of Christ – all demonstrate Frye's point that 'it is a change of worlds that is necessary, the lifting of the whole body to a fully imaginative plane' (*FS* 194). Classical and Eastern examples of the Beulah ascent tend to be less emphatic on this point (perhaps because they faced less cultural resistance to the visionary element of myth), but the ascent can still be clearly discerned. While Adonis himself is symbolic of human life bound to the Orc cycle, the infamous 'Gardens of Adonis' of ancient ritual and Renaissance poetry attempt to restore the pastoral paradise to which he in his coupling with Aphrodite aspired. Frye observes that there may in fact be an etymological connection between the name 'Eden' and the classical *hortus adoni*, probably over the Hebrew word *Adonai*, 'lord' (*FS* 229). The cave of the Nereids, described in Book XIII of the *Odyssey*, is the source of Blake's description of Beulah in *Milton* as having a southern entrance for gods and a northern entrance for mortals (*FS* 232, Blake 123). But Blake saw the true classical counterpart of the biblical Beulahs to be the Hesperides, the Arcadian garden of nymphs, which he preferred to locate (as per some mythical accounts) at the western mouth of the Mediterranean, to associate it with his sunken Atlantis (*FS* 138, 174, 240). Guarded by the hundred-headed dragon of the matronly Hera, and accoutred with a golden-appled tree and nymphs numbering three (like the daughters of Job), the Hesperides garden aptly metaphorizes an imaginative state above Generation. It is significant that Hercules, hard at his penultimate labour, must free Prometheus

(Orc) en route to it, and take on the burden of Atlas (the fallen Albion) while he is there.

Representations of the Beulah state occur analogously in oriental myth and literature, though Frye is, given the parameters of his study, less disposed to survey them. But both the implicit eroticism of, say, the *Arabian Nights* or the Koranic afterlife of *al-janna* (in which the daughters and nymphs appears as harem girls and *houris*) and the explicit eroticism of the Vedic-era epithalamium of the *Kama Sutra* inscribe the garden setting. One of the clearest eastern depictions of Beulah is in K'un-lun, the paradise of Chinese Taoist mythology: he who ascends to the third story of this terraced garden of jade (like him who attains Beulah's 'threefold' vision) gains the prospect of heaven, is greeted by Xi Wang-mu ('royal mother of the West') and her maidens, and may eat of the peach of immortality (Birrell 171–5, 183–4). A significant narrative example of the attainment of Beulah in eastern myth is the triumph of the Buddha beneath the bo-tree, as related in the *Lalitavistara Sutra* (Bays 290): Gautama's endurance of the attacks of his adversary Kama-Mara ('love-death'), who tortures him with whirlwinds of rain and boiling mud, is analogous to the crucifixion and resurrection of Christ (with the whirlwind image also recalling the Jobian transformation). When the enlightened one lightly taps the ground with one hand, bidding the earth to witness his immunity, it is a gesture equivalent to Christ's rolling away of the stone from his tomb-door: an obviating of the empirical rock of Ulro. The garden-symbol of Beulah appears as the Buddha's perfect perceptual discipline transforms the elemental missiles of his Urizenic foe into lotus-flowers; although Buddhism's ascetic devaluation of desire is well on display in his resisting, rather than his indulging, in the three daughters of Mara who are presented to him (this complicates but hardly obscures the example, however: Christ also resists three women at his crucifixion, and three women return to his sepulchre after his resurrection, which has since become a garden).[26]

Significant as these mythical episodes are, they do not represent the full measure of human imaginative potential. Beulah is an exemplary achievement in imaginative expansion (to which, as we have shown, the religious terms 'resurrection' or 'redemption' apply) by a leading subjectivity. It evinces the redeemed form of external nature by virtue of the mind's attainment of perceptual command over it, but not the eternal form humanity might command of nature, which is actually a liberation from it or the transformation of it into the total form of humanity. A final step in imaginative growth is necessary for this. This last phase is that of anagogic interpretation, the collective recognition of the eternal forms of human desire, which is the eternal form the imagination attempts to create. The revelation of this is, as we have shown, the goal of the archetypal discourse of myth. A failure or reluctance to take this last step is a commitment to the fallen cycles of time, for in not taking it human life returns to the world of Generation. As Frye explains:

> We must ... either accept the hopeless pessimism suggested by the Orc cycle, or find some vision of life that will do what it fails to, and impose an intelligible human form both on Enitharmon's crystal house and on the time in which it persists. (*FS* 246)

To undertake this step and impose this form is to initiate the apocalypse that is the pinnacle of religious vision, the revelation of the Pauline 'fullness of time' (Galatians 4:4), and the entrance of human life into the state Blake calls Eden. In Blakean terms, the Eden of Genesis is actually only the state of Beulah, which accounts (among other things) for its garden form and the inevitability of its being lost through the Fall that was the contraction of the imagination. Blake thus reserves the name Eden for the state to be met after Beulah is passed through again, through the expansion of the imagination, in order to emphasize that the lost paradise of God is neither desirable nor attainable compared to the created paradise of 'Divine Humanity.'

Where Generation brings the elements of concrete reality out of the abstract void of Ulro and into the field of time and space, and Beulah brings those scattered objects into the field of the imagination, Eden is their transformation into Frye's 'archetypes of the human mind' through the universally intelligible discourse of myth. Eden is the bringing of those objects into eternity, in other words, into identity with each other in and with consciousness, for the phenomenological reach of imagination is now unified and total. Eden is the complete transformation of cosmos into human consciousness: where individual consciousness once stood at the centre of reality, collective consciousness now spans from its centre to its circumference. Fulfilling as it does the phenomenological intentionality of the objects of consciousness as perceived in the three lower imaginative states (the implications of which will be delineated shortly), Eden constitutes what Blake calls the 'fourfold' world or vision. But it is not only the completion of intentionality that makes the attainment of Eden 'apocalyptic': it is also the dissolution of lesser modes of consciousness, particularly those which presume something as absurd as ontological objectivity. Frye deduces that

> The whole point about an apocalypse is that the darkening sun and the falling stars and the rest of the fireworks represent a kind of vision that is disappearing because it is unreal, whereas what takes its place is permanent because it is real, and if real, familiar. With a deafening clangor of trumpets and a blinding flash of light, Man comes awake with the sun in his eyes and his alarm clock ringing beside him, and finds himself in what he now sees to have been all the time his own home. (*FS* 306)

Where the lower paradise of Beulah is the model of human life as *culture*, an expansion of the imaginative field in which the objects of consciousness may be 'cultivated,' the upper paradise of Eden is the model of human life as *civilization*, in the original sense of the word, as *civitas*: the construction of the city and the civil society extensive of it. The city, as the pre-eminent object that humanity collectively builds up out of nature (but which is not at all an 'object' since it is dwelled-in or inhabited), is the central image of Blake's Eden. All acts of imaginative identification that recreate the objects of nature, or which infold human beings into larger bodies (the latter of which, as we have suggested, turn on the presence of love or sympathy), are contributions to the civilization of Eden. What Blake utilizes and Frye theorizes as the archetype is, in other words, the building block of the eternal city of Man. '[I]f we do not see a city behind the garden of Eden,' explains Frye, 'we are bound in consistency to regard civilization as a decline from an ideal state of nature which was uncivilized, a line of thought leading directly to the natural religion of Rousseau' (*FS* 231); or, one hastens to add, the morally pragmatic philosophy of Nietzsche. This principle is clear even without an appeal to social theory, however, for since Beulah is the ideal state of nature but not the recreation of it, a state beyond Beulah must be attained if we are to be free of the jaws of Generation. '[U]nless we visualize the unfallen state as a city it will always seem to be impotent and transient compared to the fallen world. As an ideal the Utopia is much more human than the Arcadia' (*FS* 237). Blake calls the archetypal city of Eden 'Golgonooza,'[27] which he describes in *Jerusalem* as containing

> all that has existed in the space of six thousand years:
> Permanent, & not lost not lost nor vanishd, & every little act,
> Word, work, & wish, that has existed, all remaining still

> In those Churches ever consuming & ever building by the Spectres
> Of all the inhabitants of Earth wailing to be Created:
> Shadowy to those who dwell not in them, meer possibilities:
> But to those who enter into them they seem the only substances
> For every thing exists ... (Blake 157–8)

Having theorized the potential of such a state, where 'word, work and wish' have equal and total phenomenological reality, Frye is able to outline the real significance of this highest level of imaginative vision:

> All imaginative and creative acts, being eternal, go to build up a permanent structure ... above time, and, when this structure is finished, nature, its scaffolding, will be knocked away and man will live in it. Golgonooza will then be the city of God, the New Jerusalem which is the total form of all human culture and civilization. Nothing that the heroes, martyrs, prophets and poets of the past have done for it has been wasted; no anonymous or unrecognized contribution to it has been overlooked. In it is conserved all the good man has done, and in it is completed all that he hoped and intended to do. And the artist who uses the same energy and genius that Homer and Isaiah had will find that he not only lives in the same palace of art as Homer and Isaiah, but lives in it at the same time. (*FS* 91)

Crucial to the state of Eden are a number of archetypal symbols drawn from important cultural objects. The function of these symbols is well accounted for in Frye's theory of myth, whereas they were scarcely or unsystematically explained by theories that rest on the presumption of metaphysical realities or forms of consciousness. Eliade's theory, as we saw earlier in this study, is hard pressed to theorize the archetypal significance of the sword, for instance, as the idea of its originating in 'the sacred' is dubious. Jung and Campbell accept the conventional interpretation of the sword, by Freud, Frazer, and other early anthropologists, as an obvious phallic symbol, but this reading does not follow naturally from theories that root archetypes in an abstract stratum of the mind (even if such symbols are, as these thinkers hold, ultimately fuelled by some kind of bodily libido). Even Freud's voluminous theorizing does not systematically account for how bodily form and desire actually structure certain objects and develop their archetypal significance in art. But when Frye confirms that in Blake the 'spear and the arrow' (to which we may fairly add the sword, as per the preface to *Milton*) are 'quasi-phallic symbols of the release of imaginative power,' and that 'the bow is the tense energy of the human body,' these interpretations follow logically from a theory of myth that understands archetypes as expressive of the desire, experience, and the very form of corporeal consciousness (*FS* 215). With the metaphorization of these literal objects into symbolic form, furthermore, they no longer evince the death drive of the constrained ego (as they do in their originally objective or literal form), but are redeemed as ecstatic extensions or expressions of the imagination or body image. These symbols thus figure prominently in the magnificent wars to establish or hold Eden and Golgonooza that are depicted in Blake's verse. Anyone suggesting, however, that the importance of these archetypes means that Eden must be an exclusively masculine imaginative state would do well to observe the similar prominence of gate images in Blake's poetry; the massively ornate gates of Golgonooza, described in the first chapter of *Jerusalem*, are equated with the 'bright loins' of the daughters of Beulah, 'beautiful golden gates which open into the vegetative world' (Blake 158).

This same principle holds for another crucial archetype of the Eden state: that core technology of *homo faber*, the wheel. The tragic vision of human life as unavoidably cyclical, which is conventionally symbolized by the wheel of fortune or fate, is expressed in Blake's poetry in circular imagery of machinery and industry. It appears locally in the spinning wheels and looms of Vala or the 'dark Satanic mills' of the *Milton* preface, and is writ large in the stellar orbits (or what Blake calls 'starry wheels') of the abstract heavens of Ulro and the unending *ouroboros* of Generation. Such images connote the perception of time and space as an 'inscrutable fate' and as an 'external compelling power' (*FS* 380, 246); they articulate the phenomenologically constrained experience of human life tied to the rotating cycles of time and our unknowing duplications of them. But as Frye explains, 'we invented the wheel ourselves to spin our garments and propel our vehicles': 'the wheel is a tool of human civilization,' and as such cannot signify an absolute or objective form of the universe, only metaphorize our chosen perception of it. If indeed we determine the phenomenology of perception through metaphor, as we have shown, then 'we can seize this universal wheel and run it ourselves,' a truth well conveyed in Ezekiel's vision of the countervailing 'wheel within a wheel' (*FS* 246, Ezekiel 1:16). Blake uses precisely this image in *Jerusalem* to distinguish between the oppressive, mechanistic wheel of cyclic or fallen experience and the liberating archetypal wheel of Eden:

> behold the Loom of Locke whose Woof rages dire
> Washd by the Water-wheels of Newton. black the cloth
> In heavy wreathes folds over every Nation; cruel Works
> Of many Wheels I view, wheel without wheel, with cogs tyrannic
> Moving by compulsion each other: not as those in Eden: which
> Wheel within Wheel in freedom revolve in harmony & peace. (Blake 159)

The most prominent form of this redeeming wheel is found in Blake's well-known figure of the chariot, a particularization of what he calls the 'Vehicular Form' of the imagination (which Frye in turn elucidates as 'the body which is the form of the soul's energy' [*FS* 272]). Blake's famous 'chariots of fire' is an image adapted from the ascent of the prophet Elijah (2 Kings 2:11), but the real significance of the figure is in its recurrence in the poet's longer works, where it constitutes his 'infernal' or 'diabolical' reading of Ezekiel's chariot of God. In Ezekiel God is imaged as a chariot drawn by four angelic animals or 'living creatures' (Ezekiel 1:5). 'The reason why the animals who draw the chariot become symbols of the driver,' Frye discerns, 'is that otherwise the suggestion is that the driver is actually dependent on an external power for his energy.' In the radically humanist mythography of Blake and Frye,

> The chariot is actually the vehicular form of the driver himself, or his own body ... [I]f we consolidate the image ... the distinction between the physical power of the engine and the mental power of the man who drives it ... disappears. The real chariot-furnace is the flaming energy of the spiritual or risen body, and it is the automotive power of the heart and lungs and bowels and brain of this body which we try to represent when we depict angels as winged. (*FS* 273)

This is, of course, the main thrust of *The Four Zoas*: the apocalyptic importance of harnessing the various powers, faculties, and modes of human consciousness (including the material or 'animal' body; *zoa* in Greek means 'beast') in order to drive the resurrected body of Man, or Christ. The image of the chariot is essential to an evocation of the Eden state for its provision of a cultural symbol of the ecstatic body in full expansion (or in full flight, as it were). Like all significant images of effortless or miraculous conveyance in myth and art, from steeds and stagecoaches to station wagons and starships, it envisions the recreated body of humanity (i.e., civilization) wielding imaginative control over time and space.

The enclosing or containing counterpart of the projective symbol of the chariot is the archetype of the furnace, which is related to and sometimes identified with the chariot by virtue of its status as a source of power, or engine. Where the chariot symbolizes the recreation of reality by the outward-bound circumference of the imagination, the furnace symbolizes the infolding of reality into the centre of the imagination for the purpose of recreation (their simultaneous function in the same object thus constitutes extremely potent symbolism). In a sense, the furnace archetype has been operative since Ulro, where the furnace-like 'dens of Urthona' signify the repressed imagination, human life in bondage (recall, again, the description of the biblical Egypt as a 'furnace of iron'). As human life moves into Generation and Beulah through the expansion of the body image, more and more of the objects of nature or reality are consumed by the imagination. What finally brings humanity into Eden is the collective recreation or re-forging of reality, and here the real significance of the furnace becomes clear and takes on apocalyptic proportions. The image, as Frye explains, is an essential symbol of the body itself:

> The clearest symbol of the natural body, life imprisoned in death, is the furnace ... in which the heat of energy is confined in an abstract husk with its light shut out. This image of the furnace or prison of lightless heat is the core of the orthodox conception of hell, which traditionally has heat without light, and it exactly fits the eternal torment of life in the Selfhood, 'the being shut up in the possession of corporeal desires which shortly weary the man,' which is Blake's hell. As the natural man is born as this kind of furnace, he is born in hell, and if he has any intelligence he looks for a way of escape. (*FS* 288)

He has only to look within himself for this, as we have shown, for the means of escape are the means of production latent in his own body-consciousness. Frye delineates this through a series of precise phenomenological equations between the body and the furnace (adapted from chapter 3, plate 53 of *Jerusalem*) that culminates in an outline of the archetype's importance to the Eden state:

> On the level of an unconscious will to live, the hammer is the heart-beat, the bellows the lungs and the furnace the whole metabolism of a warm-blooded animal. The same is true of the risen or spiritual body, but that body is part of Golgonooza, which is conceived as a huge machine shop or foundry, a

> vast crucible into which the whole physical world has to be thrown before the refined gold of the New Jerusalem can emerge from it. (*FS* 253)

Just as the physical body is the source of power and forms for individual consciousness or imagination, the furnace is the source of power and forms for the collective consciousness or imagination that is civilization *in toto,* Blake's Eden. The second stanza of Blake's 'A Divine Image,' for example, runs:

> The Human Dress, is forged Iron
> The Human Form, a fiery Forge.
> The Human Face, a Furnace seal'd
> The Human Heart, its hungry Gorge. (Blake 32)

In the first book of *Milton,* however, Blake speaks of the greater furnace that awaits

> Where Jerusalems foundations began; where they were laid in ruins
> Where they were laid in ruins from every Nation & Oak Groves rooted
> Dark gleams before the Furnace-mouth a heap of burning ashes
> When shall Jerusalem return ... (Blake 99–100)

The imaginative function of the body at the level of the individual, which is to absorb and recreate reality, is the imaginative function of the furnace at the level of civilization. The metaphorical association of the body with the furnace therefore fulfils the essential purpose of the archetype, which is to identify the individual consciousness with the total form of humanity, which (for Blake and Frye) is a fully unified civilization, or God.

This discussion of the furnace archetype brings us to the charactero-logical dimensions of Eden. If the furnace is an archetype of the human body, it is also Blake's character Orc. Since a furnace requires someone to work it, there must be someone else, some other character or being, that works through Orc, forging the objects of nature in the imagination as a smith does with a furnace. This, as Frye explains, is precisely the case:

> Orc himself is a monster of natural life ... who must in turn be overcome, or shaped into a form, by someone else. And as Orc shapes life out of death, so this someone else shapes the conscious vision out of life which is the

> imagination proper, the character or identity, and so constructs a Being from the Becoming. Orc brings life into time; the shaper of Orc brings life in time into eternity, and as Orc is the driving power of Generation, so his shaper is the power of 'Regeneration.' This shaper is the hero of all Blake's later poems, Los the blacksmith, the divine artificer, the spiritual form of time, the Holy Spirit which spoke by the prophets ... Los is the builder of the eternal form of human civilization, and is therefore a smith, a worker in metal and fire, the two great instruments of civilized life. (*FS* 251–2)

Los is the Romantic principle of poet-as-prophet, but pushed to the very limits of the divine and human natures: Frye describes the figure in both religious and biological terms as 'the Holy Spirit' and yet also as the 'incubating power from whom all life proceeds' (*FS* 251). In phenomenological terms, Los is the recognition that the impulses and appetites of organic life, given the time and space to unfold but also the proper disciplining and conditioning, articulate a total form. In Blake's *The Book of Urizen*, it is revealed that Los is actually the father of Orc, and that it is Los who chains him at birth under the dominion of Urizen. In the later prophecies, where the role of Los as the (re)creative imagination is emphasized to an 'almost wearisome' degree (*FS* 252), the dispensation of Urizen and the explicit tempering of Orc by Los have the resonance of recognition scenes. In fact, the way in which the fiercely rebellious heroism of Orc in Blake's early poems is replaced by the fiercely prolific heroism of Los in the later poems makes available the interpretation that one character metaphorically evolves into the other, as a child, previously unawares, might mature into his or her birthright. Indeed, Los is in many ways the agent of an evolutionary process; 'After laying the foundation of unconscious life,' Frye writes, 'Los evolves consciousness and human forms take shape,' often through such 'remarkable piece[s] of embryology' as that contained in the sixth chapter of *The Book of Urizen* (*FS* 258):

> Many sorrows and dismal throes
> Many forms of fish, bird & beast
> Brought forth an Infant form
> Where was a worm before. (Blake 79)

'As soon as humanity appears, Los confines his attention to it, and strives to develop a visionary imagination out of the human mind and to reconstruct the arts of civilized life' (*FS* 258). The rebelliousness of Orc touches off the wars depicted in many of Blake's works, but it is the wisdom of Los that turns this energy into the 'mental fight,' the imaginative wars fought with the bows of burning gold and the arrows of desire that he creates. It is Los who builds the anagogic palace of art that is Golgonooza. Where Orc is the phenomenological fact of the body's desire, Los is the revelation of the deeper principle concealed in that fact, that desire is itself creative and carries the seed of its own fulfilment. If Orc is corporeal desire, Los is the concealed and revealed form of corporeal desire made manifest through wisdom of the spirit.

With a name that is a near-anagram of 'soul' and more than halfway to *logos,* Los is, admittedly, the closest thing in Blake and the mythic theory of *Fearful Symmetry* to a metaphysical principle; but it cannot be properly called such, since it is ultimately inseparable from phenomenal manifestation, even as it inclines teleologically toward the unification of phenomena. Los is the personification of a principle or law of creation, proceeding from the physical law or fact of the body's energy; just as gravity and magnetism and organic growth are apt to be misunderstood as indicative of a transcendent order, but are actually potentials abiding in and among phenomena themselves for change, expansion, or union with other phenomena. The attraction of a falling hammer to the earth or of a growing plant toward the sun cannot be said to be teleological in any metaphysical sense, and yet it is no less than a destiny that the hammer will fall and that the plant will grow; so it is with the fulfilment of human corporeal desire, or Orc, through the imagination, or Los, though of course this creative law applies to the phenomena of human perception and not to the provisional order of the empirical universe (which it shortly dispenses with).

The sciences have long been aware of a principle of creative entelechy operating in the lower biological forms of life (which is commonly called 'instinct'), but have been ham-handed in theorizing its conscious equivalent in human beings, and handcuffed altogether in relating it to the higher, thought-to-be-purely-speculative question of spiritual being. Frye's clarification of Blake's Los is very much a supposition directed into these sparse quarters from the better-manned watchtowers of art and religion. Lest it be objected that the metaphorizing of Los as a blacksmith implies that the principle he represents is not universal but historically specific, and excludes societies that have not developed metalworking (or that have, though it is difficult to conceive, evolved beyond it), we should recognize that this is merely the broadest possible symbolization of the human restructuring of nature in which every culture and civilization by definition participates. The essential point is this: there are in the order of nature such things as mud, trees, grain, and iron ore. These things become, in the order of culture, brick, wood, bread, and steel, which were impossibilities before the human presence, but which are now different but equally real phenomenal objects with nothing abstract or metaphysical about them. It stands to reason that, if a higher level of phenomenological being exists beyond empirical awareness, as we have shown, such objects await another stage of phenomenal transformation (into the spiritual dimension that we have hitherto assumed excludes phenomena). Things so transformed are what Frye understands as archetypes, and they take up a place in Blake's world of Eden through the work of Los, whose name is really an anagram of 'sol,' the ancient word for the sun as the singular physical source of life, and echoes the word 'low' before it suggests anything of the transcendent. Just as the totality of humanity is the phenomenological reality of the resurrected body of Christ, so Los is the phenomenological reality of what Christian theology knows as the Holy Spirit. But as it originates in and is inseparable from the creative action of human life in the phenomenal world, it is also what we conventionally call the imagination. Frye is spanning both criteria when he explains that 'Los, with the hammer of the smith and the sickle of Time, is Blake's Demiourgos, a word that means both the Creator of the universe and a worker for the people' (*FS* 259).

As the analogy above reminds us, however, and as Frye confirms, 'the true and eternal God is not the Creator ... but the total form of his creation, which is the larger body of Man' (*FS* 250–1). Los is the worker of the furnace of Orc, with which he drives the chariots of fire and casts the bows of burning gold and the arrows of desire; he is not the form of God but rather its agent. His archetypes of Eden are aspects of the totality emergent from (and as) his forge, which is the eternal city of Golgonooza. But since such archetypes are also dimensions of the human body, we should recognize that Golgonooza itself, as the totality of archetypes, must also be the re-forged body of humanity. Thus we are reminded that it is Albion who is the true God or totality of man, and that Los's real task is to reassemble the fallen Titan's body which was scattered as the diversity of objects and beings at the Creation-Fall (just as it is the work of the Holy Spirit to evince the resurrected body of Christ en route to the apocalypse). This is the point of the sexual unions, marriages, family reconciliations, alliances, and assumptions that occur among the various characters of Blake's poetry, and the reason why his later prophecies culminate with images of their being melted down and mingled together in the furnaces of Los (along with everything else) as Golgonooza is constructed. '[T]he imagination exists immortally not only as a person but as part of a growing and consolidating city, the Golgonooza which when complete will be the emanation or total created achievement of Albion' (*FS* 248).

Keeping in mind that the scattered pieces of the body of Albion are the formerly disparate phenomena of reality, ready to be re-formed by Los, we are now poised to take stock of all the ways in which Blake's Eden is 'fourfold,' and to understand why Albion's resurrection, our entrance to Eden, is really a unified or total phenomenology. The fragmented body of the empirical universe, to the fallen understanding, consists of the differentiated Empedoclean elements of earth, water, and air, which are the general symbols of Ulro, Generation, and Beulah, respectively: these things are progressively united in and animated (in the essential sense of the word, 'brought to life') by the fourth element of fire: fire is the energy of corporeal desire in Generation, love and sympathy (*eros* and *agape*) in Beulah, and the creative imagination proper, the furnace-chariot of Los, in Eden (the latter two in particular are connected through the word 'consummation' as it applies to the biblical apocalypse, where it means both sexual union and dissolution in flame [*FS* 196, 351]). Where the elements are unified, so too must be the four Aristotelian qualities of which they consist, and so cold, hot, moist, and dry are also harmonized, as per the Galenic theory of bodily humours. Where the elements and qualities are contained, so then the four directions of the compass must also be, for there is no longer any differentiated denotation of movement after a total perception of space has been achieved. This coordination of the elements, qualities, and displacements of material space is attained because the four senses of the physical body – sight, hearing, smell, touch (which includes taste, since it is really the inward specification of touch, and, as mentioned earlier, likewise metaphorizes cultural possession) – have combined in the total imaginative apprehension called vision (*FS* 274). With the unified vision of space by the unified body comes, finally, the unification of time, and thus in Eden the three temporal perspectives of past, present, and future (which also roughly correspond to Ulro, Generation, and Beulah) are simultaneously apprehended in a fourth perspective, that which we call the eternal (*FS* 300). The entire process means that man has changed from 'a centre to a circumference of perception,' such that we recognize that

> What we see in nature is our own body turned inside out. From our natural perspective we cannot see this for the same reason that a fly crawling on a fresco cannot see the picture: we are too small, too close, too unintelligent, and have naturally the wrong kind of eye. But the imagination sees that the labyrinthine intricacies of the movements of the heavenly bodies reflect the labyrinth of our brains ... It sees that the revolving and warming sun is the beating and flaming heart of the fallen Albion ... It sees that the ridges of mountains across the world are Albion's fractured spine. It sees that the natural circulation of water is a human circulation of blood. It sees that nature is the fossilized form of a God-Man who has, unlike other fossils, the power to come to life again. It sees that what vibration-frequencies are to color, what a prosodic analysis is to a poem, what an anatomized cadaver is to a body, so the physical world is to the mental one, the seamy side of its reality. (*FS* 349–50)

Depictions of the total apocalypse that rights the world, and turns it outside in again, are understandably quite rare in myth and art. 'There are great visions of hell, of the Creation, of the Fall, of the unfallen state,' Frye explains, 'but English poets have been inclined to fight shy of the *Dies Irae*.' The same may be said for artists and thinkers in general, and for the immemorial purveyors of myth. Leaving aside questions of representation and cultural resistance, the scarcity of this final phase of myth has to do with the presence of residual Cartesianism and egocentricism that may be sufficiently weakened so as to admit the desire for apocalypse, but remains stubborn enough to pre-empt actual participation in it. As Frye explains,

> The City of God has often enough appeared in the distance to the earth-bound visionary: it has often been described, and even reached at the end of a personal pilgrimage; but as an eternal form remote from the world of time, not as a phoenix arising in the human mind from the ashes of the burned mysterious universe. (*FS* 305)

A total perceptual and perspectival reversal, the transformation of consciousness that the koine Greek of the New Testament calls *metanoia* ('changed mind' or 'conversion';[28] cf. *GC* 130–1, 193), is necessary for this latter, which explains why the apocalypse is often only timidly hinted at through a few key archetypes, or presented in an otherwise attenuated form.

As the experiences of Elijah and Ezekiel have suggested, it behooves the divine and the human to herald their (re)union through the vehicle of the chariot. In classical myth, Venus, Juno, and Bacchus are infamous charioteers. Blake's metaphor from *The Four Zoas* of the harnessing a chariot as the disciplining and unification of consciousness is important in Hindu mythology: it functions identically in the *Katha Upanishad* (1.3.3–6)[29] and figures prominently in the *Bhagavadgita*, where the relationship of Arjuna to his charioteer Krishna symbolizes the coordination of human action with divine wisdom (*FS* 272–3). One is hard pressed generally to find a mythological or religious pantheon which has not, at one time or other, metaphorized the sun's daily arc as the track of a fiery chariot, such that it is perhaps the prime example of the perception of a natural object as cultural phenomenon (and recalls our Los-sol anagram). The blacksmith as supreme demiurge, where the figure can be observed, appears in a manner remarkably consistent with Blake's usage: the binding of the philanthropic smith Prometheus by the divine smith Hephaistos in Aeschylus has something of the Orc-Los progression (*FS* 252). It may not be insignificant, then, that Prometheus, as mentioned earlier, is eventually freed by Hercules, a god-man who as a fellow son of Zeus is the half-brother of Hephaistos (as an Orc figure that evolves into a Los, Prometheus becomes, along with Christ, the prototypical agent of the imagination in Frye's later works). Had Frye been disposed to survey behind (or, rather, before) his general association of Blake's Albïon with the Purusha or cosmic man of Hinduism, he might well have called attention to an earlier hymn in the *Rig-Veda* (10.72.1–9) that reveals creation and restoration to be the work of a divine blacksmith: the demiurgic Brahmanaspati, who creates through 'blast and smelting,' moves about (like Los) by or as a chariot drawn by eight horses, and animates the world through his chanting. Frye does call attention to Isaiah's prophecy that the New Jerusalem will be the work of a divine smith (Isaiah 54:11–16, *FS* 254), which is another example of the simultaneous presence of a second element of the apocalyptic vision, in this case, the eternal city. This broad archetype is often reduced to an image of *ecclesia*, however, such as may be observed in the Augustinian *Civitas Dei* or the Camelot of Arthurian mythology, which tends to be held out as distant ideal or perpetual future rather than something to be entered into and unified within. For this reason, the sunken Atlantis, with its connotation of imminent return from the sea of time (Generation), was to Blake's thinking a better example of the type.

All the major elements of apocalyptic vision, it seems, are functionally present in only one mythic source, the Bible's Book of Revelation, which thus becomes the precise template for the two great climaxes of Blake's work, the ninth night of *The Four Zoas* and the fourth chapter of *Jerusalem*. 'Both deal with the apocalypse,' Frye explains (*FS* 357), and he describes the former in particular as a 'colossal explosion of creative power' unlike anything else in English poetry (*FS* 305). Not only are the key archetypes of apocalypse present in these visions, but many of the earlier stages of imaginative growth are also recapitulated in what is a steadily intensifying depiction of the concrete forms of human desire: the natural, objective world, symbolized by the beast or dragon, and the whore of Babylon (images of Generation), is dissolved, and the bride of the new earth is wed; both are 'consummated' in the appropriate manner (by fire and marriage, respectively) by the imagination. Built among and around restored gardens, the New Jerusalem of Golgonooza then coheres, as the new home or dwelling-place of the man who is all men and finally God – Albion or Christ, the latter of whom is now also the Los or Holy Spirit who built it, who presides over his abode from a throne which is the divine chariot still.

Having completed this survey of Blake's and Frye's total mythic structure, we are finally in a position to say how it outstrips those of Eliade, Jung, and Campbell. The Blakean mythic cosmos not only swallows and assigns appropriate places and roles to Eliade's natural hierophanies, Jung's personae, and Campbell's initiatory phases; more importantly, it uses the constituents of these lesser threefold structures as the basis from which to generate the fourfold experience of eternity. Each of these other mythic complexes, we must recall, is trinary: Eliade's elemental cosmos consists of three levels, the celestial or ouranic, the chthonic, and the aquatic; Jung felt that in counting his archetype of the self he had a fourfold arrangement of personae that 'squared the circle' of the mandala, but we must note that his collective unconscious also consists of only three levels,[30] those of the shadow/trickster archetype, the wise old man, and the deep-seated anima; and the ritual rhythm of Campbell's monomyth is, of course, infamously tripartite, being made up of the phases of departure, initiation, and return. Each of these aligns variously with the imaginative states of Ulro, Generation, and Beulah. What Blake recognized, and what Frye ramifies, however, is that 'four and three ... are respectively the numbers of infinite extension and cyclic recurrence' (*FS* 300). The final epiphany, therefore, lies not in the circumambulation of three, but the discovery of a visionary fourth that is concealed in, or interpenetrates, the three, which unifies them and extends them into another dimension. For Eliade, this concealed fourth would be the human-profane which, having denied its own worth, abjects itself before the elemental and makes it absolute. For Jung, it would be the archetypal self, not as the besieged centre of a mandala, the object of desire and power, but as its subject at the mandala's circumference, coordinating rather than controlled by the other archetypes of the collective unconscious.[31] For Campbell, it would be a recognition that the peak experience of the hero's goal is always literally (and metaphorically) available, but never as the self-dissolving transcendence he mistakenly believes it to be. The missing insight, in each case, is really an oversight of the essentially phenomenological or imaginative condition of consciousness, of which all thought and reality is a function, and myth the perennial expression. It is the omnipresent awareness of this condition in the work of Northrop Frye that distinguishes his theory of myth, such that he himself may aptly if whimsically be characterized as the unacknowledged visionary fourth of the Eranos group.

This phenomenological condition is the extensive or unifying fourth in all its contexts. Nothing exists until it is apprehended by consciousness in perception, and only in this do things exist. Consciousness is the fire of desire, or love, or the creative imagination, that dissolves and recreates earth, water, or air into new objects on the broadening levels of culture. Consciousness is the alighting and enlightened eye that, united with the other senses, develops into vision. Consciousness is the body that provides the space or presence into which time is gathered (as when we speak of an occasion or event as being 'at hand'); space is the fourth dimension of time, the simultaneous or visually extensive apprehension of past, present, and future that is eternity (which is usually depicted as a verticalization of a horizontal 'time line'). The hallmark of consciousness is the unfolding or fulfilment of some potential form already abiding in itself and its object on the common material plane of their interaction; it has nothing to do with the substitution or imposition of an abstraction, which is arbitrary and unreal, and in fact sabotages the creative processes of consciousness.

The proper phenomenological grounding of the Blakean-Frygian mythic cosmos thus gives it a distinctive structure, as compared with those of our other mythologists. Eliade, Jung, and Campbell cleave to the basic form of the mandala, which, inflected by their assumptions about the sanction of the archetype, becomes the cipher or key to recognizing what the real function or effect of myth is in their respective theories. These are examples of what Frye in his diaries of the period calls the 'geometry of vision,' disclosures of 'diagrammatic patterns present in thought' through metaphors and particularly in prepositions indicating movement in space ('up, down, beside' [*D* 78]). Eliade's theory of myth configures it as a cycle of abstraction from the natural element, a process that ultimately excluded *homo religiosus*; his mandala is therefore the closed circuit of the Möbius loop. Jung's theory of myth configures it as an archetypal cycle in which man is very much involved, but to his inevitable dissolution at the hands of greater powers; his mandala is therefore the ravenous *ouroboros*. Campbell's theory of myth configures it as a journey of ascent, but with no means of ascent, only an unreachable destination; his mandala is therefore actually two different ones, the separate planes of the *parallelepipedon*. Each of these is an depiction of myth as alienating, dominating, or frustrating the effort to experience the fuller vision of human life it seems to depict, the results of presuming that it originates beyond human consciousness (i.e., metaphysically) and is fundamentally 'other' to it.

By replacing metaphysical assumption with phenomenological fact, Blake was able to demonstrate, and Frye to clarify, that myth originates in consciousness and possesses a productive shape. There is no mention of the mandala by name in *Fearful Symmetry*, but Blake's and Frye's metaphors of centre and circumference indicate they are thinking in terms of circular totality. Guided by Blake's 'apocalyptic theory of perception' and his poetic cosmology, Frye theorizes myth as a progressive broadening and intensifying (which is to say *heightening*) of consciousness across the continuous plane of real phenomenological experience. The only circular form that simultaneously broadens and heightens as a continuous plane is the conical, or if we are to speak of traversing that plane, an ascending spiral: this is the total form of myth in Blake's verse and in the mythic theory of *Fearful Symmetry*, the 'spiral or cone of existence,' or what Blake in *Milton* calls a 'vortex' (*FS* 350). In the experience of myth, human consciousness ascends the vortex, uniting with objects and beings on broader levels, from a single, constrained point of time and space that is the prison of Ulro, through Generation and Beulah, until

> when once a traveller thro Eternity
> Has passd that Vortex, he perceives it roll backward behind
> His path, into a globe itself infolding ...
> Thus is the earth one infinite plane. (Blake 109)

This 'one infinite plane' is Eden attained, the apprehended totality of all things on a single level of consciousness that is the paradise of eternity. Frye thus speaks of the whole structure in his diaries as the 'apocalyptic vortex of animal to conscious perception, nature to imagination" (*D* 81). The Blakean-Frygian vortex is the traditional mandala, but with the addition of not merely the third dimension (vertical space, as provided in the form of the upright human body), but the fourth dimension of which we have been speaking (time, as movement in and of space, the unfolding and infolding of space). Indeed, the interpenetration or exchange of centre and circumference in the spiral form illustrates that time is not merely an additional dimension of space, but its factor, and an inverse one at that, such that when time and space are gathered together in perception they collapse into each other and vanish. As Frye explains:

> [E]very act of the imagination, every such union of existence and perception, is a time-space complex, not time plus space, but times *times* space, so to speak, in which time and space as we know them disappear, as hydrogen and oxygen disappear when they become water. (*FS* 46)

If there is a geometry of apocalypse, it can only be found in the form or structure of the vortex: the upward spiral of Blake and Frye fulfils the mythic dream of the ascent of consciousness to the perception of eternity (as the mandala of conventional mythography, in ignoring ground of human consciousness, records its failure).

That the phenomenology of mythic consciousness should turn out to have a spiral shape should come as no surprise, since it is the base structure of both being and becoming, product and process, on the phenomenal plane. Observing whirlwinds and whirlpools, meteorology and hydrology confirm the discovery of physics that the natural and most efficient means of moving matter through a vertical space is in a spiral (something that anyone who has ever drained a sink or uncorked a bottle already knows). At the same time the structure is also the ultimate in stability: engineering and carpentry alike inform us that the interpenetrating action of a screw creates a bond that can only be broken by destroying the bound objects themselves. All organic matter and energy, we theorize, enters the universe through the double spiral or helix of the DNA molecule, and all matter and energy whatever leaves it again only through the vortex of the quantum singularity or 'black hole.' At every level, in other words, we are confronted with evidence that the spiral may be the essential form, the alpha and omega, of existence itself.[32] The frequent occurrence of this structure in mythic discourse, in the whirlwind of Job or Ezekiel's wheel within a wheel, in *metanoia* as turn-of-mind or metaphor as turn-of-phrase, bodes nothing less than an exchange of context between consciousness and cosmos.

In conceding any truth in this hypothesis, human beings would have to acknowledge, as Frye starkly puts it, that 'they are barred from Paradise only by their own cowardice, and cannot shift the responsibility for their misfortunes to God, nature, fate, or the Devil, all of which are within them' (*FS* 259). The outright acceptance of it would be the discovery of an apocalyptic element in culture that is capable of achieving what the most profound physical science or the most potent political ideology can scarcely conceive, and would hopelessly bungle, in its garish literalism, if it dared to:

> A larger human brain will be developed by Man when the whole of human life is seen and understood as a single mental form. This single mental form is a drama of creation, struggle, redemption and restoration in the fallen life of a divine Man. This drama is the archetype of all prophecy and art, the universal form which art reveals in pieces, and it is also the Word of God, the end of the journey of our intellectual powers. (*FS* 340)

This apocalyptic element is myth, in other words, but myth only when understood as 'a single mental form,' as the divine word unfolding through and as human consciousness and the transubstantiation of reality into art. To interpret or approach myth otherwise is to deal in half measures, to quite literally sell myth 'short.' In his conclusion to *Fearful Symmetry*, Northrop Frye thus commends the various scholarly branches of mythography for doing their part in helping to illuminate this 'single mental form.' The names and mythic structures of the Eranos mythologists (as well as figures like Frazer and Freud) are all but present by implication:

> [A] study of comparative religion, a morphology of myths, rituals and theologies, will lead us to a single visionary conception which the mind of man is trying to express, a vision of a created and fallen world which has been redeemed by a divine sacrifice and is proceeding to regeneration. In our day psychology and anthropology have worked great changes in our study of literature strongly suggestive of a development in this direction,

> and many of the symbols studied in the unconscious, the primitive and the hieratic minds are expanding into patterns of great comprehensiveness, the relevance of which to literary symbolism is not open to question. Anthropology tells us that the primitive imaginative gropings which take the forms of ceremonies and of myths invented to explain them show striking similarities all over the world. Psychology tells us that these ritual patterns have their counterpart in dreams elaborated by the subconscious. (*FS* 424)

But Frye then goes on to explain that there is a major shortcoming to these various approaches, which is a limitation of vision having to do with their necessarily Epimethean or backward-looking posture as scholarly fields. Another perspective, Frye argues, is necessary to reveal the true nature and relevance of myth:

> Neither the study of ritual nor of mythopoeic dreams takes us above a subconscious mental level, nor does such a study ... suggest anything more than a subconscious unity among men. But if we can find such impressive archetypal forms emerging from sleeping or savage minds, it is surely possible that they would emerge more clearly in the concentrated visions of genius. These myths and dreams are crude art-forms, blurred and dim visions, rough drafts of the more accurate work of the artist. In time the communal myth precedes the individual one, but the latter focuses and clarifies the former, and when a work of art deals with a primitive myth, the essential meaning of that myth is not disguised or sublimated, or refined, but revealed. A comparative study of dreams and rituals can lead us only to a vague and intuitive sense of the unity of the human mind; a comparative study of works of art should demonstrate it beyond conjecture. (*FS* 424–5)

This Promethean or forward-looking perspective in mythography is art and the creative imagination itself, which can be seen here, as always, functioning as the extensive fourth; hidden in and among psychology, anthropology, and religion, art as the study of the imagination unifies the field of mythography and reveals its forms as lived experience. If art and the imagination are the concealed fourth of myth, they are the real or eternal form of it, and thus the particular field of study we have called the phenomenology of myth is as much what Frye would years later call the 'phenomenology of the imagination' (*LN* 20).

This particular branch of mythography, which Frye in *Fearful Symmetry* calls 'the study of anagogy' (*FS* 425), is one that he would make his own over the course of his life, in the steadily broadening and heightening contexts that the imagination creates. Having brought out of Blake a theory of mythic consciousness, Frye abided for a time in his own cyclical Generation-world with *Anatomy of Criticism* (1957) where his purview widened to encompass all of literature, but his ascent halted to consider a theory of metaphor as mimetic and representational rather than phenomenological and existential. This period saw him subtly redefine anagogy as a hypothetical or potential apocalypse, as opposed to an actual, perceptual one, a proposition which did nothing to hinder (and, indeed, may have helped) his mapping of the literary cosmos. But his spiral progress eventually continued in the *The Great Code: The Bible and Literature* (1982) and its initial theorization of *kerygma*, a refinement to his phenomenology of myth and metaphor which accounts for the Christian Bible's otherwise elusive authority. Then, in the last year of his life, Frye developed a theory of the unity of Western culture in *Words with Power: Being a Second Study of the Bible and Literature* (1990) and its elegant abridgment *The Double Vision* (1991), a theory which offered a full conceptualization of kerygma, as a revision of his original notion of anagogy and a more precise phenomenology, in the terms of postmodern thought. Thus, as Robert Denham observes:

> [W]hat is fundamental to [Frye's] work is not so much the principles outlined in the *Anatomy*, though that is surely a book that will remain with us, but the principles we find in those books that serve as the bookends of his career, *Fearful Symmetry* at the beginning and fifty years later, the two Bible books and *The Double Vision*. (*LN* xxxvii)

With our survey of the first of these texts now complete, we shall therefore conclude our study of Frye's phenomenology of myth with a look at its final incarnation in his last and perhaps most evocative book, *Words with Power*.

Conclusion

Phenomenology and Postmodern Mythography: Northrop Frye's *Words with Power* and the Theory of Kerygma

For a long time I've been preoccupied by the theme of the reality of the spiritual world, including its substantial reality.

[T]he whole book turns on the thesis that the spirit is substantial; it's the realizing of primary concerns out of the language (Word) of primary mythology.

Northrop Frye, *Late Notebooks, 1982–1990* (720, 9)

The usual pattern of an intellectual life is one that sees the idealism and radicalism of youth gradually replaced by the pragmatism and conservatism of maturity, the process Northrop Frye in his study of Blake called the Orc cycle, in reference to the submission of the rebellious Orc to the aging, tyrannical Urizen. Having studied the dangers of this cycle, Frye made sure that his own career avoided the pattern. During the final years of his life, he wrote as radically about the nature and importance of myth and metaphor as he had in *Fearful Symmetry*, and came again to avow that these fundamentals of literature are the *sine qua non* of a genuine human life. This renewed existential focus is evident in the descriptive subtitles of the books he published after *Anatomy of Criticism*: *The Stubborn Structure* (1970) is subtitled 'Essays on Criticism and Society'; *The Critical Path* (1971), 'An Essay on the Social Context of Literary Criticism'; and *Spiritus Mundi* (1976), 'Essays on Literature, Myth and Society.' In an essay published in 1985, he describes his resumed interest as an inquiry into the cultural (as opposed to the specifically literary) function of metaphor:

> The hypothetical nature of literature, its ironic separation from all statements of assertion, was as far as I got in my *Anatomy of Criticism* ... The literary

> imagination seemed to me then, as in large part it does now, to be primarily a kind of model-thinking, an infinite set of possibilities of experience to expand and intensify our actual experience. But the *Anatomy* had led me to the scripture or sacred book as the furthest boundary to be explored in the imaginative direction, and then I became increasingly fascinated with the Bible, a book dominated by metaphor throughout, yet obviously not content with an ironic removal from experience or assertion. Clearly one had to look at other aspects of the question, and reconsider the cultural context of metaphor, as something that not only once had but may still have its roots in ecstatic experience. (*MM* 114)

As the last line above implies, Frye's reconsideration of the 'cultural context' of metaphor was really a deeper examination of its phenomenological nature and function. As early as 1970, his notebooks speak of the 'need to get the phenomenological basis of metaphor clear' and even of something called 'phenomenological metaphor,' the latter of which he describes as 'the deepest & most teasing problem (*RT* 107, 109). As we can see above and will see again, however, he favours the term 'ecstatic' in his published works.[1] In his last major book, *Words with Power* (1990), Frye offers a full delineation of the cultural context in question, demonstrating how its material grounding on one hand enables a spiritual dimension on the other. The result is a thorough affirmation of his belief that all significant experience of culture, and the only means of integrating its material and spiritual aspects, depend upon our capacity to experience the reality of myth and metaphor. His first principle, as he puts it in the book's introduction, is that mythometaphorical thinking, despite all arguments to the contrary, 'cannot be superseded, because it forms the ... context of all thinking' (*WP* xvi). In the far-reaching discussion that follows this statement, Frye's intention is to provide a detailed phenomenology of the cultural context, as an expansion and revision of the theory of myth he brought out of Blake forty years earlier, and to provide for literary and cultural criticism something broadly analogous to a unified field theory in physics.

To this end, Frye opens *Words with Power* with a survey of the various modes or uses of language, a semiotic sequence or spectrum that phenomenologically grounds the schema he presents in the second essay of *Anatomy of Criticism* (the 'Theory of Symbols'), and potently refines the one which opens *The Great Code*. The schema of the *Anatomy* consists of four phases of signification (the literal and descriptive, the formal, the mythic or archetypal, and the anagogic), and derives its form primarily from the medieval theory of polysemous meaning used in the exegesis of biblical text (*AC* 71–128): charting the different levels of mimetic representation and formal referentiality, it is intended primarily as a 'systematizing of literary symbolism' (*AC* 71). By the time Frye turned to writing *The Great Code*, the first fruits of his deeper inquiry into 'the phenomenological basis of metaphor' had transformed this schema into a phased distinction between the concrete 'language of immanence' and the abstract 'language of transcendence' (*GC* 15): but this Viconian progression of the metaphoric, metonymic, and descriptive linguistic modes (*GC* 5–30) is ambiguated somewhat by its dual purpose as both a general history of language and a phenomenology of metaphor, and leads only to sparse conjecture about the possibility of a fourth, revelatory mode.[2] The sequence that opens *Words with Power*, however, is a more extensive if not complete survey of 'the different idioms of linguistic expression' that culminates in a demonstration of 'the authority of poetic language' (*WP* xxi), which is theorized in precisely phenomenological terms. It is a collation of linguistic modes, in other words, that not merely identifies the contexts in which the literary symbol operates, or general phases in the historical development of language, but also theorizes in detail the capacity of language and symbolism to create different realities for human consciousness.

The sequence consists of five successive modes, each of which has a primary focus or explicit purpose, as well as an 'excluded initiative,' an unacknowledged motivation which emerges in, and becomes the focus of, the following mode. The sequence thus unfolds as a dialectical process, with each new mode becoming a fuller realization of language's creative potential (the modes 'are not so much hierarchical,' Frye explains, 'as progressing from the less to the more inclusive' [*WP* 4]). The process begins with the *descriptive* mode, in which language is used to create an accurate verbal replica of a reality that is assumed to exist outside it, to which it ostensibly refers; its excluded initiative is the reconstitutive word-ordering process of language itself, the principle that language really does 'put things *into* words,' the fact that our perception of reality depends on how it is structured in language. The *conceptual* mode makes this word-ordering process its focus, and thus resigns the task of referring to an external world in order to posit abstract concepts; its excluded initiative is the human subjectivity that is necessarily concealed behind the presumably objective posture of conceptual discussion or argument. In the *rhetorical* or *ideological* mode, this hidden subjectivity becomes the focus, as language is used to articulate and rationalize structures of social authority to the human subject; its excluded initiative is myth, the metaphors of which ideology manipulates and selectively literalizes to accomplish that purpose. The *imaginative* or *metaphoric* mode makes the hypothetical postulates of myth and literature its focus; its excluded initiative is the radical notion that such postulates need not remain hypothetical, but are posed with the prospect of being actualized. When the reality of myth and metaphor becomes the focus of a final mode, the apotheosis of language is reached in what Frye calls *kerygma* (Greek, 'proclamation'), the mode which creates a 'myth to live by' (*WP* 117). In kerygma, we encounter 'verbal formula[e] that insist on becoming part of us,' and experience 'a resurrection of the original speaking presence' or a merging of the human subject with a linguistic object in 'a single area of verbal recognition' (*WP* 114). A process that began with the simple recapitulation of reality in descriptive language, something which every functional, articulate human being practises, ends in the recreation of reality in the *kerygmatic* mode.

The phenomenological guarantor of this process (and of Frye's entire late mythography) is the deceptively simple notion of 'primary concern.' This is an idea that can be traced back to *Fearful Symmetry*'s axiom that the physical body is 'the form of the soul' (*FS* 200) and to the various experiences that are met in the Blakean imaginative states. It first emerges as a theoretical principle, however, in the *Anatomy of Criticism*, amid Frye's speculation that there must be an array of universal symbols or images that underwrite the archetypes of myth. There he surmises that:

> If archetypes are communicable symbols, and there is a center of archetypes, we should expect to find, at that center, a group of universal symbols. I do not mean by this phrase that there is any archetypal code book which has been memorized by all human societies without exception. I mean that some symbols are images common to all men, and therefore have a communicable power which is potentially unlimited. Such symbols include those of food and drink, of the quest or journey, of light and darkness, and of sexual fulfillment, which would usually take the form of marriage. It is inadvisable to assume that an Adonis or Oedipus myth is universal, or that certain associations, such as the serpent with the phallus, are universal, because when we discover a group of people who know nothing of such matters we must assume that they did know and have forgotten, or do know and won't tell, or are not members of the human race. On the other hand, they may be confidently excluded from the human race if they cannot understand the conception of food, and so any symbolism founded on food is universal in

> the sense of having an indefinitely extensive scope. That is, there are no limits to its intelligibility. (*AC* 118)

Frye's focus here, we should observe, is less on the existential basis of the root-images of archetypal symbolism, and more on the signifying power of their universality, as the means by which archetypes are intelligibly communicated: it is a priority that is entirely consistent with the representational semiotic of the volume and its intention to provide instruction in 'the techniques of literary criticism' (*AC* 3).

Several years later, however, in *The Critical Path*, Frye begins placing more emphasis on the existential roots of myth, and myth's tendency to pass through contexts of representation and knowledge and return to existential practice. This shift of focus is marked by his frequent use of the word 'concern,' which becomes his preferred term for a more profound element of, or engagement with, myth. Early in this transitional book, for example, he explains that:

> A fully developed or encyclopedic myth comprises everything that it most concerns a society to know, and I shall therefore speak of it as a mythology of concern, or more briefly as a myth of concern.
>
> A myth of concern exists to hold a society together, so far as words can help to do this. For it, truth and reality are not directly connected with reasoning or evidence, but are socially established. What is true, for concern, is what society does and believes ... The typical language of concern therefore tends to become the language of belief. (*CP* 36)

While Frye does not explain more precisely than this in *The Critical Path* what he means by 'concern,' it becomes clear that he is speaking of some element or quality of myth that commissions literature to be more than a communicative medium or a discourse of the hypothetical. In 'concern,' he seems to be trying to identify a ground or root of myth that bolsters the production and reception of literature, and constitutes for it a recessed but definitive existential context or mandate:

> It is ... true that literature is an embodiment of a language rather than a belief or thought. But there is a point at which the analogy with language breaks down. Nobody would accept a conception of literature as a mere dictionary or grammar of symbols and images which tells us nothing in itself. Everyone deeply devoted to literature knows that it says something, and says something as a whole, not only in its individual works. In turning

> from formulated belief to imagination we get glimpses of a concern behind concern, of intuitions of human nature and destiny that inspired great religious and revolutionary movements in history. (*CP* 103)

Later still, in *The Great Code*, Frye can be observed attributing even greater importance and immediacy to 'concern' as an aspect of myth, as when he speaks of myth as being 'charged with a special seriousness and importance ... a specific social concern' (*GC* 33); or when he describes myth, as he does in *The Critical Path*, as both verbally manifest in literature, and also the existential context of literature: 'There are and remain two aspects of myth: one is its story-structure, which attaches it to literature, the other is its social function as concerned knowledge' (*GC* 47). 'A society ... cannot keep its myths of concern constantly in mind unless they are continually being re-presented' (*GC* 48).[3] 'The primary function of a mythology is to face inward toward the concerns of the society that possesses it,' explains Frye. '[M]ythology,' he insists, 'tends to cover all the essential concerns of its society' (*GC* 51).

In *Words with Power*, finally, Frye resolves to configure definitions of and the relationship between myth and 'concern,' and to work out the particulars of his earlier characterizations, such as this last one from *The Great Code* (i.e. the question of what these 'essential concerns' are, and how exactly myth 'covers' them). Following his intuition that the roots of myth are the irreducible or essential conditions and elements of human life (which by necessity includes our various material needs and experiences), Frye finds that he has returned to where he had started: the 'essential concerns' he has been trying to identify are generally those depicted in the universal images upon which he suspected the archetypes of myth were based. This realization, however, has since been recontextualized by his renewed existential and phenomenological focus. The result is the theory of primary concern.

In the first chapter of *Words with Power*, Frye explains that there are four primary concerns that comprise a satisfactory human life: 'food and drink, along with related bodily needs; sex; property (i.e. money, possessions, shelter, clothing, and everything that constitutes property in the sense of what is "proper" to one's life) [and] liberty of movement' (*WP* 42). The four primary concerns are, in other words, the needs and experiences that are met through the perpetual and unchanging human occupations of 'making a living, making love, and struggling to stay free and alive' (*WP* 43). These primary concerns are readily distinguishable from what Frye calls the 'secondary concerns,' which, conversely, are considerations that

> arise from the social contract, and include patriotic and other attachments of loyalty, religious beliefs, and class-conditioned attitudes and behavior. They develop from the ideological aspect of myth, and consequently tend to be directly expressed in ideological prose language. (*WP* 42)

The secondary concerns are the variable ideological pressures and demands on our lives that often override or take precedence over the primary concerns. Secondary concerns typically convey the sentiment 'Your social order is not always the way you would have it, but it is the best you can hope for at present, as well as the one the gods have decreed for you. Obey and work' (*WP* 24). Attendance to the primary concerns, however, is as close as we can come in our experience to an absolute moral good and a participation in a universal humanity (through the particular). As Frye writes:

> The general object of primary concern is expressed in the Biblical phrase 'life more abundantly.' In origin, primary concerns are not individual or social in reference so much as generic, anterior to the conflicting claims of the singular and the plural. But as society develops they become the claims of the individual body as distinct from those of the body politic. A famine is a social problem, but only the individual starves ... The axioms of primary concern are the simplest and baldest platitudes it is possible to formulate: that life is better than death, happiness better than misery, health better than sickness, freedom better than bondage, for all people without significant exception. (*WP* 42)

In spite of this, he observes,

> All through history secondary concerns have taken precedence over primary ones. We want to live, but we go to war; we want freedom, but permit, in varying degrees of complacency, an immense amount of exploitation, of ourselves as well as of others; we want happiness, but allow most of our lives to go to waste. The twentieth century, with its nuclear weaponry and its pollution that threatens the supply of air to breathe and water to drink, may be the first time in history when it is really obvious that primary concerns must become primary, or else. (*WP* 43–4)

'Myth,' Frye explains, 'exerts a counterbalancing force to such history' (*WP* 26). The theory of primary concern suggests that what is responsible for the discourse of myth is not some transcendent or metaphysical being, or any conceptual truth or ideological factor. It is, rather, the universal need to have these four bodily requirements satisfied, and the anxiety that they might not be (Frye even refers to the primary concerns in his notebooks as 'primary anxieties' [*LN* 165]). When cultural historian Morris Berman notes that 'History gets written with the mind holding the pen,' and asks 'what would it look like, what would it read like, if it got written with the body holding the pen?' (Berman 110), Frye's response would be that it would not be history at all, but myth. For example, in what is perhaps a staggeringly obvious but previously untheorized connection, Frye observes that the material concern for food and drink is what produces the *sparagmos* archetype and the metaphor of communion:

> [T]he vast number of 'dying god' myths assembled by Frazer, whatever the variety of anthropological contexts they may fit into, seem to have a common origin in anxiety about the food supply, which becomes linked to sexual anxieties through a quasi-magical association of fertility and virility. (*WP* 43)

> [The] direction of development ... is toward the metaphorical, as the concern for food and drink develops into the Eucharist symbolism of the New Testament ... [T]he metaphorical or 'spiritual' direction is thought of as fulfilling the physical need in another dimension of existence: it may require sublimation, but does not cut off or abandon its physical roots. (*WP* 45)

Proceeding from specific observations such as this, Frye concludes that it is the 'rooting of ... myth in primary concern [that] accounts for the fact that mythical themes, as distinct from individual myths and stories, are limited in number' (*WP* 44–5).

We shall return to the important question of how exactly the primary concerns generate the archetypes of myth, and what is accomplished in their production. The more relevant point at this juncture is that, in suggesting a demonstrable connection between archetypes and a set of human universals like the primary concerns, Frye is poised to seize what has hitherto been the donkey's carrot of archetypal theory, if not a good deal of philosophical and semiotic inquiry at large: a conception of myth as a stable discourse grounded in a set of phenomenological and ethical constants, which exists, therefore, beyond the vagaries of history and ideology, and which holds out, as a consequence, the prospect of universal human consciousness. A major implication of this, from the point of view of cultural theory, is that if myth originates in primary concern, the common denominators of all human life and experience, it speaks to and for everyone's essential interests, and not to or for anyone's *particular* interest (as theories of ideology have hitherto assumed that every discourse does). From the perspective of mythography, the salient issue, however, is that Frye's principle of primary concern provides a more convincing mythogenetic theory than any offered by the other theorists we have studied, as it solves many of the problems cited by them and their critics and even clarifies his own more tenable theory from *Fearful Symmetry*.

Primary concern provides an obvious solution, for instance, to the 'double difficulty' outlined by Mircea Eliade in *Patterns of Comparative Religion*; that of 'accepting that there is something sacred about all physiological life and ... that of looking at certain patterns of thought ... as hierophanies' (*Patterns* 31). What was the Achilles' heel of Eliade's metaphysical mythography, the much-maligned material-profane, has become the very starting point of Frye's theory, and, as we shall see, the fulcrum with which he overturns all anti-humanist propositions or hierarchies.

The principle of primary concern also closes a major gap in the mythogenetic assumptions of Jung as surveyed by Eric Gould. One of Gould's chief criticisms of Jung, we may recall, is that he provides no explanation for how the archetype makes the transition from its original abstract state in the collective unconscious into language in the conscious mind (Gould 22–3). While we have yet to examine precisely how the primary concerns give rise to archetypes, we can already see that this is not going to be a theoretical problem that Frye will encounter. For Frye, there is no distance between the archetype's origin and its entry into language, because his archetypes are first and foremost structures in language, and in the theory of primary concern, the physical body is at once the ground of language and the source of archetypal form. There is, in other words, no gap to be crossed.[4]

The notion of primary concern does, however, meet and make good upon a memorable claim put forth by Joseph Campbell in *The Power of Myth* interviews: 'myth is a manifestation in symbolic images, in metaphorical images, of the energies of the organs of the body,' Campbell suggests. 'This organ wants this, that organ wants that. The brain is one of those organs' (*Power* 46). As we discovered in our survey of Campbell's mythography, his nostalgia for the metaphysical typically prevents him from substantiating assertions of this kind.[5] Frye's principle of primary concern, on the other hand, seems as if it were meant to back up this very premise as stated.

We have no indications, of course, that it is among Frye's intentions to correct these phenomenological misconfigurations of the other second-generation modern mythologists when he postulates primary concern as a foundation for his late mythic theory. But several passages in his notebooks suggest he is conscious that, in doing so, he is bringing together the seemingly disparate existential foci of the foremost mythologist of the first-generation and at least two of his school. Such entries subtly imply an awareness that he therefore represents the fulfilment of the phenomenological imperative of modern mythography. On one such occasion, for example, Frye ponders

> Why was I so fascinated by Frazer? Because he linked mythology with anxiety about the food supply – a primary concern. Why am I fascinated by *The White Goddess*, a wrong-headed book in many ways? Because it links mythology with sexual anxiety, a primary concern. Why did I get so fascinated by that sibyl G.R. Levy?[6] Because she linked mythology to shelter & buildings, a primary concern. Food, sex, shelter *are* the primary concerns. (*LN* 77; cf. *MM* 89–90, *LN* 599)

For all of this, Frye's principle of primary concern does not merely close out the modern mythographic tradition. His theorizing of a connection between the physical existence and metaphoric language opens into and is fully contemporary with the work of several influential postmodern thinkers, such as psychoanalyst Jacques Lacan, feminists Hélène Cixous and Julia Kristeva, and the foremost theorists of cognitive linguistics and 'cultural phenomenology,' George Lakoff and Mark Johnson. All of these thinkers are involved in a recent theoretical trend aimed at correcting the failure of poststructuralism to configure a relationship between language and what has been called the 'actuality' of 'the embodied subject' (Falck 12). What they share is a rejection of the residual Cartesianism in analytic philosophy and faculty psychology, which has propped up the assumption of poststructuralism that the mind, as the disembodied seat of consciousness, is free (or condemned, depending on one's perspective) to generate arbitrary systems of meaning in language. For these theorists, the body is not inconsequential to thought and signification, nor is the mind a mere *tabula rasa* upon which culture inscribes itself. Their common intention is, among other things, to demonstrate that the material conditions of the body, as the irreducible ground of language, necessarily structure 'discursive space' and influence the formation of 'the symbolic order.'

Central to Lacan's thinking, for example, is his notion of phallogocentricism, a complex metaphorization of the phallus that functions as the presumed locus of power or authority in writing (Grosz, *Jacques Lacan* 104–48). As a feminist alternative to this, Cixous offers the idea of *écriture féminine*, which theorizes the influence of the female body on women's writing, to the point where, in her essay 'The Laugh of the Medusa,' she suggests it is metaphorically informed by the processes of menstruation and lactation (Cixous 245–64). More directly congruent with Frye's thinking is Julia Kristeva's theory of 'abjection' as she applies it to the *Oedipus* plays of Sophocles, where she argues that the *pharmakos* or 'scapegoat' archetype and the ritual of royal exile is driven by the desire for bodily purification (Kristeva 84–9). Still more in line with and quite comparable to Frye's theory is the work of Lakoff and Johnson: it is their conjecture that *all* abstract and conceptual thought is metaphorically structured, and that the metaphors used to structure it are drawn from concrete bodily experience (thus throwing the entire notion of 'abstraction' itself into question). Though phrased in the language of cognitive linguistics rather than that of cultural or literary theory, their hypothesis that 'concepts are developed via metaphorical extensions of ... basic sensimotor structures' (Johnson 85) will, as we shall see, be of considerable use in demonstrating how Frye's notion of primary concern underwrites his theory of kerygma.

But elucidating the particulars of Frye's thinking on myth and metaphor in the context of postmodernism requires that we first return to the question raised earlier: how exactly do the primary concerns produce the archetypes of myth? The primary concerns are physical needs, and a need consciously recognized and linguistically configured becomes what postmodern theory by way of psychoanalysis calls 'desire.' This is the progression from 'need' to 'demand' that one finds in the theories of Lacan (Lacan 270), or from 'animal desire' to 'anthropogenetic desire' in the writings of Kojève (Kojève 6). 'Desire,' of course, is a term of great importance in *Fearful Symmetry*, where it functions as a motivating factor analogous to the primary concerns in *Words with Power* (the primary concerns could be characterized, in fact, as a delineation of the specific categories of human desire). As we discovered in the previous chapter, archetypes are metaphors collectively held and conventionally used in myth, originating in desire. Only metaphorical language, the phenomenological language of images and sensations, is natural to the expression of desire. As Mervyn Nicholson observes (in a series of very Frye-like aphorisms), 'Desire creates images and is guided by images; it *thinks* in images. Images are thus the natural idiom of desire ... The form of desire can not be anything other than an image' (Nicholson 57). The development of a bodily need into a desire (or primary concern) in consciousness and language is inevitably accompanied by the image of the object or experience required to satisfy that desire. Desire speaks in a language, in other words, that envisions its own fulfilment. It conceives of images, not concepts or arguments. The only possible reason for this can be that, despite what deconstructionists have said about the inherent instability and inefficacy of language, something of desire is genuinely satisfied in metaphor. Otherwise, among other problems, it becomes difficult to account for the omnipresence of myth, religion, and literature in human culture, all of which are discourses and activities reliant upon metaphorical language.

A metaphor, as we well know, is a verbal equation or formula that identifies one thing with another thing. The deconstructive principle of non-coincidence, Frye would concede, theoretically adheres to the non-metaphorical modes of language (such as the descriptive, the conceptual, and the ideological). The inability of these linguistic modes to deliver the object of desire means that when desire is expressed in these modes, it inevitably falls into Derrida's chain of *différance*, an anti-epistemological system of perpetual differentiation and deferral in which desire is constantly relocated in language but never fulfilled, and susceptible if not destined to be dragged about by some ideological concern which dangles the promise of fulfilment before it in order to control it (Derrida, *Margins* 3–27). This process is neatly paralleled in the history of literary theory itself in the development from deconstruction to new historicism and cultural materialism, where the system of language advanced by the first theoretical movement led inevitably to the second. Such problematics of language, however, pose themselves only if we accept the profoundly anti-humanist exile of the conscious human subject and his relations in the world of signifieds from our linguistic models and presumptions. This acceptance allows an incomplete and limited sense of language as simply a closed system of rebounding signifiers to dictate limits to human consciousness. But as the notion of primary concern is intended to remind us, such a model of language has little fidelity to actual conditions of human life. When we recall the centrality of the embodied human subject in language, we remember that there are other forces and fields of reference to be considered; we have to take into account the intense desire 'to unite human consciousness with its own perceptions,' which includes language itself and the metaphors born of desire (*WP* 250). Such a consideration obviously goes beyond questions of commonplace literary metaphor, the theory of metaphor as Aristotelian *mimesis* used in *Anatomy of Criticism*. 'We have to ... consider an extension of the use of metaphor,' Frye explains, 'that not merely identifies one thing with another in words, but something of ourselves with both' (*WP* 75).

The human subject at the centre of language brings with it not only the physical body whose needs and experiences provide the concrete metaphorical grammar of myth and literature, but also a consciousness which is indivisible but distinguishable from it. This constitutes another referential plane to that upon which that body exists (while interpenetrating with it). In the theories of Lakoff and Johnson, the sensimotor functions and experiences of the physical body (seeing, feeling, grasping, pushing, [re]collecting, penetrating, consuming, etc.) provide the metaphors with which consciousness possesses and organizes concepts, thoughts, and images. We speak of 'seeing the light,' 'grasping an idea,' 'food for thought,' or 'an intellectual movement,' not simply to provide these ideas with rhetorical or imagistic window-dressing, but because it is only through the use of such physically derived metaphors that these ideas possess any reality or meaning and serve any function for us. The first principle of cognitive linguistics is that there is no *con*ception without *per*ception, and, while Lakoff and Johnson are loath to state the case so emphatically, their implication is clearly that without such metaphors, there can be no consciousness (and hence no 'reality') whatsoever. Lakoff and Johnson define metaphor itself as 'a tool for conceptualizing one domain of experience in terms of another' (Lakoff and Johnson 46); they refer to the body and its sensimotor functions as the 'source domain,' and consciousness, which engages metaphors of those functions in order to structure thought and reality, as the 'target domain' (Johnson 97). 'One major consequence of this research,' Johnson observes, 'is that it provides a major critique of any view that treats meaning and conceptual structure as radically ungrounded and arbitrary' (Johnson 85). 'The mind is not merely embodied, but embodied in such a way that our conceptual systems draw largely upon the commonalities of our bodies ... The result is that much of a person's conceptual system is either universal or widespread across languages and cultures' (Lakoff and Johnson 6). Frye's theory of kerygma turns upon a similar physical-metaphorical exchange between body and consciousness, although he finds the result of the exchange to have greater phenomenological potency than any that could be attributed to it through cognitive linguistics.

Frye associates body and consciousness with what Paul in Corinthians calls the *soma psychikon* ('mortal' or 'natural man')[7] and the *soma pneumatikon* ('spiritual man'), respectively (*WP* 124, 1 Corinthians 15:44); but he is quick to remind us (as he has before) that the word 'spiritual' need not carry any precise theological connotations, but can be taken simply as referring to 'the highest intensity of consciousness' (*WP* 128). He acknowledges that there is no question of uniting subject and object in any ontological sense, on the field of objective reality where the *tertium non datur* principle and other empirical limitations apply. But consciousness is not subject to such principles and limitations, because this is never a reality it can access and never the reality which it inhabits. Post-Einsteinian physics, in fact, has repeatedly demonstrated the inaccessibility of 'objective' reality to the point of being able to discount its very existence through the Heisenberg Indeterminacy Principle of quantum theory ('the observer determines the observed')[8] and the work of Erwin Schrödinger and David Bohm.[9] Similarly, if the human sciences have consistently shown one thing, it is that the first order of business for human consciousness, individually and collectively, is to get clear of 'objective' reality and begin constructing something more suitable, that which we call 'culture.' In other words, consciousness naturally creates and perceives (which is the same thing, as Lakoff and Johnson demonstrate) its own reality, a reality which necessarily becomes the foundation of our experience and society. This creation of a human reality by consciousness is its primary function, in fact, and its fundamental tool for doing so, as we have suggested, is metaphor. Frye thus describes metaphors in one entry in his notebooks as 'verbal energy-currents' which carry out 'the first act of consciousness,' the effort 'to overcome the gap between subject and object' (*LN* 426).

In *Words with Power*, Frye calls metaphor engaged to this end with the full intensity of consciousness *ecstatic metaphor*, a term he adapts from Longinus and Heidegger that has traditionally been used in the discussion of religious and mystical experience (*WP* 82). For Frye, the term retains all the connotations of its Greek original *ekstasis*; 'lifted out of one's place,' leaving the limitations of mere subjectivity behind. 'The central axiom [of ecstatic metaphor] is ... something like "One becomes what one beholds,"' he writes, rewording the Hindu Upanishadic maxim *Tat tvam asi* (Sanskrit, 'Thou art that')[10] into something that sounds as if it might (or should) be found in the Gospels. His point is that 'consistent and disciplined vision ends in ... identification,' which involves an upward journey of consciousness into a world where subject and object are at one (*WP* 86). What takes place through ecstatic metaphor, Frye explains, is 'an interchange of illusion and reality. Illusion, something created by human imagination ... becomes real; reality, most of which in our experience is a fossilized former human creation from the past, becomes illusory' (*WP* 85). Extraordinary as such forms of *participation mystique* (to use Lévy-Bruhl's term) might initially appear, Frye maintains that the idea of ecstatic identification should not be an unfamiliar concept:

> In the last dozen years or so, with all the emphasis on separate realities, altered states of consciousness, and the like, we should be able at least to conceive the possibility of thinking in such terms ... [T]his ecstatic power [is] not something separate from conscious intelligence but ... simply an additional dimension of experience. (*NFR* 20)

As Michael Dolzani soberly reminds us, ecstatic identification is in fact commonplace, and implied in many of the assumptions of our daily lives: 'Not all forms of ecstatic experience are ... epiphanic: every time we identify ourselves with something else – a cause, a country, even our name – we bind together with that which we know is also other than ourselves' (Dolzani 100).

What *is* potentially epiphanic, however, as well as a surpassing of the conceptual and ideological continuums, is the occasion when that which is ecstatically engaged is not a transient aspect of human life such as cause, country, or name (which are secondary concerns), but a metaphor born of primary concern, an archetype of myth or literature: the occasion, in other words, when the essential, universal experience of the *soma psychikon,* Frye's equivalent of the 'source domain' of cognitive linguistics, structures and informs experienced reality for the *soma pneumatikon,* the 'target domain' of the spirit-consciousness. This is the process Paul is speaking of in Corinthians when he explains that the Word of God must be 'spiritually discerned' (1 Corinthians 2:14). 'The physical body is a metaphorical crucible for the spiritual body that arises from it,' Frye explains (*WP* 297). Passages in his notebooks often describe the result of this phenomenological exchange more directly and unabashedly than *Words with Power* does, however, and so we may turn to them for particularly concise accounts. In one such passage, Frye posits that, on these occasions,

> what's below consciousness, traditionally called the body, may suddenly fuse with what's above [ordinary] consciousness, or spirit. These are the moments of inspiration, insight, intuition, enlightenment, whatever: no matter what they're called or what their context is, they invariably by-pass ordinary consciousness. (*LN* 661)

In a later entry, he explains the dynamic more fully, and leaves no doubt that he is theorizing anything less than a total transformation of consciousness and reality, a perceptual apocalypse:

> The 'body' is preoccupied with primary concerns on the physical level ... It 'knows' nothing except that the ... mind or consciousness that keeps bullying it is all wrong about everything. Above ... is the spirit, and when the 'body' makes contact with that, man possesses for an instant a spiritual body, in which he moves into a world of life and light and understanding that seemed miraculous to him before, as well as totally unreal. This world is usually called 'timeless,' which is a beggary of language: there ought to be some such word as 'timeful' to express a present moment that includes immense vistas of past and future. I myself have spent the greater part of seventy-eight years in writing out the implications of insights that occupied at most only a few seconds of all that time. (*LN* 663)

This experience is, of course, the substantiation of metaphor that Frye calls *kerygma*. Engaged kerygmatically, metaphor becomes 'an instrument of spirituality' which sees 'the direct transmutation of desires and emotions into presences and powers that become "realities" in themselves' (*WP* 128). Kerygma 'extend[s] bodily experience into another dimension,' fulfilling the primary concerns of the *spiritual* body in the expanded forms that human consciousness (as distinct from the body) requires. Indeed, the spiritual body, as its etymology suggests, not only has primary concerns, but is itself the central one; '[t]he metaphorical kernel of spirit, in all languages,' Frye reminds us, 'is air or breath,' and 'breathing is the most primary of all primary concerns' (*WP* 126). Beyond this, as we shall see, the pattern of expansion and development from the primary concerns of the body to those of the consciousness/ spirit is readily apparent, as is the connection between the metaphorical image that desire generates to satisfy the spiritual dimension of primary concern and the 'literal' or 'actual' object or experience that satisfies the physical component of it. In kerygma, in fact, the archetypal metaphor is to the satisfaction of the spiritual aspect of primary concern what the actual object is to the satisfaction of its physical aspect.

Frye devotes the entire second half of *Words with Power* to surveying how the archetypes of myth become, through kerygma, the spiritual, intellectual, aesthetic, and communal experiences that are the primary concerns of human consciousness. To meet the full range of primary concern, nothing less than a complete archetypal world is required, and this is, of course, the metaphorical cosmos of myth and literature. Frye adopts the traditional mythographic term *axis mundi* for this structure, which he sees as consisting of four vertically arranged archetypal spaces or clusters. He refers to these as 'variations,' and names them the Mountain, the Garden, the Cave, and the Furnace, respectively; the structure overlays, to some extent, the four imaginative levels of Blake, but in the reverse order. Each 'variation' relates to one of the primary concerns, which is either fulfilled, manipulated, or denied altogether, depending on whether its archetypes are produced and received in the kerygmatic, the ideological, or the conceptual mode. The *axis mundi* thus appears to human consciousness in any of (and in up to) three different aspects, based upon which mode of language is allowed to speak for and address the primary concerns (*WP* 184, *LN* 240). There is, first, the axis of 'authentic myth,' the apocalyptic world created as kerygmatic experience fulfils primary concern; the models or archetypes of this cosmology are the gods, epiphanic states, and comic resolutions of biblical and classical mythology. Second, there is the axis formed by the 'demonic parody' of these authentic myths, a nightmare vision of the denial of primary concern that results from its being approached through abstract or conceptual language; its models are the various tragedies and antagonists of mythology. Last, there is the axis created via 'ideological adaptation,' the forms and experiences that result from the archetypes of myth being co-opted to secondary concern through ideological language, and used to rationalize structures of political or social authority.

The human concern for freedom of movement creates metaphors and images of upward or heavenly ascent, such as mountains, towers, ladders, staircases, upward spirals, and 'world trees.' The kerygmatic engagement of such metaphors enables experiences of being in harmony or accord with the primary categories of perception, time and space. Such experiences include aesthetic epiphanies in music (time) and dance (space), an uninhibited participation in play, unfettered communication and travel, and, importantly, freedom of religion and intellectual inquiry. The great biblical archetype of the concern for freedom of movement is the ladder or staircase to heaven depicted in Jacob's dream of Genesis 28 (*WP* 151–2). A major classical example (and the most significant, insofar as Frye sees each variation as having a 'presiding deity' or 'informing presence' [WP 277]) is the god Hermes in his role as psychopomp, or conductor of souls to higher realms of being. An abstract or conceptual approach to the concern for movement creates the demonic parody of these states, the experience of falling into complete discord with time and space and the perception of them as oppressive and alienating categories of being. The chief biblical examples of this demonic state are the collapsing Tower of Babel and its concomitant world of babble and conflict, and the melancholy wanderings of the exiled Cain (*WP* 154, 185). The classical counterparts of these include the failed revolt of the Titans and the fall of Icarus (*WP* 159). The ideological adaptation of the metaphors of ascent establish what in the Renaissance was called 'the chain of being,' a concretizing of a metaphorical-spiritual ladder to heaven into a static social hierarchy (*WP* 167–74). Such structures typically serve to rationalize the high standing of tyrants and political leaders, and to fix the subject to a lower station, rather than encourage freedom of movement.

The concern for sexual fulfilment generates imagery of gardens and other natural, earthly paradises; in kerygma, these metaphors guide the development of erotic love, create the *hierogamy* or sacred marriage of lovers, and allow for an equally sacred sense of concern for the ecology of 'Mother Earth.' These are relationships of ecstatic union that liberate rather than subordinate, and which are therefore more aptly imaged as the unity of centre and circumference than as vertical or hierarchical structures. The biblical archetypes of such states are the harmonious relationship of Adam and the feminized Garden of Eden and of Adam and Eve before the Fall (*WP* 189–91), and the major antitypes of these; the relationship of Solomon and his bride in the Song of Songs and of Christ as Bridegroom to humanity itself (what organized religion calls 'the Church') as Bride (*WP* 196–7). The classical emissary of this concern is, of course, Eros as the god of erotic love. The demonic parody of erotic love, the consequence of abstraction, is 'the sado-masochistic cycle, in which the female may tyrannize over the male or vice versa' (*WP* 218). This includes the double edge of the Oedipal complex, with the son's possessive lust for the mother cutting one way, and the mother's domination of the son the other. Frye describes this condition as the 'inferno of damned lovers in the setting of a bleak landscape of exhausted fertility' (*WP* 219). Examples of this demonic state (in addition to the experience of Oedipus and Jocasta) include the fiery, doomed relationships of Samson and Delilah in the Bible, and that of Hercules and Deianeira from classical mythology (*WP* 218–22). Ideological adaptation of the archetypes of erotic love creates social institutions and movements that are dominated by incest-taboo imagery and metaphors of rigid maternal and paternal authority (*WP* 223). Among these are all the socialized forms of censorship and prudery that attempt to separate sex from spiritual life, foster the attitude that sex should serve only a reproductive purpose, or which promote the exploitation (i.e. 'rape') of the natural world.

The concern for food and drink brings forth images of descent into and return from caves, underworlds, waters, and other 'lower kingdoms.' These are metaphors derived from the disappearance of vegetable life into the ground in winter and its rebirth in spring, as well as from the water cycle and the taking of fish from the sea. In kerygma, these metaphors cultivate the experience of *katabasis*, the quest into a lower world of death to recover some object or wisdom that has been suppressed, repressed, or otherwise lost, but which is essential to the life or fertility of the upper world. Where this involves a representative journey or solitary sacrifice on behalf of collective health, we can discern the outline of the Frazerian dying, rising god sequence, and recognize that its purpose is the kerygmatic transformation of communion meal into community. The best-known classical example of this is the death and revival of this variation's presiding deity, Adonis; other models include the *nekyia* or summoning of the prophet Tiresias by Odysseus in the *Odyssey*, the image of the sunken Atlantis, and the pronouncements of the oracle at Delphi (*WP* 231, 247–9, 251). The biblical archetypes of this variation cast its revolutionary potential into sharper relief, as they include the descent and exodus from Egypt, the experience of Jonah, and, most significantly, the crucifixion and resurrection of Christ (*WP* 237–9, 245, 257–65). There are several demonic parodies that can result from this concern being abstractly approached: one occurs when the spiritual elements of faith and wisdom are missing from the descent structure and thus, as with vegetable life, the descent must be made over and over again in an endless cycle that resolves nothing (the devouring and regurgitating vortex of the *Odyssey*'s Charybdis is an apt image of this). Another is the inversion of the sacrificed fertility god whom we eucharistically eat and drink (or otherwise associate with the miraculous provision of food), and who galvanizes a community with his return: this is the figure of death that instead devours us, the representative of the consuming hell lurking behind all the demons, cannibal giants, gaping sea-monsters, and ravenous tyrants of myth, from Egypt's Pharaoh to Jonah's 'great fish' to the Hell that Christ harrows (*WP* 260). When mobilized in ideological language, the archetypes of the food concern are often used to rationalize an obsessive desire to create and preserve continuity in social institutions and political causes, which typically results in the devaluation or sacrifice (consumption) of the individual (without any hope of kerygmatic resurrection).

The concern for property produces images of furnaces, fire, and other spaces and voids at the very bottom of the cosmos (of 'creation'). Such imagery involves metaphorical descents into and returns from worlds located below even the 'lower kingdoms' of the previous variation. The kerygmatic engagement of these metaphors is what drives and inspires our higher achievements in technology, education, and the arts: the human activities and vocations that produce the very 'properties' of civilization itself. The classical agent of such work is the Titan Prometheus, the bringer of fire to mankind (technology), the god of forethought (education), and the creator of man (the arts). The biblical archetypes of these achievements are the miracle of God's creation of the universe *ex nihilo,* and the experience of Job, stripped of every scrap of property and human dignity and then miraculously restored to an abundant material and spiritual life. When this concern is considered abstractly, the demonic parody that results is not merely a consuming demon and tyrant as in the previous level, but Satan or Lucifer, the Antichrist himself; a figure-complex whose origin lies at the outset of creation and who enters it through the void, not to construct but to corrupt and destroy. The ideological adaptation of the archetypes of property results in the anxious aligning of our Promethean powers and civil achievements with specific ideological and political positions. This culminates in the central dystopic concession, the radical social *skepsis* that insists that all the properties of civilization are inevitably corrupted by the nature of power itself, and, of course, that absolute power corrupts absolutely.

As we can see, the spiralling ascent and descent of human consciousness through the kerygmatic experiences provided by the apocalyptic variants of the *axis mundi* would constitute 'the revelation of a paradisal state ... where all primary concerns are fulfilled' (*WP* 88). Driven by the ecstatic production of and response to the archetypes of myth, the experience of kerygma is the creation of a reality and a society that shatters the binary categories of what we have previously known as reality and society. This includes, obviously, such binaries as the 'master-slave dialectic' that thinkers from Nietzsche to Foucault to Said have argued or assumed is our fundamental mode of thought and being. Other, even more basic binaries also fall away in the verbal and perceptual apocalypse of kerygma:

> [T]he principle that opens the way into the kerygmatic is the principle of the reality of what is created in the production and response to literature. Such a reality would neither be objective nor subjective, but essentially both at once, and would of course leave the old opposition of idealism and materialism a long way behind. (*WP* 128).

In what may be the climactic passage of *Words with Power,* in fact, we can find Frye struggling to evade even the binaries of grammar itself as he characterizes kerygma: '[A]s the subject-object cleavage becomes increasingly unsatisfactory, subject and object merge in an intermediate verbal world, where a Word not our own, though also our own, proclaims and a Spirit not our own, though also our own, responds' (*WP* 118).

Frye's frequent use of the subjunctive mood ('such a reality *would*') and his description of himself in his late notebooks as 'an architect of the spiritual world' remind us that this visionary reality is nothing preexistent to kerygmatic consciousness (*LN* 414). If it were, he would use the indicative consistently and refer to himself as a cartographer or cosmologist. His theme is, rather, the world we are free to build and create in kerygma, the reality we may speak, write, construct, and experience through what he describes as a dialectic of word and spirit (*WP* 89, 251). Protests that this and that part of his theory do not correspond to this and that aspect of our literary or cultural experience are pointless in this regard, for he is not articulating something that *is* in the (now irrelevant) 'objective' sense, but something that *could and should be,* and is within our power to manifest through the untapped resources of consciousness and language.

Frye meditates on this very issue, in specifically phenomenological terms, in one of the notebooks written as he was beginning the existential revision of his theories, around the time of *The Critical Path.* The passages constitute a fitting coda to our study of his thought: '[M]yth doesn't *exist,*' Frye states emphatically; 'it's an intentional object, something there to be thought about: so are genres & conventions.' Continuing the thought in an entry entitled 'Further on phenomenology,' he speculates that his mytho-metaphorical theories actually begin where traditional phenomenology ends, with the reduction of reality to consciousness, because they push on to develop the full implications of this process, the full identification of reality and consciousness in metaphor:

> [M]etaphor is that which annuls reduction and leads us back to existence, not directly, but within the genres & conventions formed by the myth, which has the metaphor at its core. The point of reduction is not so much to cut off existence as to cut off *objective* existence: one then returns to it with the language, which *has* to be metaphorical language, of the world behind subjects & objects. (*TBN* 97)

In the years that followed, Frye came to recognize that this identity of consciousness and reality, this return to 'the world behind subjects and objects,' amounts to a substantiation of what had previously been understood as only a spiritual world, and that this substantiation is the fulfilment of the essential human concerns expressed in myth. In a striking passage from his late notebooks, Frye realizes that the tenable theorization of this process is the real achievement of *Words with Power*, if not his whole intellectual project, and one which belongs to or establishes a field of human inquiry and endeavour beyond that of traditional phenomenology:

> [T]he whole book turns on the thesis that the spirit is substantial: it's the realizing of primary concern out of the language (Word) of primary mythology. Only the total Word can make the spirit substantial. Everything else ... is ideological. I don't want to become a conservative Hegelian, and my goal is not absolute knowledge, whatever that is, but the Word & Spirit set free by each other and united in one substance with the Other detached from Nature and identified as the Father. (*LN* 9)

If we are provoked by these last lines, as indeed we must be, to see Frye's theories as operating far in excess of what he modestly maintained was his native context, that of literary criticism, as well as beyond that of phenomenology, it may be wise of us to regard his work as what Robert Denham calls 'the record of a religious quest' (*LN* xxxvii). This perspective has the virtue of accounting for the most far-reaching aspects of his theory; its massive ordering of our mythological heritage, its poignant concern for redemption, and its profound consideration of the nature of humanity and divinity. The only other alternative may be to see Frye's milieu as an emergent unification of disciplines on the far side of philosophy, the result of his having journeyed through those disciplines, ingesting the priorities and yet avoiding the presumptions of the same array of fields we have observed informing the study of myth, until he himself is able to summarize:

> The 'religio' element in religion is, or first appears, as an external compulsory bond, acting first through the mysterious power of nature, later through the communal hypnosis of the state. Existentialism has worked out the theory of *religio* for the subject. When Hegel, & Marx after him, places the absolute in the subject instead of in the (projected and objectified) conception of 'substance,' the history of philosophy takes a fateful turn. (*TBN* 86)

The fullest vista to be encountered after this 'fateful turn' is in fact that presented in the work of Northrop Frye himself, for that work represents the plateau toward which these other fields and disciplines have been reaching, and the furthest prospect ever offered to consciousness. We have yet to, quite literally, 'come to terms' with that work, as we have said, for it seems to exceed whatever terms are applied to it and demand the formulation of new ones. Frye's ideas and theories, we may decide, should rightly be called by the distinctive terms he developed for them: the study of anagogy, or the kerygmatic. But if these terms prove too forbidding for us, we shall have to content ourselves with the narrower labels that arise from our difficulty in seeing his work as the singular achievement it is; phrases like 'apocalyptic humanism,' the study of imagination, archetypal theory, or the phenomenology of myth.

Notes

Introduction: Phenomenology and Modern Mythography

1 These are included in the 'Emmanuel College essays' section of *SE.*

2 Frye apparently waited until 1947–8 before he 'seriously returned' to reading Jung (Ayre 425). A diary Frye wrote during the first half of 1949 is filled with references to him, and includes one brash entry where Frye announces 'I think I've pretty well got the hang of Jung' (*D* 184).

3 See Edith Sitwell's review of *Fearful Symmetry.* See also Ayre 205.

4 This study by Jung was originally published in German in 1912 under the title *Wandlungen und Symbole der Libido* ('Transformations and Symbols of the Libido'), which became *Psychology of the Unconscious* in its first English translation of 1916. It eventually became volume 5 of *The Collected Works of C.G. Jung: Symbols of Transformation.*

5 Freud's *Totem and Taboo,* it should be recalled, announces its position with regard to this point in its subtitle, *Some Points of Agreement between the Mental Lives of Savages and Neurotics.*

6 Frye would later write in *The Great Code* that 'Frazer was a Classical and Biblical scholar who thought he was a scientist because he had read so much anthropology, and hence was subject to fits of rationalism, which seemed to attack him like a disease' (*GC* 35). A critique of Frazer's progressivism is resonant in Frye's comment that *The Golden Bough*'s 'escalator philosophy of progress, from magic through religion to science, made him think of his symbolic pattern as immemorially archaic, rather than something latent in the human mind' (*NFCL* 100).

7 Although Campbell was a member of the English department of Sarah Lawrence College in New York for most of his career, his contributions to literary studies are limited to *A Skeleton Key to Finnegans Wake,* and those of

his essays on myth which discuss the importance of myth to literature. After *The Hero with a Thousand Faces,* he is consistently referred to as a 'comparative mythologist' working in a field called 'comparative mythology,' although one would be hard pressed to find many academic programs, departments, or associations that actually carry that designation.

8 It is interesting to note that Frye may have been partly responsible for ensuring that *Patterns in Comparative Religion* obtained English-language publication in 1958. As John Ayre reports, 'Karl Miller, who was a virtual one-man operation managing Beacon Press paperbacks in Boston, put Frye on his editorial board to tap his knowledge. As a result, Frye managed to make accessible such ostensibly unpromising items as Austin Farrer's *A Rebirth of Images,* Mircea Eliade's *Patterns in Comparative Religion,* Gaston Bachelard's *The Psychoanalysis of Fire* and Hans Jonas's *The Gnostic Religion*' (Ayre 278).

9 Northrop Frye to Andrew Brink, in a letter of 1 April 1971.

10 As Guilford Dudley writes, 'Eliade has given us an *antihistory* of religions. He does not give us a causal nexus to explain the progression of religious thought and behavior. Instead, he gives us a paradigmatic relationship between archetypes, symbols and hierophanies' (Dudley 151–2). Numerous scholars have pointed out that Eliade's aim appears to have been to transplant to North America the European academic discipline known as *Religionswissenschaft,* with which most historians of religion identified themselves (see Dudley 3–42). It is also worth noting that the original French title of *Patterns in Comparative Religion* was *Traité d'Histoire des Religion.*

11 For instance, *The Columbia Dictionary of Modern Literary and Cultural Criticism* names Frazer, Jung, Campbell, and Frye as the primary theorists of myth in its entry on 'Myth Criticism.' Frazer, Jung, Campbell, Eliade, and Frye are also chief among the many myth theorists listed in the entry on 'Myth' in Holman and Harmon's *A Handbook to Literature.* The summary of 'Archetypal Criticism' in M.H. Abrams's *A Glossary of Literary Terms* mentions Jung and Campbell, and emphasizes Frye's contribution to the study of myth and literature, but largely conflates their thought. *The Johns Hopkins Guide to Literary Theory* (Groden and Kreiswirth) gives priority to Jung in its entry on 'Archetypal Theory and Criticism,' but does mention Frye prominently. Its entry on 'Myth Theory and Criticism' refers to Frye as 'the most influential' of a group of literary critics concerned with myth, but focuses more on the theories of Jung and Freud (with Campbell and Eliade conspicuously represented in the entry's bibliography). The only examples of summaries that adequately register both Frye's involvement and his uniqueness in

modern mythography are the entries on 'Archetype' and 'Archetypal Criticism' in Makaryk's *Encyclopedia of Contemporary Literary Theory.*

12 *Fearful Symmetry, The Hero with a Thousand Faces, The Myth of the Eternal Return,* and almost all of Jung's works were published by Princeton University Press. Eliade's *Patterns in Comparative Religion,* however, was first published in English by Beacon Press (see n.8 above). Campbell's book, and Frye's *Anatomy of Criticism,* are, apparently, the two best-selling titles of Princeton University Press.

13 The Bollingen Foundation, whose name was benefactor Mary Mellon's oblique way of honouring Jung (who had a country retreat in the Swiss village of Bollingen), was embroiled in controversy in 1948 when it awarded a thousand-dollar literary prize to Ezra Pound for his *Pisan Cantos.* Many writers, reviewers, and politicians vehemently objected to the prize going to a poet who had been committed to a psychiatric hospital and whose tendency to make anti-democratic and anti-Semitic remarks was well documented. Being at the centre of the Foundation's activities, Jung was dragged into the controversy as an apparent Fascist sympathizer. While Frye was fascinated by the remarkable poetic visions that emerged from the disturbed mind and life of Pound, and would not likely have objected to the award (he would remind us that it celebrated a literary work, not the life or actions of an author), his name was obviously not connected with the controversy as it was not affiliated with the Bollingen Foundation.

14 The footnote, referring to the phrase 'central unifying myth' (*AC* 192), reads: 'Cf. Joseph Campbell, *The Hero with a Thousand Faces* (1949); Lord Raglan, *The Hero* (1936); C.G. Jung, *Wandlungen und Symbole der Libido* ... and the account of the "eniautos-daimon" in Jane Harrison, *Themis.* To these perhaps I may add my own account of Blake's Orc symbolism in *Fearful Symmetry* (1947), Ch. VII' (*AC* 361).

15 Frye reviewed several of Eliade's works in 'World Enough without Time,' and several of Jung's in 'Forming Fours'; both reviews are reprinted in *Northrop Frye on Culture and Literature* (95–106 and 117–29, respectively). He also reviewed the third volume (*Occidental Mythology*) of Joseph Campbell's *The Masks of God* ('After the Invocation' 6, 19).

16 Strenski's basic thesis, which he applies to Eliade, Cassirer, Lévi-Strauss, and Malinowski, is remarkably sceptical, even by the standards of cultural materialism: 'Instead of there being a real thing, myth, there is a thriving *industry,* manufacturing and marketing what is *called* "myth." "Myth" is an "illusion" – an appearance conjured or "construct" created by artists and intellectuals toiling in the workshops of the myth industry. Masquerading as an "im-

porter" of the exotic and the archaic, the myth industry in fact fabricates one of the most sought-after "exports" from the human sciences and humanities. In its myriad confusing forms, that "export" supports the modern literature of "myth"' (Strenski 1–2).

17 The Canadian political party known as the CCF (Cooperative Commonwealth Federation) merged with the CLC (Canadian Labour Congress) in 1961 and became the NDP (New Democratic Party).

18 See *D* 237 and *LN* 632, for instance.

19 See Ayre 122 for an account of these events and attitudes.

1. *De Caelis:* The Platonic Patterns of Mircea Eliade

1 Eliade writes that 'primitive spirituality lives on ... as a nostalgia which creates things that become values in themselves: art, the sciences, social theory, and all the other things to which men will give the whole of themselves' (*Patterns* 433–4).

2 This phrase usually occurs in Eliade's writings in its locative case, as *in illo tempore* ('in that time'). Eliade seems to have adopted the phrase from the Vulgate of St Jerome. Some of Eliade's critics translate the phrase as 'the other time' instead of 'that time,' probably to emphasize its alterity to history. Bryan Rennie suggests that it is intended to suggest the common fairy-tale phrase 'once upon a time,' but this seems to be inconsistent with Eliade's dissatisfaction with the primarily literary connotation of the word 'myth' (Rennie, *Reconstructing* 81).

3 Eliade argues that 'the cosmic myth serves as the exemplary model ... of any ceremony whose end is the restoration of integral wholeness; this is why the myth of the Creation of the World is recited in connection with cures, fecundity, childbirth, agricultural activities and so on. The cosmogony first of all represents Creation' (*Eternal Return* 25).

4 Augustine's discussion of *de ideis* in *De diversis quaestionibus octoginta tribus* begins with his attributing his terms and concepts to Plato: *Ideas Plato primus appellasse perhibetur,* he writes ('Plato is said to have been the first to use the name ideas' [46.1]).

5 In the *Phaedrus* particularly, Plato presents the notion that ideas and ideal forms (*eidos*) are contained *en hyperouranio topo,* 'in a region above the heavens' (*Phaedrus* 247c).

6 As Dudley observes, 'Critical studies of Eliade almost never refer to his work on Renaissance philosophy in Italy; this omission of this early phase of his career implies that the roots of his thought are in India and that his work on Italian philosophy may be regarded as essentially irrelevant ... But Eliade's

early work may be doubly significant. First, it signaled his interest in philosophy, and second, it oriented his thought to Platonism and Renaissance humanism' (Dudley 43).

7 It is worth noting that *Das Heilige* is translated just as often as 'The Sacred' as it is as 'The Holy.' Eliade's *The Sacred and the Profane* was published in German as *Das Heilige und Das Profane,* perhaps as an explicit titular recognition of Otto's influence.

8 I am relying here upon Bryan Rennie's translation of Penner from German (Rennie, *Reconstructing* 205).

9 Eliade writes that 'Sky divinities gradually turn into sun divinities ... the same sort of process which results, in other situations, in their transformation into gods of atmosphere and fecundation' (*Patterns* 127).

10 See Abdul JanMohamed's influential theorizing of the 'Manichean Allegory' of colonialist literature (JanMohamed 18–23).

2. *De Profundis:* C.G. Jung and the Archetypes of the Collective Unconscious

1 Freud's focus on pathology can be detected behind Jung's characterizing of his own book as 'really only an extended commentary of the prodromal stages of schizophrenia' (*CW 5* xxv). Indeed, the subtitle of *Symbols of Transformation* is 'An Analysis of the Prelude to a Case of Schizophrenia.' The book is closely concerned with the psychological problem of the incest drive, as well, such that the index records an entire column of page references where it is discussed.

2 To cite but one example of this aspiration, Jung qualifies a set of remarks in his essay 'Archetypes of the Collective Unconscious' by stating that '[t]his is not a new discovery in the realm of medical psychology, but the age-old truth that out of the richness of a man's experience there comes a teaching which the father can pass on to the son' (*CW 9i* 31).

3 Kant writes, for instance, that 'things as objects of our senses exist outside us, but we know nothing of what they may be in themselves, knowing only their appearances, i.e. the representations which they cause in us by affecting our senses' (*Prolegomena* 289).

4 '[O]ur manner of perceiving,' Kant writes, is 'peculiar to us, and not necessarily shared by every being, though, no doubt, by every human being' (*Critique* 37).

5 Jung writes: 'If we apply our admittedly peculiar point of view consistently, we are driven to conclude that Wotan must, in time, reveal not only the restless, violent, stormy side of his character, but also his ecstatic and mantic qualities – a very different aspect of his nature. If this is correct, National

Socialism would not be the last word. Things must be concealed in the background which we cannot imagine at present, but we may expect them to appear in the course of the next few years or decades. Wotan's reawakening is a stepping back into the past; the stream was dammed up and has broken into its old channel. But the obstruction will not last forever ... Then at last we shall know what Wotan is saying when he "murmurs with Mimir's head"' (*CW 10* 192).

6 See Marie-Louise von Franz's *Patterns of Creativity Mirrored in Creation Myths* (1972).

7 Odajynk is here quoting *CW 8* 360.

8 'Jung, like Freud,' Frye observes, 'has no form of society: he just says the individual has to adjust himself to it' (*D* 188).

3. The Inner Reaches of Outer Space: Joseph Campbell and the Two Faces of Myth

1 Sales of *The Hero with a Thousand Faces* have likely exceeded one million copies by now, as the figure of 'nearly one million copies' is derived from the rear jacket of the third Princeton reprinting of 1973.

2 For a discussion on the similarities and differences between Frazer's and Weston's impact on literature and Campbell's impact on film, see Harold Schechter and Jonna Gormely Semeiks's essay 'Campbell and the "Vanilla-Frosted Temple": From Myth to Multiplex.'

3 Campbell was raised as a Catholic. Frye was raised in the Methodist church.

4 Cf. Husserl's oft-used term *Lebenswelt* ('life-world'), and Heidegger's concept of *Dasein* ('being-there' or 'being-in-the-world').

5 In citing Jung's and Campbell's resignations on this point, I do not want to be misunderstood as endorsing the bourgeois empirical conceit that everything in the human life and experience can be critically understood, that every mystery is solvable. Rather, I am evoking a principle periodically cited by Frye that the premature declaration of something as incomprehensible or unknowable from a human perspective is a favourite rhetorical gesture of 'mystery religions' which have ideologically abused their authority throughout human history.

6 It is this presupposition that prompts Manganaro to put Northrop Frye in the company of Frazer, T.S. Eliot, and Campbell as a group of mythic thinkers concerned with the acquisition of cultural authority through the advancement of the metaphysics of presence (Manganaro 111–50). Eric Gould proceeds from a similar prejudice, which allows him to implicate Frye in Jung's project, even to shallowly label Frye's theories 'applied Jungianism'

(Gould 25): a characterization that any close reader of Frye's works would find absurd, and which ignores Frye's own comments on Jung (some of which are cited in chapter 1: see pp. 13–14 and 16–17). If Manganaro and Gould had given proper consideration to the phenomenological dimensions of Frye's mythography, they would not have included his work so readily in their critiques (and the present study would have been considerably less necessary). Insofar as Manganaro's and Gould's respective critiques of Campbell and Jung find warrant in the readily discernible metaphysical bases of their theories, their criticisms of the two mythologists are useful. But insofar as their critiques of Frye extend from an erroneous presumption derived more from these other mythologists than Frye's own writings, their criticism of him is not. Manganaro approvingly quotes Gould's assertion that 'there can be no myth without an ontological gap between event and meaning' (Gould 6, Manganaro 160). In a metaphysical theory of myth, which necessarily posits an extra-linguistic ontology, this is true, and that theory of myth becomes subject to poststructuralist critique. If the criterion of reality is shifted from an ontological to a phenomenological basis, as Frye's theories demonstrate, mythic event and mythic meaning become simultaneous: a myth is born or lived (or reborn and relived) in the experience of its being read or written. The mythic event and the configuration of its meaning coincide in the consciousness of the subject.

7 Dundes seems not to have noticed that Campbell concedes this point when he calls the monomyth a 'composite adventure' (*Hero* 36).

8 Dundes's complaint that the monomyth cannot be applied to a single hero's biography is made more complicated but also more answerable by another caveat in *Hero* that he seems to have overlooked: 'If one or another of the basic elements of the archetypal pattern is omitted from a given fairy tale, legend, ritual or myth, it is bound to be somehow or other implied – and the omission itself can speak volumes for the history and pathology of the example' (*Hero* 38).

9 Campbell, like Jung, does provide some provision for the experience of the heroine, although his remarks are less extensive and more cryptic in this context. In his discussion of the 'Meeting with the Goddess,' for example, Campbell writes: 'And when the adventurer, in this context, is not a youth but a maid, she is the one who, by her qualities, her beauty, or her yearning, is fit to become the consort of an immortal. Then the heavenly husband descends to her and conducts her to his bed – whether she will or no. And if she has shunned him, the scales fall from her eyes; if she has sought him, her desire finds its peace' (*Hero* 119). Campbell provides no female equivalent of the 'Woman as Temptress' experience, but one assumes that the

corresponding (or inverted) archetypal experience for the heroine of the hero's endurance of the material world of the mother would be her endurance of the logocentric vacuity of the patriarchal world.

4. Cleansing the Doors of Perception: Northrop Frye's *Fearful Symmetry*

1 It is worth noting, and consistent with Baker's observation, that *Fearful Symmetry* is divided into 12 parts, like the classical epic. Frye's original intention, however, seems to have been that *Fearful Symmetry* should consist of one hundred short parts (*TBN* 130, 196). In any event, when Frye speaks in *Fearful Symmetry* of 'philosophical epics which ... deal with cosmological themes,' one speculates that he might include his own work in such a category (*FS* 111).

2 For the only major dissenting opinion on the obvious accord between Blake and Frye, see David Cook's *Northrop Frye: A Vision of the New World* (48–54). Cook argues that Frye theorizes the imagination as more sensory-based and corporeal than Blake intended, in order to give it a more acceptable and immediate social grounding. While this was certainly Frye's intention, a careful reading of the passages of Blake quoted by Frye suggests that the claim of considerable difference between their theories is spurious. Blake himself constantly assumed the corporeal grounding of his poetics: the first line of *There Is No Natural Religion*, for example, reads 'Man cannot naturally perceive but through his natural or bodily organs.' Later in that piece, he writes that 'Mans desires are limited by his perceptions. None can desire what he has not perceiv'd' (Blake 2). A subtler reading of the space between Frye and Blake is that posed by Imre Salusinszky in his essay 'Frye and Romanticism': Salusinszky argues that Frye functions as a Bloomian *tessera* who 'extends' the project of the Romantic imagination (Salusinszky 58). A more tenable stance than Cook's, Salusinszky's position is actually quite compatible with the critical consensus cited here, and particularly the approach of the present study to the issue: Frye's 'extension' of Blake's agenda is how his identification with Blake appears from the perspective of literary history, which is the primary critical context of Salusinszky's essay.

3 It is important to observe that Frye goes on say: 'I am not by any means sure it is possible really to get free of presuppositions, but it is obvious that all genuine advance in knowledge goes along with a continued attempt to objectify and become aware of the assumptions that one is starting from' (*SM* 18).

4 Because many of the parenthetical citations in this chapter cross-reference Frye's quotations of Blake in *Fearful Symmetry* with the corresponding pas-

sages from Erdman's edition of Blake's poetry and prose, references to Blake have been made by page number (rather than title and line number) to avoid citations of inordinate length.

5 Frye's comments on Coleridge register this ambiguity in the poet's theory of imagination: 'Coleridge, as is well known, intended the climax of the *Biographia Literaria* to be a demonstration of the "esemplastic" or structural nature of the imagination, only to discover when the great chapter arrived that he was unable to write it. There were doubtless many reasons for this, but one was that he does not think of the imagination as a constructive power at all ... Coleridge is in the tradition of critical naturalism, which bases its values on the immediacy of contact between art and nature that we continuously feel in the texture of mimetic fiction' (*FI* 29–30). For a set of more appreciative comments on Coleridge, see *NFCL* 175–6 (and note also the epigraph of *WP*). Frye's observation that Coleridge's theory of imagination is less radical and complete than Blake's accounts for why Coleridge, in the words of M.H. Abrams, 'does not make special cognitive claims for poetry' (Abrams, *Mirror* 314). Blakean poetics, however, as the present work attests, do indeed appear to have productive 'cognitive' effects. Coleridge himself once wrote of Blake, 'verily I am in the very mire of common-place common-sense compared with Mr. Blake, apo- or rather ana-calyptic Poet and Painter!' (Coleridge, *Collected Letters* 833).

6 Merleau-Ponty's *Phenomenology of Perception* was written in 1945, though it did not appear in English translation until 1962.

7 Frye writes: 'The product of "beauty" is art; art is civilization; and it is only civilization that can give any value or any meaning to those impersonalizing tendencies of the mind which build up the imaginative forms of science and morality. Thus Blake's identification of religion with art is utterly different from the Romantic identification of the religious and aesthetic experiences. There is no place in his thought for aesthetics, or theories of abstract beauty' (*FS* 51).

8 Frye's point here, of course, is that mytho-metaphorical experience is contingent upon being able to think associatively outside the envelope of empirical thought and beyond rigid, logical definitions. But it is nevertheless an interesting stipulation from a theorist whose later books, particularly *Anatomy of Criticism*, would be criticized as being cluttered with an excess of definitions and critical jargon. The unspoken assumption behind such criticism, that there is a compulsive orderliness to Frye's work, is clearly invalid, given the open posture and liberality of his literary and cultural theory and the much greater amount of jargon theory and criticism that would develop after Frye. But it is curious to see this statement from a

thinker who would later pen a book that included a three-page glossary of terms, and who would acknowledge 'the necessity of being a terminological buccaneer' (though one may alternatively read this as demonstrating his point about the need for definitions to remain fluid and unfixed [*AC* 365–8, 362]).

9 The Blakean phrase 'corporeal understanding,' which he uses to refer to the Lockean process of reflecting on the passive reception of sensory data, has here been changed to 'Selfhood' (his term for the ego-persona which perceives in this fashion), so as to avoid confusion with Merleau-Ponty's positive use of 'corporeal' and 'corporeality' in reference to the body as the basis of the 'body image' and the root of imaginative consciousness.

10 Frye would later clarify his use here of the word 'conquest,' obviously aware of the potential for its being misunderstood if the nature of mytho-metaphoric thought is not properly grasped. 'I wouldn't use the word *conquest* now,' Frye explained in an interview in 1983. 'I would speak of identification. I was thinking very largely of Blake's "where man is not, nature is barren" ... I would put a much stronger emphasis now on the participation of man in nature. Largely through my work on Canadian literature, I've become more and more impressed with the baroque hostility to nature as something mindless, as something just to be parcelled out by the consciousness. I can see how very sinister some of the results of that have been' (*WGS* 250).

11 Merleau-Ponty has here used the French verb *lire*, to read, which Colin Smith translates as such: but it is obvious he is referring to a more extended consideration than simple reading. By his own phenomenology, a word would have to be read for it to be a word at all; it could not possibly have the effect he refers to if it had not been read. Merleau-Ponty seems rather to be referring here to the process he speaks of later in the passage, of the 'secondary' phase of apprehension or interpretation through which the word assumes 'the appearance of a sign'; in other words, the process of reflection or abstraction.

12 In addition to 'The Case against Locke,' a somewhat whimsical but relevant example of Frye's corporeal phenomenology of reading may be found in his essay 'Literature as Therapy' (*EAC* 21–36).

13 Plotinus avows, for instance, that 'the sphere of sense [is] the Soul in its slumber; for all of the Soul that is in the body is asleep and the true getting-up is not bodily but from the body: in any movement that takes the body with it there is no more than a passage from sleep to sleep ... the veritable waking or rising is from corporeal things; for these [are] directly opposed to Soul' (Plotinus 208). In *The Double Vision,* Frye describes Plotinus as 'an

ascetic ashamed of being in a body' (*DV* 73), echoing the opening of Porphyry's biography of Plotinus, which attributes this attitude to him (*DV* 88).

14 In *The Double Vision*, Frye cites Plotinus as a purveyor of religion's self-defeating tendency to find God distant or absent altogether through the application of abstract language: '[R]eligion tends to outgrow the notion of a personal god in order to reach its loftiest ideals. Or, to put it another way, we can build a higher tower of Babel with a god so transcendent that he transcends first personality and then himself, eventually disappearing beyond the bounds of human categories of thought. Even in Plotinus, who retains a personal god, that god is so remote that language cannot say what he is except "one"' (*DV* 64).

15 Cotrupi maintains that 'Frye was aware of Vico as early as the mid-1930's, even though, as he tells us, he did not actually read Vico until years later.' Despite her recognition of a 'paucity of direct published reference to Vico' by Frye prior to *The Great Code* (1982), and her admission that translations of and works on Vico did not become widely available until the mid- to late-1940s (by which time Frye had already developed the theory of *Fearful Symmetry*), Cotrupi, curiously, finds that 'it is probably safe to assume' that Vico's influence was active in Frye's thought during the late 1940s and early 1950s (Cotrupi 15–16).

16 See *NFCL* 100, *AC* 108–9, *SM* 116, *GC* 35, for instance. See also the quotation from *NFCL* 121 on p. 17.

17 Frye, for his own part, confirms something of this consolidating intention in his diaries of the period, which speak of his desire to 'link' up 'several categories' of archetypes ('I don't just mean Jung's archetypes either,' he says). Elsewhere he confides, in a rare example of awkward syntax, that being 'in quest of what I am in quest of I have to unite Jung as well as add Freud' (*D* 244, 185). The latter is yet another theorist whose mythography Frye seems to have absorbed, as we will see later in this chapter.

18 Note the etymology of 'consensus': Latin, *con* (with, together) + *sensus* (sense); literally, 'sensing together.'

19 Frye writes, 'surely there are many layers of unconsciousness. On top, below the personal unconscious, is the family & racial unconscious; our heritage from parents & the mental & physical makeup that says I, for instance, will resemble the English and not the Zulus or Siamese. Below that is the human unconscious, then the animal unconsciousness, then the organic unconscious & finally the material unconscious' (*RT* 39).

20 It is significant that the Greek verb *agein* is where the English word 'agency' originates.

21 Frye explains: 'the Fall ... begins in Beulah, the divine garden ... Once he takes the final step of thinking the object world independent of him, Albion sinks into a sleep symbolizing the passivity of his mind, and his creation separates and becomes the "female will" or Mother Nature, the remote and inaccessible universe of tantalizing mystery we now see' (*FS* 126). He later adds that 'the Fall is completed when Jacob and his eleven other sons follow Joseph into Egypt, and the Hebrews sink under all the tyrannies of the Selfhood, the "furnace of iron," as Egypt is called' (*FS* 364). In the interest of efficient explication and to emphasize the significance of the 'upward thrust' of Blake's and Frye's mythography, however, we have left our discussion of Beulah and the maternal/natural world of Generation until they are reattained by imaginative effort later in the overall *mythos.*

22 Other explanations for the origin of Blake's name Orc include the suggestion that it is derived from the Latin *orca* ('whale') and that it is an anagram from the French *cor* ('heart').

23 The analogy of Frye's understanding of Blake's Orc with the Jungian self is by no means exact, however. For Frye, Orc is not simply a centre of consciousness, it is the epicentre of desire, which for Jung is well diffused among the archetypes of the collective unconscious. Frye thus remarks in his diaries that he is 'very dissatisfied with the way Jung jumped over the libido Orc-hero to his archetypes without incorporating him' adequately (*D* 184).

24 This progression probably contains, or is analogous to, the Jungian development of the shadow into the trickster and the wise old man (although there is something of the trickster in the late-emergent Los).

25 In quoting the phrases 'dialectic of love' and 'the domineering male in erection,' O'Hara is repeating Frye's approbation of the former and his disapprobation of the latter as found in *SR* 121–2.

26 In John 19:25–7, Jesus' mother, 'his mother's sister, Mary the wife of Cleophas, and Mary Magdalene' come to the cross, and are dismissed. In Mark 16:1, 'Mary Magdalene, and Mary the mother of James, and Salome' bring 'sweet spices' to the sepulchre, 'that they might come and anoint him.' In John 19:41, we are told 'Now in the place where he was crucified there was a garden; and in the garden a new sepulchre, wherein was never man yet laid.'

27 Frye does not attempt in *Fearful Symmetry* to discern the origins of Blake's name Golgonooza or whether it follows his habit of inventing words for his characters, places, and states. He does speculate in an endnote that '[a]part from the echo of "Golconda,"' the name has 'a vaguely Indian look' (*FS* 445, n. 43). Harold Bloom states that it is 'evidently an anagram for New Golgotha,' to replace or correct the scene of the crucifixion (Bloom 115).

One speculates that it also involves a fusion of the word 'gone' and the Greek word for mind *nous* to suggest a disappearance and recreation of reality in a more comprehensive mental or spiritual state.

28 One of the minor tragedies in the history of biblical translation must be the AV's translation of such a visionary term as *metanoia* as merely 'repentance' (cf. Romans 2:4, for example).

29 'Know the Self to be sitting in the chariot, the body to be the chariot, the intellect the charioteer, and the mind the reins. The senses they call the horses, the objects of the senses their roads. When the Highest Self is in union with the body, the senses, and the mind, then wise people call him the Enjoyer. He who has no understanding and whose mind (the reins) is never firmly held, his senses (horses) are unmanageable, like vicious horses of a charioteer. But he who has understanding and whose mind is always firmly held, his senses are under control, like good horses of a charioteer' (*Katha Upanishad* 1.3.3–6).

30 Jung was aware of what he called 'the problem of the fourth,' recognizing it as 'an absolutely essential ingredient of totality' (*CW 11* 127). If we consider Frye's remarks in his diaries that the '[s]ame 3-4 symbolism' is 'in Blake & Jung,' that 'in Jung too, & perhaps in Blake, the form of the fourth is demonic' (*D* 78), alongside his complaint about Jung's failure to incorporate the libido-centre of the 'self' or 'Orc-hero' into his structure (see n. 23 above), we can see that Jung was not ignorant of the importance of the fourth; he just failed to properly integrate it into his array of archetypes. The structure of Jung's unconscious, like Eliade's cosmology and Campbell's monomyth, is thus only threefold, with the revolutionary fourth marginalized in each case.

31 'Jung's self,' Frye observes, 'takes form at the centre of a wheel, instead of being one of the foci of an ellipse' (*D* 61).

32 There are several detailed studies that explore this proposition, including Sir Cook Theodore Andrea's *The Curves of Life,* Matila Costiescu Ghyka's *The Geometry of Art and Life,* and Vladimir B. Ginzburg's *Grain of the Universe* and *Unified Spiral Field and Matter.* For a survey of the importance of the spiral form to myth, see Walter L. Brenneman's *Spirals: A Study in Symbol, Myth and Ritual.*

Conclusion: Phenomenology and Postmodern Mythography

1 This is not to imply that Frye had difficulty with the word 'phenomenological.' In a notebook believed to date back to 1961, in fact, Frye writes that, for his purposes, 'the word "phenomenological" is a good one, because it's

an even longer word than "metaphysical"' (NB18.48). Frye also uses, on at least one occasion, the provocative phrase 'directly experienced metaphor' (*MM* 17).

2 This is not a critique or reduction of *The Great Code,* merely a recognition of the fact that it, like *Anatomy of Criticism,* is less intended as phenomenology of myth than *Fearful Symmetry* or *Words with Power.* Frye's specific concerns in *The Great Code* include not only the structure and historical formation of the Christian Bible, but the structure and historical formation of its reception, the way the Bible 'has traditionally been read' (*GC* xiii). The sequence of the metaphoric, metonymic, and descriptive modes may well be better suited and more applicable to this task (a point also worth considering in relation to the *Anatomy,* whose 'Theory of Symbols' may well be better suited to the specific demands of literary criticism as opposed to the broader concerns of cultural theory). At the same time, however, there can be little disputing that Frye deliberately relaxed the historical imperative of the linguistic sequence in *Words with Power* ('my sequence is not historical,' he announces early in the book [*WP* 4]), or that the theory of a fourth, revelatory linguistic mode, kerygma, is embryonic in *The Great Code* (the word itself, for example, appears only a handful of times [*GC* 26, 29, 30, 231], once in a diagram that indicates some uncertainty about its nature through the schematic use of a series of question marks).

3 It is my opinion that Frye is using the word 're-presented' here not in the semiotic sense, and certainly not in any mere aesthetic sense, but in the root sense of the word as it persists in social and political contexts: 'to act for' or 'on behalf of.'

4 Frye addresses this 'gap' in Jung's thought (which he refers to as a 'paradox') in a notebook entry: 'Jung went farther than Freud, and posited a collective unconscious that comes closer to explaining the origin of myth. But ... he's tied up in the paradox of an "unconscious" that we are supposed to know about. You have to advance into a collective consciousness ... [T]here are two forms of this: one is ideological; the other is the spiritual aspect of primary concern' (*LN* 638).

5 To be fair, we must concede that Campbell does make an effort to do so in the first chapter of *The Masks of God: Primitive Mythology* (1959), where he attempts to theorize what he calls 'the enigma of the inherited image' (*Primitive Mythology* 30–8). There Campbell links the notion of the archetype to the 'innate releasing mechanism' or IRM, a concept originating in the study of animal behaviour that attempts to identify the site of stimulus reception and instinctual response. In doing so, Campbell is thus bringing his archetype closer to Jung's, who consistently suggested a connection

between archetypes and instincts. The linkage does not so much resolve the ambiguity that adhered to Jung's original speculations, however, as simply provide it with another nomenclature. The most Campbell can say is that 'in the central nervous system of all animals there exist innate structures that are *somehow* counterparts of the proper environment of the species' (*Primitive Mythology* 35, italics added). In any case, Campbell's attempt to account for the archetype through the IRM seems to have won little ground for his theories, perhaps because the concept of the IRM has itself been criticized, outmoded, and replaced by other hypotheses in animal ethology. This is in contrast to Frye's phenomenological orientation, which seems to have come into its own with the advent and intersection of cognitive linguistics, cultural phenomenology, and quantum physics (see nn. 8 and 9 below).

6 Frye is speaking here of Gertrude Rachel Levy, author of *The Gate of Horn* and *The Sword from the Rock: An Investigation into the Origins of Epic Literature and the Development of the Hero.*

7 The root meaning of the Greek word *psychikos* ('of the senses' or 'sensual') is relevant here.

8 The Heisenberg Indeterminacy Principle is a theoretical ramification of the discovery of physicist Werner Heisenberg (1901–76) that precise measurements of certain sub-atomic events and quantum phenomena are impossible, because of interference to the measured quantity by the presence of a measuring instrument. The most common example of this cited by physicists is the impossibility of observing a sub-atomic particle: electron microscopes shower their subjects with electrons and invariably alter the image in the very process of compositing it. A macroscopic example is the way in which a thermometer, immersed in a cup of tea, lowers the tea's temperature slightly in the process of measuring it. The implications of this seemingly innocuous discovery are considerable. Reality, for science, is a function of its quantification: where such quantification was once assumed to be empirical and objective, Heisenberg's discovery suggests that quantification occurs in the interrelationship of the observer and the observed (cf. Capra 79–80). Many interpreters of Heisenberg have gone so far as to suggest that the real implication of his discovery is that the observer actually *determines* the observed; a notion which, if applied to the human sciences, would endorse the first principle of phenomenology, that reality is a function of the presence and engagement of human consciousness.

Frye references post-Einsteinian physics in general, and the Heisenberg Principle in particular, in *The Great Code* when he speaks of how 'Einstein is the great symbol for a new realization that matter, which up to the twentieth century had been the great bastion of the objectivity of the world, was an illusion of energy. With this, however, the sense of the clear separation of subject and object, which was so marked a feature of the scientific attitude up to that point, overreached itself and began to come to an end. It was no longer possible to separate the observer from what he observes' (*GC* 14). Frye goes on to suggest that his own metaphorical theory is 'oddly contemporary with post-Einsteinian physics' (*GC* 17).

9 Some of the deeper inquiries of theoretical physicists Erwin Schrödinger and David Bohm (who are considered part of Heisenberg's so-called 'Copenhagen school' of quantum theory) are understood by Frye as analogous to some of the questions he is pursuing in the context of literary and cultural theory. Frye frequently implies that his notion of kerygma is, to some extent, an effort to answer Schrödinger's speculation that 'consciousness is the singular of which the plural is unknown,' and David Bohm's that the seemingly chaotic universe contains a hidden or 'implicate order' that needs only the right mode of measurement or perception to be discovered (cf. *DV* 84, *LN* 26, 105–6, 291, 416, 545, 595, 713–14, *MM* 122).

10 *Chandogya Upanishad* 6.8.7; cf. *LN* 290, 428.

Works Cited and Consulted

Abrams, M.H. *A Glossary of Literary Terms.* New York: Harcourt Brace Jovanovich, 1993.

– *The Mirror and the Lamp: Romantic Theory and the Critical Tradition.* New York: Oxford University Press, 1953.

Adamson, Joseph. *Northrop Frye: A Visionary Life.* Toronto: ECW Press, 1993.

Aithal S. Krishnamoorthy, ed. *The Importance of Northrop Frye.* Kanpur, India: Humanities Research Centre, 1993.

Allen, Douglas. *Structure and Creativity in Religion: Hermeneutics in Mircea Eliade's Phenomenology and New Directions.* The Hague: Mouton, 1978.

Aristotle. *Aristotle's Poetics.* Trans. James Hutton. New York: Norton, 1982.

Augustine, Saint. *De diversis quaestionibus octoginta tribus (Eighty-three different questions).* Trans. David L. Mosher. Washington, DC: Catholic University of America Press, 1982.

Ayre, John. *Northrop Frye: A Biography.* Toronto: Random House, 1989.

Balfour, Ian. *Northrop Frye.* Boston: Twayne, 1988.

Baird, Robert. *Category Formation and the History of Religion.* The Hague: Mouton, 1971.

Barthes, Roland. *Mythologies.* Paris: Editions du Seuil, 1957.

Bates, Ronald. *Northrop Frye.* Toronto: McClelland and Stewart, 1971.

Bays, Gwendolyn, trans. *The Voice of the Buddha: The Beauty of Compassion (The Lalitavistara-sutra).* Berkeley, Calif.: Dharma, 1983.

Bentley, G.E. *Blake Books.* Oxford: Clarendon Press, 1977.

Berman, Morris. *Coming to Our Senses: Body and Spirit in the Hidden History of the West.* Toronto: Simon and Schuster, 1989.

Birrell, Anne. *Chinese Mythology: An Introduction.* London: Johns Hopkins University Press, 1993.

Blake, William. *The Poetry and Prose of William Blake.* Ed. David V. Erdman. Garden City, NY: Doubleday and Company, 1970.

Bloom, Harold. 'States of Being: *The Four Zoas.*' *Blake: A Collection of Critical Essays.* Ed. Northrop Frye. Englewood Cliffs, NJ: Prentice-Hall, 1966. 104–18.

Bodkin, Maud. *Archetypal Patterns in Poetry.* Oxford: Oxford University Press, 1934.

Boyd, David, and Imre Salusinszky, eds. *Rereading Frye: The Published and Unpublished Works.* Toronto: University of Toronto Press, 1999.

Brenneman, Walter L. *Spirals: A Study in Symbol, Myth and Ritual.* Washington, DC: University Press of America, 1979.

Bultmann, Rudolph. *Theology of the New Testament.* Trans. Kendrick Grobel. New York: Scribner's, 1951.

Butler, Judith. 'Sexual Ideology and Phenomenological Description: A Feminist Critique of Merleau-Ponty's *Phenomenology of Perception.*' *The Thinking Muse: Feminism and Modern French Philosophy.* Ed. Jeffner Allen and Marion Young. Bloomington: Indiana University Press, 1989. 85–100.

Campbell, Joseph. *The Flight of the Wild Gander: Explorations in the Mythological Dimension.* New York: Viking, 1969.

– *The Hero's Journey: The World of Joseph Campbell.* Ed. Phil Cousineau. San Francisco: Harper and Row, 1990.

– *The Hero with a Thousand Faces.* Princeton: Princeton University Press, 1949.

– *The Inner Reaches of Outer Space: Metaphor as Myth and as Religion.* New York: Harper and Row, 1986.

– *The Masks of God: Primitive Mythology.* New York: Viking Press, 1959.

– *The Power of Myth.* Ed. Betty Sue Flowers. New York: Doubleday, 1988.

Capra, Fritjof. *The Web of Life: A New Scientific Understanding of Living Systems.* New York: Anchor, 1996.

Carmody, Denise Lardner, ed. *Eastern Ways to the Center: An Introduction to Asian Religions.* Belmont, Calif.: Wadsworth Publishing, 1992.

Cave, John. *Mircea Eliade's Vision of a New Humanism.* New York: Oxford University Press, 1993.

Cayley, David. *Northrop Frye in Conversation.* Concord, ON: Anansi, 1992.

Cixous, Hélène. 'The Laugh of the Medusa.' *New French Feminisms.* Ed. Elaine Marks and Isabelle de Courtivron. New York: Schocken Books, 1981. 245–64.

Childers, Joseph, and Gary Hentzi, eds. *The Columbia Dictionary of Modern Literary and Cultural Criticism.* New York: Columbia University Press, 1995.

Clarke, J.J. *In Search of Jung: Historical and Philosophical Enquiries.* London: Routledge, 1992.

Coleridge, Samuel Taylor. *Collected Letters (Vol. 4).* Ed. Earl Leslie Griggs. Oxford: Clarendon, 1959.

– *The Oxford Authors: Samuel Taylor Coleridge.* Ed. H.J. Jackson. Oxford: Oxford University Press, 1985.

Cook, David. *Northrop Frye: A Vision of the New World.* New York: St Martin's, 1985.
Cook, Eleanor, et al., eds. *Centre and Labyrinth: Essays in Honour of Northrop Frye.* University of Toronto Press, 1983.
Cotrupi, Caterina Nella. *Northrop Frye and the Poetics of Process.* Toronto: University of Toronto Press, 2000.
Dante Alighieri. *The Convivio of Dante Alighieri.* London: Dent and Sons, 1931.
Denham, Robert D. *Northrop Frye: An Annotated Bibliography of Primary and Secondary Sources.* Toronto: University of Toronto Press, 1990.
– *Northrop Frye and Critical Method.* University Park: Pennsylvania State University Press, 1978.
Denham, Robert D., and Thomas Willard, eds. *Visionary Poetics: Essays on Northrop Frye's Criticism.* New York: Peter Lang, 1991.
Derrida, Jacques. *The Margins of Philosophy.* Trans. Alan Bass. Chicago: University of Chicago Press, 1982.
– *Of Grammatology.* Trans. Gayatri Chakravorty Spivak. Baltimore: Johns Hopkins University Press, 1976.
– *Specters of Marx.* Trans. Peggy Kamuf. London: Routledge 1994.
Dolzani, Michael. 'Wrestling with Powers: The Social Thought of Frye.' *The Legacy of Northrop Frye.* Ed. Alvin A. Lee and Robert D. Denham. Toronto: University of Toronto Press, 1994. 97–102.
Donaldson, Jeffery, and Alan Mendelson, eds. *Frye and the Word: Religious Contexts in the Criticism of Northrop Frye.* Toronto: University of Toronto Press, 2004.
Doty, William. 'Dancing to the Music of the Spheres: The Religion in Joseph Campbell's "Non-Religious" Mythography.' *Paths to the Power of Myth: Joseph Campbell and the Study of Religion.* Ed. Daniel C. Noel. New York: Crossroad, 1994. 3–12.
– *Mythography: A Study of Myths and Rituals.* Tuscaloosa: University of Alabama Press, 1986.
Dudley, Guilford. *Religion on Trial: Mircea Eliade and His Critics.* Philadelphia: Temple University Press, 1977.
Dundes, Alan. *Interpreting Folklore.* Bloomington: Indiana University Press, 1980.
Durkheim, Emile. *The Elementary Forms of the Religious Life.* Trans. Joseph Ward Swain. London: Allen and Unwin, 1915.
Eagleton, Terry. *Literary Theory: An Introduction.* London: Blackwell, 1983.
– *Marxism and Literary Criticism.* London: Methuen, 1976.
Eliade, Mircea. *Images and Symbols: Studies in Religious Symbolism.* Princeton: Princeton University Press, 1991.
– *The Myth of the Eternal Return: or, Cosmos and History.* Princeton: Princeton University Press, 1954.
– *Patterns in Comparative Religion.* New York: Sheed and Ward, 1958.

– *The Sacred and the Profane: The Nature of Religion.* New York: Harcourt Brace, 1959.
– *Shamanism: Archaic Techniques of Ecstasy.* Princeton: Princeton University Press, 1964.
Eliade, Mircea, ed. *The Encyclopedia of Religion.* Vol. 6. New York: Macmillan, 1987.
Eliot, T.S. *Complete Poems and Plays, 1909–1950.* New York: Harcourt, Brace and World, 1971.
Ellwood, Robert. *The Politics of Myth: A Study of C.G. Jung, Mircea Eliade, and Joseph Campbell.* Albany: State University of New York Press, 1999.
Fagles, Robert, trans. *The Iliad.* New York: Penguin, 1990.
– *The Odyssey.* New York: Penguin, 1996.
Falck, Colin. *Myth, Truth and Literature: Towards a True Post-Modernism.* Cambridge: Cambridge University Press, 1989.
Fish, Stanley. *Is There a Text in This Class? The Authority of Interpretive Communities.* Cambridge, Mass.: Harvard University Press, 1980.
Foucault, Michel. *The Foucault Reader.* Ed. Paul Rabinow. New York: Pantheon Books, 1984.
Frazer, James George. *The Golden Bough: A Study of Magic and Religion.* Abridged ed. London: Macmillan, 1922.
Freud, Sigmund. *The Origins of Religion: Totem and Taboo, Moses and Monotheism, and Other Works.* Ed. Albert Dickson. Markham, Ont.: Penguin Books Canada, 1985.
Frye, Northrop. 'After the Invocation, a Lapse into Litany.' *Book Week,* 22 March 1964: 6, 19.
– *Anatomy of Criticism: Four Essays.* Princeton: Princeton University Press, 1957.
– 'Blake's Treatment of the Archetype.' *Discussions of William Blake.* Ed. John E. Grant. Boston: D.C. Heath, 1961. 6–16.
– *The Correspondence of Northrop Frye and Helen Kemp, 1932–1939.* Ed. Robert D. Denham. 2 vols. Toronto: University of Toronto Press, 1996.
– *The Critical Path: An Essay on the Social Context of Literary Criticism.* Bloomington: Indiana University Press, 1971.
– *Creation and Recreation.* Toronto: University of Toronto Press, 1980.
– *The Diaries of Northrop Frye, 1942–1955.* Ed. Robert D. Denham. Toronto: University of Toronto Press, 2001.
– *The Double Vision: Language and Meaning in Religion.* Toronto: University of Toronto Press, 1991.
– *The Eternal Act of Creation: Essays, 1979–1990.* Ed. Robert D. Denham. Bloomington: Indiana University Press, 1993.
– *Fables of Identity: Studies in Poetic Mythology.* New York: Harcourt, Brace and World, 1963.

– *Fearful Symmetry: A Study of William Blake.* Princeton: Princeton University Press, 1947.
– *Fearful Symmetry: A Study of William Blake.* Boston: Beacon Press, 1962.
– *The Great Code: The Bible and Literature.* New York: Harcourt Brace Jovanovich, 1982.
– 'Literature and Myth.' *Relations of Literary Study: Essays on Interdisciplinary Study.* Ed. James Thorpe. New York: Modern Language Association, 1967. 27–54.
– *Myth and Metaphor: Selected Essays, 1974–1988.* Ed. Robert D. Denham. Charlottesville: University Press of Virginia, 1990.
– *Northrop Frye in Conversation.* Ed. David Cayley. Concord, Ont.: Anansi, 1992.
– *Northrop Frye on Culture and Literature: A Collection of Review Essays.* Ed. Robert D. Denham. Chicago: University of Chicago Press, 1978.
– *Northrop Frye on Literature and Society, 1936–1989.* Ed. Robert D. Denham. Toronto: University of Toronto Press, 2002.
– *Northrop Frye on Religion: Excluding 'The Great Code' and 'Words with Power.'* Ed. Alvin A. Lee and Jean O'Grady. Toronto: University of Toronto Press, 2000.
– *Northrop Frye's Late Notebooks, 1982–1990: The Architecture of the Spiritual World.* 2 vols. Ed. Robert D. Denham. Toronto: University of Toronto Press, 2000.
– *Northrop Frye's Notebooks and Lectures on the Bible and Other Religious Texts.* Ed. Robert D. Denham. Toronto: University of Toronto Press, 2003.
– *Northrop Frye's Student Essays, 1932–1938.* Ed. Robert D. Denham. Toronto: University of Toronto Press, 1997.
– *The Secular Scripture: A Study of the Structure of Romance.* Cambridge, Mass.: Harvard University Press, 1976.
– *Reading the World. Selected Writings, 1935–1976.* Ed. Robert D. Denham. New York: Peter Lang, 1990.
– *Spiritus Mundi: Essays on Myth, Literature, and Society.* Bloomington: Indiana University Press, 1976.
– *The Stubborn Structure: Essays on Criticism and Society.* Ithaca: Cornell University Press, 1970.
– *A Study of English Romanticism.* New York: Random House, 1968.
– *The 'Third Book' Notebooks of Northrop Frye.* Ed. Michael Dolzani. Toronto: University of Toronto Press, 2002.
– *Words with Power: Being a Second Study of the Bible and Literature.* New York: Harcourt Brace Jovanovich, 1990.
– *A World in a Grain of Sand: Twenty-Two Interviews with Northrop Frye.* Ed. Robert D. Denham. New York: Peter Lang, 1991.

Garfield, Eugene. 'Is Information Retrieval in the Arts and Humanities Inherently Different from That of Science?: The Effect that ISI's Citation Index on the Arts and Humanities Is Expected to Have on Future Scholarship.' *Library Quarterly* 50 (1980): 40–57.

George, Andrew, trans. *The Epic of Gilgamesh.* London: Penguin, 1999.

Ghyka, Matila Costiescu. *The Geometry of Art and Life.* New York: Dover, 1978.

Ginzburg, Vladimir B. *Grain of the Universe: In Search of the Archimedes File.* Pittsburgh: Helicola Press, 1996.

– *Unified Spiral Field and Matter: A Story of a Great Discovery.* Pittsburgh: Helicola Press, 1999.

Gould, Eric. *Mythical Intentions in Modern Literature.* Princeton: Princeton University Press, 1981.

Graves, Robert. *The White Goddess: A Historical Grammar of Poetic Myth.* London: Faber and Faber, 1948.

Griffith, Ralph T.H., trans. *The Hymns of the Rig-Veda.* 1896. Delhi: Motilal Banarsidass, 1973.

Groden, Michael, and Martin Kreiswirth, eds. *The Johns Hopkins Guide to Literary Theory and Criticism.* Baltimore: Johns Hopkins University Press, 1994.

Grosz, Elizabeth. *Jacques Lacan: A Feminist Introduction.* New York: Routledge, 1990.

– *Volatile Bodies: Toward a Corporeal Feminism.* Bloomington: Indiana University Press, 1994.

Gulick, Walter B. 'The Thousand and First Face.' *Paths to the Power of Myth: Joseph Campbell and the Study of Religion.* Ed. Daniel C. Noel. New York: Crossroads, 1994. 29–44.

Hamilton, A.C. *Northrop Frye: Anatomy of His Criticism.* Toronto: University of Toronto Press, 1990.

Harrison, Jane Ellen. *Themis: A Study of the Social Origins of Greek Religion.* 1912. Cambridge: Cambridge University Press, 1927.

Hart, Jonathan. 'Northrop Frye and the Poetics of Context.' *New Directions in Northrop Frye Studies.* Ed. Wang Ning and Jean O'Grady. Shanghai: Shanghai Educational Press, 2001. 21–56.

– *Northrop Frye: The Theoretical Imagination.* New York: Routledge, 1994.

Heath, Sir Thomas Little. *The Thirteen Books of Euclid's Elements, translated from the text of Heiberg with introduction and commentary.* New York: Dover, 1956.

Heidegger, Martin. *Basic Writings.* Ed. David Farrell Krell. San Francisco: Harper and Row, 1993.

– *Being and Time.* San Francisco: Harper and Row, 1962.

Herbert, J. 'Hindu Mythology.' *Larousse: World Mythology.* Ed. Pierre Grimal. New York: Gallery Books, 1989. 208–48.

Holman, C. Hugh, and William Harmon, eds. *A Handbook to Literature.* Englewood Cliffs, NJ: Macmillan, 1992.

Husserl, Edmund. *Cartesian Meditations: An Introduction to Phenomenology.* Trans. Dorion Cairns. The Hague: Martinus Nijhoff, 1973.

– *Logical Investigations.* 1901. Trans. J.N. Findlay. Amherst, NY: Humanity Books, 2000.

Hyman, Stanley Edgar. 'Myth, Ritual and Nonsense.' *Kenyon Review* 11.2 (1949): 455–75.

Irigaray, Luce. *Etre Deux.* Paris: Bernard Grasset, 1997.

James, William. *The Varieties of Religious Experience.* New York: Collier Macmillan, 1961.

Jameson. Fredric. *The Political Unconscious: Narrative as a Socially Symbolic Act.* Ithaca: Cornell University Press, 1981.

JanMohamed, Abdul. 'The Economy of Manichean Allegory: The Function of Racial Difference in Colonialist Literature.' *Critical Inquiry* 12.1 (1985): 18–23.

Jaynes, Julian. *The Origins of Consciousness in the Breakdown of the Bicameral Mind.* New York: Houghton Mifflin, 2000.

Johnson, Mark L. 'Embodied Reason.' *Perspectives on Embodiment: The Intersection of Nature and Culture.* Ed. Gail Weiss and Honi Fern Haber. New York: Routledge, 1999. 81–102.

Jung, C.G. *Alchemical Studies (CW 13).* Princeton: Princeton University Press, 1968.

– *The Archetypes and the Collective Unconscious (CW 9i).* Princeton: Princeton University Press, 1958.

– *Civilization in Transition* (*CW 10*). Princeton: Princeton University Press, 1964.

– *Experimental Researches* (*CW 2*). Princeton: Princeton University Press, 1973.

– *Freud and Psychoanalysis (CW 4).* Princeton: Princeton University Press, 1967.

– *Letters, Volume I: 1906–1950.* Princeton: Princeton University Press, 1973.

– *Memories, Dreams, Reflections.* Ed. Aniela Jaffé. New York: Vintage, 1965.

– *Mysterium Coniunctionis (CW 14).* Princeton: Princeton University Press, 1970.

– *The Practice of Psychotherapy (CW 16).* Princeton: Princeton University Press, 1954.

– *Psychological Types (CW 6).* Princeton: Princeton University Press, 1921.

– *Psychology and Alchemy (CW 12*). Princeton: Princeton University Press, 1944.

– *Psychology and Religion: East and West (CW 11).* Princeton: Princeton University Press, 1958.

– *The Structure and Dynamics of the Psyche (CW 8).* Princeton: Princeton University Press, 1960.

– *The Symbolic Life: Miscellaneous Writings* (*CW 18*). Princeton: Princeton University Press, 1955.

– *Symbols of Transformation (CW 5).* Princeton: Princeton University Press, 1956.

– *Two Essays on Analytical Psychology (CW 7).* Princeton: Princeton University Press, 1953.

Kant, Immanuel. *Critique of Pure Reason*. Trans. F. Max Müller. London: Macmillan, 1881.

– *Prolegomena to Any Future Metaphysics*. Trans. James W. Ellington. Indianapolis: Hackett, 1977.

Kerrigan, William. 'The Raw, the Cooked, and the Half-Baked.' *Virginia Quarterly Review* 51 (1975): 651–5.

King, Jeff. *Where the Two Came to Their Father: A Navaho War Ceremonial, with Commentary by Joseph Campbell*. 1943. Princeton: Princeton University Press, 1969.

King, Karen L. 'Social Factors in Mythic Knowing: Joseph Campbell and Christian Gnosis.' *Paths to the Power of Myth: Joseph Campbell and the Study of Religion*. Ed. Daniel C. Noel. New York: Crossroad, 1994. 68–80.

Knight, G. Wilson. *The Starlit Dome: Studies in the Poetry of Vision*. Oxford: Oxford University Press, 1941.

– *The Wheel of Fire: Interpretations of Shakespearian Tragedy*. Oxford: Oxford University Press, 1930.

Knight, W.F. Jackson. *The Cumaean Gates: A Reference of the Sixth Aeneid to the Initiation Pattern*. Oxford: Blackwell, 1936.

Kogan, Pauline. *Northrop Frye: The High Priest of Clerical Obscurantism*. Montreal: Progressive Books and Periodicals, 1969.

Kojève, Alexandre. *Introduction to the Reading of Hegel: Lectures on the Phenomenology of the Spirit*. Ed. Allan Bloom. Ithaca: Cornell University Press, 1980.

Krieger, Murray, ed. *Northrop Frye in Modern Criticism: Selected Papers from the English Institute*. New York: Columbia University Press, 1966.

Kristeva, Julia. *Powers of Horror: An Essay on Abjection*. New York: Columbia University Press, 1982.

Kugler, Paul. 'Psychic Imaging: A Bridge between Subject and Object.' *The Cambridge Companion to Jung*. Ed. Polly Young-Eisendrath and Terence Dawson. Cambridge: Cambridge University Press, 1997. 71–85.

Lacan, Jacques. *Écrits: A Selection*. New York: Norton, 1977.

Lakoff, George, and Mark Johnson. *Philosophy in the Flesh: The Embodied Mind and Its Challenge to Western Thought*. New York: Basic Books, 1999.

Lentricchia, Frank. *After the New Criticism*. Chicago: University of Chicago Press, 1980.

Levy, Gertrude Rachel. *The Gate of Horn*. London: Faber and Faber, 1948.

– *The Sword from the Rock: An Investigation into the Origins of Epic Literature and the Development of the Hero*. London: Faber and Faber, 1953.

Lévy-Bruhl, Lucien. *Primitive Mentality*. London: Gresham Press, 1923.

Locke, John. *An Essay Concerning Human Understanding*. 1690. New York: Dutton, 1974.

Makaryk, Irena R. *Encyclopedia of Contemporary Literary Theory: Approaches, Scholars, Terms.* Toronto: University of Toronto Press, 1993.

Manganaro, Marc. *Myth, Rhetoric, and the Voice of Authority: A Critique of Frazer, Eliot, Frye and Campbell.* New Haven: Yale University Press, 1992.

McLuhan, Herbert Marshall. 'Inside Blake and Hollywood.' *Sewanee Review* 55 (1947): 710–13.

Meier, C.A. *Soul and Body: Essays on the Theories of C.G. Jung.* San Francisco: Lapis Press, 1986.

Merleau-Ponty, Maurice. *Phenomenology of Perception.* 1945. Trans. Colin Smith. London: Routledge and Kegan Paul, 1962.

– *The Primacy of Perception and Other Essays on Phenomenological Psychology, the Philosophy of Art, History and Politics.* Ed. James M. Edie. Evanston: Northwestern University Press, 1964.

– *Sense and Non-Sense.* Trans. H. Dreyfus and P. Dreyfus. Evanston: Northwestern University Press, 1964.

Müller, F. Max, trans. *The Upanishads.* New York: Dover, 1962.

Nicholson, Mervyn. 'Cosmology and Imagination in Northrop Frye: A Further Contribution to URAM Studies on Frye.' *URAM: Interdisciplinary Studies in the Philosophy of Ultimate Reality and Meaning* 15 (1999): 45–98.

Odajynk, Volodymyr Walter. *Jung and Politics: The Political and Social Ideas of C.G. Jung.* New York: Harper Colophon, 1976.

O'Grady, Jean, and Wang Ning, eds. *Northrop Frye: Eastern and Western Perspectives.* Toronto: University of Toronto Press, 2003.

O'Hara, Daniel T. *The Romance of Interpretation: Visionary Criticism from Pater to de Man.* New York: Columbia University Press, 1985.

Penner, Hans. 'Bedeutung und Probleme der Religiosen Symbolik bei Tillich und Eliade.' *Antaios* 9 (1967): 127–43.

Pietropaolo, Domenico. 'Frye, Vico, and the Grounding of Literature and Criticism.' *Ritratto di Northrop Frye.* Ed. Agostino Lombardo. Roma: Bulzoni, 1990.

Plato. *Phaedrus.* Trans. C.J. Rowe. Wiltshire, England: Aris and Phillips, 1986.

Plotinus. *The Enneads.* Trans. Stephen MacKenna. London: Faber and Faber, 1956.

Porphyry. *Life of Plotinus and The Enneads of Plotinus.* Trans. A.H. Armstrong. Cambridge, Mass.: Harvard University Press, 1966.

Rennie, Bryan S. *Reconstructing Eliade: Making Sense of Religion.* Albany: State University of New York Press, 1996.

Rennie, Bryan S., ed. *Changing Religious Worlds: The Meaning and End of Mircea Eliade.* Albany: State University of New York Press, 2001.

Ricketts, Mac Linscott. 'In Defence of Eliade.' *Religion: Journal of Religion and Religions* 3 (Spring 1973): 24–7.

Richter, David H., ed. *The Critical Tradition: Classic Texts and Contemporary Trends.* New York: Bedford, 1989.

Russell, Ford. *Northrop Frye on Myth: An Introduction.* New York: Garland, 1998.

Said, Edward. *Orientalism.* New York: Vintage, 1979.

Salman, Sherry. 'The Creative Psyche: Jung's Major Contributions.' *The Cambridge Companion to Jung.* Ed. Polly Young-Eisendrath and Terence Dawson. Cambridge: Cambridge University Press, 1997. 52–70.

Salusinszky, Imre. 'Frye and Romanticism.' *Visionary Poetics: Essays on Northrop Frye's Criticism.* Ed. Robert D. Denham and Thomas Willard. New York: Peter Lang, 1991. 57–74.

Schechter, Harold, and Jonna Gormely Semeiks. 'Campbell and the "Vanilla-Frosted Temple": From Myth to Multiplex.' *Use of Comparative Mythology: Essays on the Work of Joseph Campbell.* Ed. Kenneth Golden. New York: Garland Publishing, 1992. 179–91.

Segal, Robert. *Encountering Jung: Jung on Mythology.* Princeton: Princeton University Press, 1998.

– *Joseph Campbell: An Introduction.* New York: Meridian, 1997.

Sitwell, Edith. 'William Blake.' *Spectator* 10 October 1947: 466.

Spengler, Oswald. *The Decline of the West.* Trans. Charles Francis Atkinson. New York: George Allen and Unwin, 1926.

Strenski, Ivan. *Four Theories of Myth in Twentieth-Century History: Cassirer, Eliade, Lévi-Strauss and Malinowski.* London: Macmillan Press, 1987.

Theodore Andrea, Sir Cook. *The Curves of Life: Being an Account of Spiral Formations and Their Application to Growth in Nature, to Science, and to Art.* New York: Dover, 1979.

Tolkien, J.R.R. *The Lord of the Rings.* London: HarperCollins, 1991.

Underwood, Richard A. 'Living by Myth: Joseph Campbell, C.G. Jung, and the Religious Life-Journey.' *Paths to the Power of Myth: Joseph Campbell and the Study of Religion.* Ed. Daniel C. Noel. New York: Crossroad, 1994. 13–28.

Vico, Giambattista. *The New Science.* Trans. Thomas Goddard and Max Harold Fisch. Ithaca: Cornell University Press, 1970.

– *On the Most Ancient Wisdom of the Italians.* Trans. L.M. Palmer. Ithaca: Cornell University Press, 1970.

von Franz, Marie-Louise. *Patterns of Creativity Mirrored in Creation Myths.* Zürich: Spring Publications, 1972.

Watkins, Calvert. *How to Kill a Dragon: Aspects of Indo-European Poetics.* Oxford: Oxford University Press, 1995.

Wehr, G. *An Illustrated Biography of C.G. Jung.* Boston: Shambhala Publications, 1989.

Weston, Jessie L. *From Ritual to Romance.* 1919. Princeton: Princeton University Press, 1993.

Willard, Thomas. 'Archetypes of the Imagination.' *The Legacy of Northrop Frye.* Ed. Alvin A. Lee and Robert D. Denham. Toronto: University of Toronto Press, 1994. 15–27.

Wilson, Colin. *Lord of the Underworld: Jung and the Twentieth Century.* Wellingborough, Northamptonshire: Aquarian Press, 1984.

Zaehner, R.C., trans. *The Bhagavad-Gita.* London: Oxford University Press, 1969.

Zimmer, Heinrich. *The King and the Corpse: Tales of the Soul's Conquest of Evil.* Ed. Joseph Campbell. Princeton: Princeton University Press, 1948.

Index